Anthropology at the Edge

Essays on Culture, Symbol, and Consciousness

J. Ian Prattis

University Press of America, Inc.
Lanham • New York • London

University Press of America, ® Inc.
4720 Boston Way
Lanham, Maryland 20706

3 Henrietta Street
London, WC2E 8LU England

Printed in the United States of America
British Cataloging in Publication Information Available

Library of Congress Cataloging-in-Publication Data

Prattis, J. I.
Anthropology at the edge : essays on culture, symbol, and consciousness / J. Ian Prattis.
p. cm.
Includes bibliographical references and index.
1. Symbolic anthropology. 2. Structural anthropology. I. Title.
GN452.5.P73 1996 301--dc20 96-43225 CIP

ISBN 0-7618-0556-7 (pbk. : alk. ppr.)

™ The paper used in this publication meets the minimum requirements of American National Standard for information Sciences—Permanence of Paper for Printed Library Materials, ANSI Z39.48—1984

Contents

List of Figures

Preface

Students and colleagues over the past decade have encouraged, and frequently insisted, that I draw my thoughts, lectures and writings on symbolic anthropology into a collection of essays. I appreciate their prodding, yet the delay was not due to procrastination. I simply did not have a coherent structure in my mind into which my seemingly disparate thoughts and writings could readily fit. I also felt I did not know enough about symbolic anthropology. In 1995, however, the intensive preparation that was necessary for the production of a twelve week television course on Culture and Symbol made me realize that the structure I was looking for was inherent in how I taught. I thought of the television course, and now this volume, as an orchestral piece with an opening movement and statement of themes, followed by other movements, themes and harmonies, then a finale that returned to the opening themes with a crescendo drawn from a radical yet consistent orchestration. More pragmatically, this book is intended as a text, a companion piece to the television course on Culture and Symbol which is designed to be syndicated for institutions other than Carleton University, and delivered through an Internet homepage:

http://www.carleton.ca/~tolaveso/cspage.html

This is an educational step into the Electronic University of the Future and these essays will then play through a different kind of orchestral score.

The first movement of the volume - I. Beyond Structuralism - was for me a formidable task, because I have a great admiration for Claude Lévi-Strauss' work and scholarship. Yet I felt something was missing in his analyses. While I understood his semiotic necessity of stripping away the cultural content of categories in order to get at the invariant structuring principles of the human mind, this was at the cost of the symbolic significance and transformative powers of the categories themselves. I felt that Lévi-Strauss had become trapped in the logic of his analytic model concerning the conception of the human mind. In Chapter 1, *"Man and Metaphor"*, which was first published in 1984 in Communication and Cognition (V.17, 2/3), I tackled the problematics of structuralism in terms of human adaptive capacities. First of all I established the logic of structuralism and then embarked on a tour-de-force through myth, science, poetry and cave art to demonstrate the inadequacies of Lévi-Strauss' approach, particularly in addressing problems of consciousness and transformation. I stretched structuralism as far as I could by making analogies between elementary structures, archetypes and meditation symbols, and placed a construction on Lévi-Strauss' axioms that perhaps may not appeal to him.

I enlarge on my disagreement with Lévi-Strauss in Chapter 2, *"Parsifal and Semiotic Structuralism"*, which was finally published in Ivan Brady's reader, *Anthropological Poetics*, in 1991. This work took an exceptionally long time to sculpt into a final form and I am still not totally satisfied with it. I include Brady's "Prelude" to this chapter as he skillfully places my endeavours with the Parsifal myth within its intellectual context and also identifies my competitors:- Roland Barthes and Claude Lévi-Strauss. In Chapter 2, the Parsifal myth is subjected to an intense scrutiny and Lévi-Strauss' analysis is criticised as permitting very limited kinds of conclusions. As an alterative I propose a mythopoetic reading of the myth that requires both an internal view of symbols as transformation vehicles and an external context of theoretical reference points. The latter are drawn first of all from Carl Jung (1959) and then significantly from the arguments of Edmund Husserl (1970) with respect to "bracketing", a notion that I consider essential for the construction of a self-aware anthropology. In the analysis of the myth I focus significantly on the interaction between Parsifal and Blanche Fleur, and consider Blanche Fleur as a paramount manifestation of what Carl Jung called the "anima" complex (1959; see also Emma Jung 1957). Furthermore, I contend that a semiotic structuralist approach can only get at certain levels of a symbolic system. It is certainly unable to penetrate the archetypal mysteries of a complex such as the anima. My mythopoetic unravelling of this myth is not so obstructed.

What lay "Beyond Structuralism" for me was a turn towards anthropological poetics, and a redefinition of subject-object relationships. This is the second movement - II. The Poetic Turn and Postmodern Reflexivity. I was moving in the direction of postmodernism long before the term became fashionable in anthropology. I also felt that anthropologists knew much more than they expressed in their monographs and articles. Furthermore, that the unlocking of this knowledge required a deep dive into epistemology and the use of language forms that had a richer semantic corpus than everyday discourse. Rather than documenting ethnographic events within a predetermined modernist structure I felt it was necessary for anthropologists to develop complementary understandings from different standpoints. Many of my colleagues *did* understand the dialogism of different cultural assumptions but relegated their understandings to poetry that remained largely private, rather than representing their knowledge in public discourse. I tried to change all that in 1985 when the American Anthropological Association published my edited work: *Reflections, the Anthropological Muse.* The last chapter of this volume is reproduced in this reader as Chapter 3, *"Dialectics and Experience in Fieldwork: The Poetic Dimension".* I began with the epistemological difficulties of fieldwork and proposed poetic expression as one solution to these difficulties as it is a signifying process that can record the dialectical relationship between the observer and other. This epistemological shift with all its attendant consequences would, I argued, eventually bring about a radicalization of anthropology, and provide a vital spark for rethinking anthropology's foundations.

There were other streams of radicalness entering the discipline at this time that I discuss in Chapters 5 and 6 but let me stay with *Reflections* for a moment. Ten years later "'Reflections' as Myth" was published in Dialectical Anthropology in 1995 (V.20: 45-69). In this postscript to *Reflections: The Anthropological Muse*, I collaborated with a number of graduate students at Carleton University to extend the postmodernist concern with the other to the pedagogic tradition of how we teach and communicate with students. The other in this instance is not the ethnographic other but the gifted students we have the privilege to teach and learn from. In a graduate class on Sign and Symbol I gave the students an exercise. It was to take one poem from each section of *Reflections*, to treat the collection as myth and express what their chosen sequence signified. I was exceedingly impressed with their insights and analyses, and they made me realize that I should explicate my intent in putting *Reflections* together and furthermore they strongly hinted that I should more clearly elaborate my views of mythology and postmodernism. "Reflections as Myth" was created from their insistence, and I am grateful that Derek Blair, Lee Grigas and Olaf Krassnitzky "stayed on my case", as it were, until the project was completed. Chapter 4, *"Reflections as Myth"*, is an excerpt from the wider collaboration, which I would recommend to the reader, and with it is attached my thanks to a gifted trio of students. In Chapter 4 I articulate my intentions behind *Reflections: The Anthropological Muse* and place it firmly within postmodern dialogue.

This placement is further elaborated on in Chapter 5, *"Reflexive Anthropology"*, which was published in the Encyclopedia of Cultural Anthropology in 1996. I take the concerns and implications of anthropological poetics and "pump-up-the-volume" by taking them to a higher level of generality. The discussion of reflexive levels is part of the process of re-evaluating what we do as scholars, in universities, in public life and the field, and I delineate in more detail the exploitative relationship inherent in modernist anthropology. The pitfalls of this kind of endeavour are discussed in Chapter 6, *"Opening Ourselves up to the Voyage of Anthropological Practise"*. This work was co-authored with Derek Blair and published in *Merging Trajectories, New Horizons*, a reader edited by Derek Blair and Bruce Cox, published by Carleton University Press in 1996. Blair's introduction to this chapter in the 1996 reader points out that our essay begins with a discussion of logos and eros as two epistemes. Logos is the realm of science and logic, and eros is the realm of affective imagery and symbols. We argue that the rational stance of science does not make it a superior episteme, and we demonstrate along with recent ethnographic literature that extraordinary field experiences constitute valid data. Part of the thrust of the argument is the recognition that anthropologists have a lot to gain by regarding their cultural counterparts as other aspects of the reality that they themselves are constituted of. Derek Blair and I refer to this as "universal similarism" in our 1994 work, "Exploitation in the Field", published in a special edition of Anthropology and Humanism (V.19, 1) edited by Edith Turner and Ivan Brady.

I begin the third movement - III. Process and Form - with Chapter 7, *"Celtic Festivals and Bilingualism Policy: The Barra Feis"*. This essay examines the symbolic significance of a Gaelic festival on the island of Barra in the Western Isles of Scotland. It was published in *A Different Drummer* (Cox et alia 1990), and demonstrates the cathartic effect of traditional symbolic values for cultural and economic transformation in the island community. The revival, presentation and internalization of these values was through the Barra *Feis* - a summer festival and year-round commitment to the Gaelic performing arts. I establish the pre-conditions for this kind of transformation by emphasizing minority language bilingualism as a major factor that reinforced a sense of cultural identity. This reverses the usual equation about community development, economics and culture, which has a primary focus on class relations of political economy. I replace this focus with the consideration that cultural symbols, and their reinforcement, can operate as a catalyst not only for community solidarity but also for economic and political change.

Then I examine two instances of mythic enactment: sacred dance and shamanism, before writing a chapter on the underlying process of symbolic transformation (Chapters 8, 9 and 10 respectively). I have always been fascinated with cultures that dance their myths, recognizing that here was a ritual process of transformation, deeply rooted in a culture's mythology and traditions. In Chapter 8, *"Sacred Dance and Cultural Bridges"*, I analyze sacred dance as mythic enactment, a process that produces a cycle of meaning between symbolic form (choreography) and symbolic structures contained in the human unconscious and the body. My assumption is that mythology provides a blueprint for the ritual performance to root itself in individual consciousness. I make a direct correlation between the precision of movement and sound in sacred dance and entry into an altered state of consciousness. Considerations of ritual preparation and breath control are taken through a brief discussion of shamanic and classical Hindu cultures to develop a model for my on-going collaboration with a modern dance group, as it moves from the secular to the sacred domain of expression. At the end of this essay I return to problems of research methodology in terms of the postmodernist concern with respecting the voice of the "other", which may well result in anticipated research endeavours being abandoned.

In Chapter 9, *"Death Breaths and Drivers"*, I move the focus of mythic enactment from sacred dance to shamanism. In this piece of research I rely on my own phenomenology of working with shamans to arrive at a data base that explicates a model of healing. The emphasis on breathwork in the preceding chapter, *"Sacred Dance and Cultural Bridges"*, is expanded in the discussion of shamanic practises to describe the use of "Death Breaths" as a driver to simulate near death experiences, thus enabling entry into an altered state of consciousness. I code the various forms of the shamanic journey in this state as a dialogue with archetypal material that accelerates the individuation process. From the result of fieldwork experiences with shamans and my participation in the healing and meditative arts over the past twenty years, I derive a healing structure designed around the principles of safety, sacredness and personal responsibility.

In Chapter 10, *"Metaphor, Vibration and Form"*, I move from the particulars of cultural festivals, sacred dance and shamanism to the general, to identify a process that I believe underlies all ritual enactments. Whether it is Joseph Campbell's analysis of the Hero's Journey (1949), Victor Turner's theoretical and experiential interest in symbols (1974), or Charles Laughlin's Cycle of Meaning (1995) to mention only a few scholars, there is at work a particular kind of behavioural transformation system. It begins with the mind and the meanings provided metaphorically for symbols, then proceeds to an intense focus on symbolic sequences in meditation or in ritual dramas so that the metaphor is taken into the body as physical experience. From this physical "ownership" and experience of the metaphor, the properties associated with it are encouraged, socially and ritually, to come to the surface and be enacted in the form of everyday behaviour. I outline instances where this process works and where it does not. The model I develop puts transformation and order in a dialectical relationship of symbolic process and inserts the phenomenological experience of the investigator into the equation of doing science. This ushers in the next movement.

In the fourth movement - IV. Paradigms - Chapter 11, *"Science and Sages: A Small Matter of Paradigms"*, discusses the bias and distortion in science in terms of a paradigm shift that is necessary to expand scientific self-awareness. (It may also support the radical shifts of emphasis in my own work!) In this essay I discuss the limitations and constraints of science as presently constituted in order to set the stage for the study of the interpenetration of physical and metaphysical properties of matter. I use this joint configuration to arrive at a different understanding of mantra - in particular the "Om" mantra, and then advocate a radically different perspective on the biology of the cell. Throughout this discussion there is an emphasis on meditation practices as the means to encourage scientific endeavour to shift into a more comprehensive level of explanation and understanding.

In the finale - V. Gaia and the Environment - are two essays that take the implications of my discussions of science, deconstruction and paradigm shift into the arena of environmental issues. Chapter 12, *"Issues of Inner Ecology"*, draws on the work of Rachel Carson, the Buddha and statements of traditional ecological knowledge. The role of human consciousness with respect to environmental issues emphasizes attitude and value shifts and brings the spiritual dimension onto centre stage. In Chapter 13, *"Myth, Meditation and Transformation of Consciousness"*, I acknowledge that the metaphysics of environmental issues attracts a great deal of scepticism particularly about the burden of proof. Mythology, however, provides a metaphorical means to support an argument about consciousness transformation with respect to the human-environment equation. I examine the Tree of Life myths as they provide a world-wide template for human-planet-universe relationships and direct attention to the nature of balance. As an antidote to a maladaptive inner ecology I form a triad of meditation, the Dalai Lama and the Little Prince to support an argument about congruence and clarity.

With these final two essays I return full circle to the concerns of Chapter 1, *"Man and Metaphor"*. In the first essay of this volume I examined human adaptive capacities from the perspective of structuralism. I found Lévi-Strauss' "Science de l'Homme" lacking because it was an inadequate tool to address the question of human consciousness. This very same human consciousness becomes the key factor in Chapters 12 and 13 concerning Gaia and the Environment. The finale of this composition thus returns to the opening themes of human adaptability but plays it out with a crescendo of consciousness, more in keeping with Joseph Campbell's music of the spheres (1990) than with Lévi-Strauss' "View from Afar" (1985).

Bibliography

Blair, D. and B. Cox

1996 (eds.): Merging Trajectories, New Horizons: Anthropology from the Capital. Ottawa: Carleton University Press

Blair, D. and J.I. Prattis

1994 Exploitation in the Field. Anthropology and Humanism, V.19, 1:36-39

1996 Opening Ourselves up to the Voyage of Anthropological Practise. In D. Blair and B. Cox (eds.): Merging Trajectories, New Horizons: Anthropology from the Capital. Ottawa: Carleton University Press

Brady, I.

1991 (ed.): Anthropological Poetics. Savage, Maryland: Rowman and Littlefield

Campbell, J.
1949 The Hero with a Thousand Faces. Princeton: Princeton University Press

1990 Transformations of Myth Through Time. N.Y.: Harper and Row

Cox, B., J. Chevalier and V. Blundell
1990 (eds.): A Different Drummer: Readings in Anthropology with a Canadian Perspective. Ottawa: Carleton University Press

Husserl, E.
1970 The Crisis of European Sciences and Transcendental Phenomenology (trans. by David Carr). Evanston: Northwestern University Press

Jung, C.G.
1959 Concerning the Archetypes, with Special Reference to the Anima Concept. In The Archetypes and the Collective Unconscious. The Collected Works of C.G. Jung, V.9. Princeton: Princeton University Press

Jung, E.
1957 Animus and Anima. N.Y.: Analytical Psychology Club of New York

Laughlin, C.D.
1995 The Cycle of Meaning: Some Methodological Implications of Biogenetic Structural Theory. In S. Glazier (ed.): Anthropology of Religion: Handbook of Theory and Method. Peterborough: Greenwood Press

Lévi-Strauss, C.
1985 The View from Afar. N.Y.: Basic Books

Prattis, J.I.
1984 Man and Metaphor: An Exploration in Entropy and Coherence. Communication and Cognition, V.17, 2/3:187-204

1985 Dialectics and Experience in Fieldwork: The Poetic Dimension. In J.I. Prattis (ed.): Reflections: The Anthropological Muse:266-281. Washington D.C.: American Anthropological Association

1990 Celtic Festivals and Bilingualism Policy: The Barra Feis. In B. Cox at alia (eds.): A Different Drummer. Ottawa: Carleton University Press

1991 Parsifal and Semiotic Structuralism. In I. Brady (ed.): Anthropological Poetics. Savage, Maryland: Rowman and Littlefield

1996 Reflexive Anthropology. In The Encyclopedia of Cultural Anthropology. N.Y.: Henry Holt and Company Inc.

Prattis, J. I., D. Blair,
L. Grigas and O. Krassnitzky
1995 "Reflections" as Myth. Dialectical Anthropology, V.20, 1:45-69

Turner, V.
1974 Dramas, Fields and Metaphors. Ithica: Cornell University Press

Acknowledgments

I would like to thank the editor and publisher of Communication and Cognition for permission to reprint *Man and Metaphor* (Chapter 1) from their V.17, 2/3, 1984. Ivan Brady kindly allowed me to reprint his introduction to my *Parsifal and Semiotic Structuralism* (Chapter 2), both of which were included in his edited work *Anthropological Poetics*. My appreciation also goes to Rowman and Littlefield, who published Brady's book in 1991. *Reflections: The Anthropological Muse* was published in 1985 by the American Anthropological Association. The Association has granted permission to reprint the last chapter *Dialectics and Experience in Fieldwork: The Poetic Dimension* (Chapter 3). An excerpt from *Reflections as Myth* (Chapter 4) is reprinted with permission of the editor and publisher of Dialectical Anthropology from their Vol. 20, 1, 1995. Chapter 5, *Reflexive Anthropology*, first appeared in the Encyclopedia of Cultural Anthropology in 1996 and is reprinted by permission of the editors and publisher. The co-authored chapter with Derek Blair, *Opening Ourselves up to the Voyage of Anthropological Practise* (Chapter 6), appears in Blair and Cox's reader *Merging Trajectories, New Horizons*. I thank them and Carleton University Press for permission to reprint this chapter. *Celtic Festivals and Bilingualism Policy: The Barra Feis* (Chapter 7), appeared in a 1991 publication, *A Different Drummer*, sponsored by the anthropology caucus at Carleton University. I thank my colleagues for their continuing support for my endeavours. My scientific preference for method in discourse involves a format similar to the triangular method of navigation, so there is often an overlap from one piece of work to another. With this in mind I have made a number of editorial changes to the previously published chapters to ensure a progressive flow of ideas and also to eliminate undue repetition. The remaining six chapters were written specifically for *Anthropology at the Edge* and I am indebted to colleagues and several generations of students too numerous to name who have provided feedback and critiques of earlier versions of these chapters. In particular Derek Blair, Lee Grigas, Olaf Krassnitsky, Tim Olaveson, Linnea Rowlatt, Bruce Dunn, Radhika Sekar, Bob Depew and Linda Rayner helped enormously with their careful copy editing and by bringing my attention to the task of explicating the more obtuse aspects of my arguments. I also benefitted enormously from the critiques of earlier drafts provided by Ivan Brady, Edith Turner, John Cove, Charles Laughlin, Sean Kelly, Jacques Chevalier, Jean-Philippe Chartrand, Kevin Karst, Ruth-Inge Heinze, John Dourley and Michael Sharpe. Final responsibility for the arguments rendered does, however, lie with me as there were numerous off-the-wall positions that I was not prepared to relinquish. My final thanks are to my friend Carolyn Hill who typed the many versions of each chapter and prepared the manuscript for publication. She also provided those extra insights that I certainly benefitted from.

Chapter 1

Man and Metaphor: An Exploration in Entropy and Coherence

Introduction

Structuralism has given us many sophisticated analyses of particular systems of kinship and myth. The reduction of an immense variety of symbolic systems to an invariant model of the human mind has been carried out by a number of practitioners who in their zeal to practice structuralism as an applied method have tended to miss the philosophical implications of Lévi-Strauss' thought. This is a curious inversion with Marx, whose thought has provided a philosophy which captures the imagination of half the globe, but at the level of practice the cogent idea of "relations of production" and their reproduction often defies analytic detail. It is the philosophical implications of Lévi-Strauss' thought that I am concerned with. I am going to argue that despite his work on Native American mythology, primitive classification, and marriage systems Lévi-Strauss is not interested in primitive cultures per se. The culture to which Lévi-Strauss speaks is his own -- and the elementary structures of primitive cultures are used as allegorical contrasts to draw out the contradictions in western culture. In other words, structuralism taken as a whole is myth, whose meaning we must piece together in order to understand more clearly the basis of paradox in our own culture. I will state the problematics of structuralism in terms of human adaptive capacities, then briefly outline my understanding of structuralism. Once the logic of structuralism is established, I intend to take that logic through myth, science, poetry and cave art, and return debate to the domain of theology. In this way one may provide a different answer to Lévi-Strauss' fundamental question -- "What is Man?"

In reviewing continuities and prospects in anthropological studies Selby (1969) voices a concern about an imminent fragmentation of anthropologists into two distinct camps -- structural anthropology on the one hand and cultural ecological studies on the other. He argues that the future lies in a partial coalescence of these points of view, a theme echoed by Ardener in his Malinowski memorial lecture on the New Anthropology and its Critics (1971:465). As yet no clearly thought out strategy for linking these two bodies of thought has been argued, so in this essay I propose to examine the arguments of structuralism in terms of their implications for the adaptive capacities of human populations and to consider the possible avenues this suggested synthesis may direct discourse to.

There are two important legacies in the thought of Lévi-Strauss. From l'Année Sociologique of Durkheim and Mauss there is the notion that symbolic orderings are systems of mental categories which are metaphorically prior to collective representations as objective social facts:

(categories: collective representations) :: (collective representations: social fact).

Second, from the Prague school of linguistics comes the notion of binary codes, deep and surface structures as part of linguistic process. An acknowledged debt to Marx and Freud is made in *Tristes Tropiques* in which Lévi-Strauss discusses his self appointed task to chart the archaeology of consciousness, and to construct a science of man that will complete the ventures of Marx and Freud and subsume them under a wider mantle (Lévi-Strauss 1961). It is thanks to Lévi-Strauss' genius that these disparate themes and legacies are developed into a coherent and compelling argument about the nature of Man's humanity -- a "science de l'homme" that Lévi-Strauss feels is complete.

Anthropology to Lévi-Strauss is no more and no less than a complete logic and science of man, covering all his activities and realities. This "science de l'homme" has to be complete as its system would be rendered invalid if anything was omitted. In following a tradition set by Aristotle and revived by Montesquieu, Lévi-Strauss' intent is to create a secular science of man -- one that is not based on a transcendental theory of religious value. It will be argued later, however, that perhaps the lasting influence of Lévi-Strauss' thought will be to redirect attention to a somewhat metaphysical, metareligious perspective on the human condition. The argument developed in Lévi-Strauss' writings is that categorization of phenomena in the external world follows similar universal paths, as the segmenting and classifying of stimuli is ordered by the structure of the apparatus through which man does his apprehending -- the human mind (Lévi-Strauss 1962). The nature of this ordering system and therefore of the process of thought, can only be understood through a consideration of the systems that it generates. Of the systems analyzed -- kinship, totemism, myth -- by far the most important is myth. Lévi-Strauss claims that myths provide in an encapsulated and coded form, documentation of the very beginnings of man, of the crucial period of transition from Nature to Culture.

There are three issues here.[1] First of all there is Lévi-Strauss' debt to Rousseau's *Discourse on the Origins of Inequality*, in terms of his concern with the passage from animality (the continuous) to humanity (the discrete). The distinction between humanity and its obverse animality gives rise to a fundamental opposition between Nature and Culture, which Lévi-Strauss argues is always latent in man's customary attitudes and behaviour. Second there is the realization of the Cultural being anchored in the Natural. Homologies, such as totemism, have the function of rooting perceptions about cultural formations within nature as a concrete model. I will argue that this business of rooting Culture in Nature is fundamental for humanity, in order that man can grasp a sense of coherence and unity within his universe of thought and action. The third issue is that myths are statements about the incompleteness of the transition between Nature and Culture. In other words transition is rarely accomplished, yet links and bridges between the two domains must be maintained, again for the function of maintaining coherence. This in my opinion is what symbolic codes and homologies are for; they ease the built in dialectical tension between Nature and Culture.

My concern with ultimate coherence is not a theme developed by Lévi-Strauss, largely because he is trapped in the logic of his own analytic model concerning the conception of mind. There is, therefore, a certain incompatibility between Lévi-Strauss' structuralism and the ideas to be developed here. I will argue that primitive man's use of systems of symbolic metaphor has an intentionality, a consciousness that accepts coherence as the natural ordering of things and this appears to lie beyond the level which is addressed by the semiotic structure of the unconscious, which is where Lévi-Strauss starts and ends. This divergence between Lévi-Strauss and myself will become more apparent as this essay unfolds.

In his analysis of myth, Lévi-Strauss seeks to reconstruct a "déjà vu" of human consciousness and find the roots of our own identity (1964, 1966, 1968, 1972). Implicit in his analysis is the notion that one can only understand the nature of man by understanding how she is related to Nature. This assumption, made explicit in the analysis of the Oedipus myth (Lévi-Strauss 1958), is that man has one foot firmly in nature and one in culture. I would go further and argue that codes, homologies and links are required in order that some kind of coherence is maintained between the natural and cultural components of humanity's consciousness. In observing how relations which exist in the human conception of nature are used to generate cultural products which incorporate the same relations, Lévi-Strauss argued that cultural products are ordered in time and space in the same way that products of nature are perceived to be ordered and segmented (1962). The process of ordering is assumed to be binary and oppositional and to operate at a level of consciousness that is considered to be innate. This process of analytical correlation, with its attendant transformational power, implies that the vast variety of cultural forms are simply transformations of universal structural characteristics of the human mind. As Sir Edmund Leach points out in his discussion of Lévi-Strauss this means that any particular set of materials from any one culture is a structure of relations which is an algebraic transformation of other possible structures. All such structures belong to a common set which reflects attributes of the unconscious models in the human mind (Leach 1970). By implication, when different institutions can be reduced to transformations of the same basic figure, the limits of human manoeuvrability and adaptive capacity may in fact be narrow.

Lévi-Strauss' tour de force through kinship, totemism and myth is a demonstration that this assumption set is capable of reducing vast bodies of material to comprehensible sets. The difficulty with coming to grips with Lévi-Strauss' structuralism is that our standard repertoire of concepts, rules of evidence and etiquette of discourse have been severely challenged. In the process of reducing material to comprehensible sets Lévi-Strauss has moved outside the rules of orthodox discourse. I have argued elsewhere that his endeavours can be viewed as an incomplete scientific revolution as the "truth" that Lévi-Strauss' structuralism is concerned with operates on a level different from that which requires falsifiability as a characterising criterion (Prattis 1972). The "truth" level of structuralism is found in the transformational grammar of semiotic structures in the human mind, a level that Lévi-Strauss claims directs and shapes our lives.

The question of what kind of science Lévi-Strauss has produced may be rendered irrelevant, however, if the full impact of Freud's view of science is to be considered. In his celebrated exchange of letters with Einstein, Freud remarked that every science comes in the end to be only a kind of mythology (Jones 1961). This implies that from the structure of mythology we may learn something of the structure of Lévi-Strauss' "science de l'homme". In other words the next step in the sociology of knowledge may be a "Principia Mythologica" which may do for structuralism what the "Principia Mathematica" did for positivism. The four volumes of Mythologiques are simply a preface.

Myth and Mediator

The idea that the structure of mythology provides a key to the structure of Lévi-Strauss' "science de l'homme" is consistent with the argument that if all cultural forms are viewed as transformations of the same basic figure, then structuralism itself as a cultural form should be amenable to the very assumptions it generates. That just as Lévi-Strauss pieced together the message in myth, in terms of its underlying structures and contradictions, then we should be able to do the same with structuralism. Structuralism as myth, then, should be able to identify the basis of paradox and contradiction within our own society.

In his analysis of myth Lévi-Strauss demonstrates an underlying structure, which uses different empirical levels -- geography, economy, social organization, cosmology -- as parameters for sensate codes to transmit messages that portray the basic contradictions in any given culture. Each level and code is a transformation of an underlying logical structure common to all of them, and they combine in any given sequence according to the particular capacity of the combination to transmit the required message. Sequences are punctuated by the appearance of mediators in the myth, which act as a form of relay switch. They change the direction of the myth, and put it onto a different level with a different code, so that other sequences are obtained which transmit the same message. Thus the same contradiction is played out on many levels. The mediators break the myth up into sequences and also provide the generating base for the next sequence. Lévi-Strauss argues that the replication and repetition on many different levels serves the function of rendering the structure of the myth apparent, as the slated structure of the myth comes to the surface through repetition (Lévi-Strauss 1958). If I may use a musical analogy it may be clearer just what sensate codes, empirical parameters, mediators and so on refer to.

Figure 1.1: Mediator in Myth

MUSIC	Note sequences within a scale	Musical Scale	Rests	Repetitions on a theme
MYTH	Sensate codes : taste smell sight touch hearing	Parameters : geography economy social organi- zation cosmology art, etc.	Mediators: (M) e.g. trickster	Slated structure of myth comes to the surface through repetition (M_4) sight-geography (M_3) soc. organisation (M_2) noise taste-economy (M_1) cosmology-smell

The five sensate codes are analogous to alternative note sequences played out on different scales. Noise and smell appear to be used much more than the other three codes which leads one to suspect that lexical concepts of noise and stink have more semantic transmitting power that the other three; just as certain scales provide composers with more musical scope than others. The codes, then, operate on different parameters until we come to a mediator -- and here there is something vital. The mediator acts as a punctuation mark, a statement that the message has been sent. It also acts as a relay switch in that the myth is switched into a different parameter and uses a different code. Furthermore the mediator provides the semantic field from which the elements of the next message in myth are drawn from. At this point the analogy of mediator with a musical rest is a poor one, as only at the level of punctuation mark does this comparison make sense. The mediator in myth is in fact much more powerful. It is a signal that the message is over, and it is also the semantic corpus for the tapping out of the same message using a different code and a different parameter. This is what Lévi-Strauss means by the notion of the slated structure of myth coming to the surface through repetition.

The idea of mediator in myth is very significant because we can begin to make sense of a few things. Let us start with the Trickster in Native American mythology. This particular role is frequently assigned to the coyote or raven (Lévi-Strauss 1963:224).

Figure 1.2: Trickster as Mediator

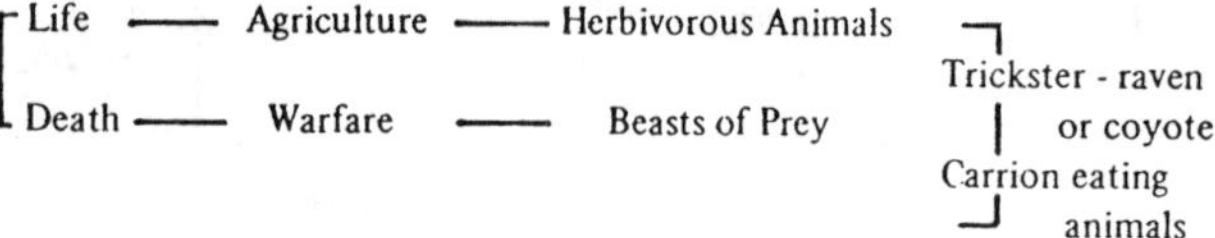

The Trickster has attributes of both the oppositional terms it replaces in the myth. As a mediator he retains an ambiguous and equivocal character in order to generate the next sequence which will end with some other mediator. The function of the mediator is to provide a basis for repetition, to render the structure of the myth apparent (Lévi-Strauss 1963:229).

In texts, poetry and cave art we find exactly the same thing going on. In the extended medieval poem - *Piers Ploughman* - Piers keeps cropping up in different forms and the recurrent introduction to this character in different form represents the punctuation marks in the poem; viz. message over; message about to be transmitted on another domain using another code. The riddle of palaeolithic cave art can be reduced to this same consideration of mediators and messages. The painted ceilings at Altimara, the magnificent friezes of animals and symbols at Lascaux do have a recognizable pattern. This was researched and documented by Leroi-Gourhan (1963). The unsolved puzzle was that between panels there always occurred a bewildering array of lines, circles, dots, squares and squiggles. In his analysis Leroi-Gourhan classifies them as variants of female and male signs -- based on the shape of the vulva and the penis. But he did not seem to realize that the variation in the configuration of these sets of symbols held the key to understanding palaeolithic art. They are mediators, and serve the same function as mediators in myth. Message over; ready for the next sequence! Palaeolithic man was using male and female symbols to punctuate the fact that in her art he was concerned to play out a fundamental opposition between Life and Death, Nature and Culture. A reinterpretation of cave art in terms of recognizing that the bewildering array of lines and circles are mediators would bring about a different and more systematic understanding of the meaning of cave art. In other words cave art is exactly the same as myth. It simply operates in a different domain. In archaeology and palaeontology no one has considered cave art in these terms but I am convinced that if someone would take this idea of mediator and messages, and reinterpret Lascaux and Altimara as total units -- everything would then make sense.

Given this analytic view of myths the message in structuralism then begins to come clear, as does my divergence from Lévi-Strauss' thought. I would argue that codes and homologies are used by man in primitive cultures to fit and complete the cosmic order of which she is a part. The symbolic and mythic codes provide coherence and unity. In non-industrial cultures symbolic codes and homologies are used to overcome the logical paradoxes that exist between Nature and Culture by reducing the dialectical tension between them. The contradiction of man in contemporary civilization is that she no longer uses codes of the same order -- the homologies appear to be forgotten or obsolete. It would seem that contemporary humanity has become the logical paradox! This consideration arises if we take Lévi-Strauss' writings as a whole and see that the contradictions which come to the surface are not so much in the material he uses, but are generated by the particular culture and historical moment that he occupies, and of which he is a product. Myth, masks, totemism and cross-cousin marriage then become allegorical dimensions along which the contradictions of industrialized, secularized culture are played out in an obverse manner by stark contrast with the elementary structures of primitive cultures. Structuralism does not, therefore, provide the means to deal with paradox, whereas the elementary structures of primitive culture do.

Lévi-Strauss uses myth as the prime document of this contrast, as it is through myth as a code of information, perception and hypotheses about the necessary conjointness of cultural and natural history that he claims to have the basis of understanding the premises of our own humanity. His analysis of the Oedipus myth (1958) shows that Oedipus limps because part of his essence will always be conjoint with organic nature, but, as a prophecy of things to come I would argue that Oedipus as the cultural creature able to answer the Sphinx's riddle regarding his own identity constitutes a destructive power. Culture unrooted in Nature provides man with a murderous, dehumanizing and alienating power made inevitable by the severing of links from the primordial world of nature. While cultures still have codes and homologies that try to bridge the Nature - Culture gap there will still be some coherence with humankind's potential humanity and grasp of unity, but where the codes have broken down and the Nature - Culture dichotomy is no longer latent in human activities, then a necessary loss of humanity ensues.

Consciousness and Entropy

The destruction of every last vestige of those cultures that had preserved a coherence with Nature that exploiting, civilized, industrial culture had renounced becomes, in Lévi-Strauss' eyes, the acid test of our humanity (1972). Lévi-Strauss is exceedingly bitter about the role of anthropology as the harbinger of destruction. For it seems that the only pure act of being left to our civilized culture is to destroy, and anthropology geared to the exigencies of professionalism is in the vanguard of this destructive process. Nature is no longer a generative base -- instead it is used for the recreational slaughter of animals and total exploitation of resources. Its rhythms and generating forms, of which human beings are a component, though sometimes glimpsed in solitude and silence are not used as models at any level. The breakdown of ritual language and oral traditions as symbolic codes that once enabled human beings to grasp that they were part of a wider and more coherent set of forces no longer serve. Contemporary culture no longer knows how to use codes that express human essence in terms of interconnectedness. Humanity has become a void papered over with rationalization and false consciousness.

On the question of rationalization one's attention is drawn to the conclusion of Weber's *Protestant Ethic and the Spirit of Capitalism* (1958:182):

> The puritan wanted to work in a calling; we are forced to do so ... when asceticism was carried out of monastic cells into everyday life, and began to dominate worldly morality, it did its part in building the tremendous cosmos of the modern economic order ... In (the puritan) view, the care for external goods should only lie on the shoulders of the 'saint' 'like a light cloak' ... But fate decreed that the cloak should become an iron cage ... Material goods have gained an increasing and finally inexorable power over the lives of men as at no previous period in history ...
>
> No one knows who will live in this cage in the future, or whether at the end of this tremendous development entirely new prophets will arise, or there will be a great rebirth of old ideas and ideals, or, if neither, mechanized putrefaction, embellished with a sort of convulsive self importance. For of the last stage of this cultural development, it might well be truly said: 'Specialists without spirit, sensualists without heart, this nullity imagines it has attained a level of civilization never before achieved.'

This prophetic view of our civilization was written in 1904, before World War I, before Stalin, before Hitler, and before Marcuse's "one dimensional man". Our advanced industrial society would appear to be Weber's cage with iron bars; and social scientists and psychiatrists are the perfect jailors, issuing a socialized pablum that puts illusion between man and her contemporary cage. Marx's views on alienation are a similar attack on the dehumanizing process inherent in industrial capitalism. In this, his least developed but I feel most important part of this thought, he demonstrates how human beings in capitalist society are progressively alienated from means of production, product and species being. Much of his discussion of capitalism is a documentation of the conditions and built-in mechanisms that prevent a movement from false consciousness to class consciousness. Within the arena of false consciousness sits the idea of a cage to which we become accustomed, as long as we escape our intellects.

In other words an avoidance of solitude, silence and reflection is a process whereby cultural man avoids those situations where contemplation on the human condition is inescapable, where he can avoid coming face to face with his own intellect. Thus the life of contemporary, civilized man is filled with senseless noise, activity and delusions which provide no scope for his grasp of coherence and unity and therefore no scope for the expression of potential humanity. This is what Lévi-Strauss inadvertently directs our attention to. In the final volume of *Mythologiques* (1972) Lévi-Strauss claims to have created a myth of myth, an epic of the twilight of man, and in doing so he attempts to bring us face to face with our own intellects. That by knowing, we realize that we are simply caught in the trap of our own history which has gone beyond the point of no return. The science of man then, according to Lévi-Strauss is perhaps not an *anthropology* but an *entropology*. As George Steiner (1972) pointed out, this is a dreadful pun because in French both words are pronounced exactly the same. Yet this pun contains the alarming realization that as scientists what we are concerned with is the logos of run-down and obsolescence -- that the real "science de l'homme" will not end up in a positive anthropology but in our comprehension of an empty and silent planet (Lévi-Strauss 1972). This is similar to the finale of Shakespeare's *King Lear*. In a desolate and dying landscape, Lear carries his dead daughter in his arms and confronts Silence. I always have the distinct impression that Lévi-Strauss and Shakespeare are writing about the same thing.

In an earlier more optimistic work Lévi-Strauss discussed the value of social anthropology in terms of stipulating that the forms of life studied -- primitive cultures as crystalline structures not antagonistic to the human condition -- had more than mere historical or comparative interest (1967). They would correspond to a permanent hope for mankind. The bitter irony is that if the later arguments of Lévi-Strauss are right, the problem arises of who will there be left to use these models? The only 'out' that Lévi-Strauss offers is through music (1972), as it has characteristics that transcend history and regenerates natural and cultural domains in the manner that Orpheus was able to do. Yet his discussion of music appears less to be a solution to human entrapment in history than the musings of a scholar struck by the full force and implications of an argument rendered. While his argument is compelling, acceptance of his conclusions of inevitable demise would be the final and irreversible rejection of any vestige of humanity. Thus I intend to disagree with a scholar I greatly admire.

There are a number of considerations that offer an alternative to the dark forbodings that emanate from Lévi-Strauss' pen. The first is to use the structure of myth to again inform one of the structure of Lévi-

Strauss' "science de l'homme". As a product of a particular historical and cultural moment, Lévi-Strauss can only speak to the contradictions generated by that moment. The antecedent forces and trajectories out of the particular moment in time and space that spawned Lévi-Strauss and form the bases of the contradictions played out in his structuralism, speak to the demise of Western, industrialized civilization and not to other moments characterized by different cultural and historical traditions. One could argue that the demise of the West does not necessarily entail the demise of the East, where there appears to exist a philosophical base that conjoins natural with cultural forces and discounts and displaces the primacy of the individual, cultural being. But even here one could be clutching at straws, as the East has become progressively enveloped within the economic confines of the West, so it should be clear that Lévi-Strauss' concern with entropy is global. There is also the consideration that for one who attempts to establish a secular "science de l'homme", that there is a discernible metaphysical or metareligious base in Lévi-Strauss' writings, that is analogous to the radical christianity of Pascal and Jansen. In documenting the fall of Man from a state of natural essence, Lévi-Strauss provides a partial and temporary redemption in primitive culture, a trial of industrial civilization and a sentence of global entropy. The last part of his conclusion does not have to follow.

Let us go back to Lévi-Strauss' model of elementary structures and depart from it into the psychology of Jung and the meditation practices of Buddhism. My differing interpretation about the elementary structures of primitive culture is that they provided man with metaphor whereby he grasped a sense of coherence and unity. These symbolic systems can be considered as an expression of the mind's dictates that correspond to Jung's concern with individuation and archetypes, and the Buddhist use of meditation symbols. In other words I will argue that archetypes and meditation symbols are homologies with exactly the same functions as the elementary structures of primitive culture.

Jung argues that as the human being matures, individuation takes place whereby a public mask or image is constructed. This public mask is known as the *persona* and Jung labelled repressed functions and attitudes as our shadow. Laughlin points out that "Because adaptation to the environment necessitates a measure of selectivity, the consolidation of the ego requires the exclusion of many aspects and relegation of them to a repressed, unconscious state within our being" (Laughlin et al. 1979:6). The shadow, therefore, is the sum of all the qualities that were repressed while the ego was being built up (Jacobi 1967:38). Repression occurs because of cultural conditioning due mainly to sexual categories which are defined in an ambiguous and contradictory way (Jung 1959:9). Jung felt that the point of individuation is to bring about an increasing dialogue between ego and being, that is to say, an incorporation of more of the repressed unconscious into the domain of conscious awareness. Other concepts in Jungian thought that are relevant to my argument are the personal unconscious and collective unconscious. The former refers to the domain of repressed, conditioned material that is *culturally* specific. The collective unconscious describes material derived from the biological, genetic realm which is considered to be *species* specific. This brings me to archetypes, which are thought to be "primordial images" that express material primarily derived from the collective unconscious. Jung argues that archetypes manifest themselves in primordial images through the phenomenology of dreams, trance, myth, art and fantasy (Jung 1959:443). The implication is that the ego engages with the unconscious through the experience of archetypes. This can occur under two kinds of circumstances. The first where the archetype spontaneously "announces" its existence by providing images and symbols that the ego then experiences; the second where the calculated and deliberate use of symbols is designed to prod or *activate* the archetype (Webber 1980:34).

Jung suspected that experiences of the unconscious, particularly of archetypes, are accelerated and structured by particular symbolic ritual systems which then become powerful tools to isolate repressed material and thus bring an enormous array of unconscious images to conscious awareness. His distinction between "natural" and "artificially" induced individuation is important here. The former occurs as part of the maturing process and the individual may be unaware of what is happening. The latter, however, occurs consciously and takes the form of a deliberate and structured communication (through symbol and with the aid of a therapist, shaman or guru) with the unconscious and is designed to heal potentially dangerous splits in the psyche (Webber 1980:34; McManus 1979). The point to be established is that the notion of a deliberate, accelerated individuation through the manipulation of symbol is vital for an understanding of what the ritual practices and elementary structures of primitive cultures actually mean (d'Aquili et al. 1979).

From the perspective argued above the whole idea of homology in the elementary structures of primitive societies then becomes analogous to a symbolic metaphor whereby the conscious and the unconscious parts of the mind are linked. One can then argue that the generating base of duality, of binary opposition which is fundamental to Lévi-Strauss' entire thought, lies in the separation of the conscious from the unconscious. Once we suspect that unity and coherence in personal, societal and global terms comes about through maintaining links between these two parts of the mind, and furthermore realize that the elementary structures of primitive society were an effective means of achieving this coherence, then we begin to realize that we are stumbling across something enormously significant with respect to our own civilization. This means making an analogy between Nature as both concrete model and generating base and the notion of the unconscious as the anchor of truth and awareness.

(Nature : Culture) :: (Unconscious : Conscious)

There is of course a deeper level yet:

(Nature : Culture) :: (Brain : Mind)

which permits me to make a connection between the arguments made so far in this essay with Buddhist philosophy and practice.

Buddhist meditation practices have the function of initially taking the initiate and slowing him down to an awareness of her own natural biology. This is an essential first step in Buddhist practice, to a realization that projections, objects and constructions are nothing other than an extension of mind. The realization of the transformation of the mind's precepts, and of a coherent unity with a wider set of forces, rests with specific practices that initially root the practitioner within an awareness of his own natural biology and cycles. (The Brain : Mind connection from above is a statement relating the Natural biology of Brain with the Cultural metaphors used by Mind). Once this initial calming and awareness is achieved further meditation practice requires the selection and concentration upon particular symbols (Yidam) and sequence of symbols in order that particular experiences from the unconscious become part of the initiate's training in awareness. The process of awakening, the path to enlightenment in Buddhist practice is guided by a progressive and cumulative series of meditational encounters with the unconscious (Chang 1963; Evans-Wentz 1958; Govinda 1960). The purpose of the practice is to accelerate, via the use of symbol (Yidam), the process that Jung termed individuation. The end is a purification of the individual in the interests of healing; a by-product is the emergence of a coherent, balanced human being closely in touch with himself, other human beings and her environment.

In the Vajrayana Buddhist practice the initiate, at a particular level of training, is given a "Yidam" to concentrate on during meditation (Govinda 1960). The Yidam is a symbol, or transformation key that enables the initiate to experience latent aspects of her own consciousness. A series of Yidams have the function of taking the initiate deeper and deeper into his unconscious, so that the individual can experience fully the pure essence of the awakened mind. It is this aspect, in Buddhist teaching, that provides growth and psychic unity, a process that rounds out and enlarges the individual's psyche, potential awareness and incidentally his humanity. Thus the Yidam is an external symbol that triggers off internal models that then penetrate unconscious structures bringing them up to conscious awareness. It becomes a psychological transformation vehicle, being part of a symbolic system designed to penetrate unconscious structures that contain experience not normally available to the conscious mind. This particular realm of experience is, however, crucial for the construction of coherence and unity as Jung, Buddhist masters and shamans in primitive societies have constantly pointed out (Eliade 1964, 1969; Govinda 1960; Jung 1959). The obverse point is that without the process of bringing the unconscious into the domain of conscious awareness, enlightenment, healing, awakening, psychic balance, etc. are impossible. Instead of coherence there is chaos, breakdown and entropy at the individual, societal and global level.

This takes us back to the second issue of myth mentioned at the beginning of this essay -- that Culture unrooted in Nature constitutes a murderous, alienating and destructive force. The analogy is that the conscious unrooted in the unconscious is similarly destructive. This would imply that structuralism can be viewed as an imperfect attempt to document the traditions, structures and codes whereby a coherent sense of unity and balance was once grasped. Codes and symbolic traditions of vocabulary use define the limit and the transformational boundaries of our comprehension. Oral and symbolic traditions stretching into antiquity, such as myth, give their users a sense of coherence at the symbolic level which becomes part of personal awareness and consciousness. The *lack* of an oral symbolic tradition and of other codes then makes it necessary to first of all rationalize symbolic worldviews in terms of established religious tradition and eventually to bypass them entirely through a total secularization of life.

Primitive cultures with their elementary structures retained a sense of coherence in worldview as it had been acted out through myth and other metaphors. Primitive cultures are thus able to grasp a timeless history articulated with an eternal present. Lévi-Strauss (1967) refers to the obsessiveness of the Savage Mind in its pursuit of an eternal present. He claims that primitive man used myth as a machine to suppress history and that this attempt is unsuccessful. In this Lévi-Strauss is wrong, history is not repressed. It is viewed in a timeless manner so that coherence is achieved. It is his modelling that sets up the dichotomy between Savage Mind: Scientific Mind; his analytic preferences that limit structuralist discourse to the semiotics of binary opposition; his epistemology that prevents discussion of coherence. The position I am developing is that semiotic structuralism - Lévi-Strauss' endeavour - provides only a partial explanation for the meaning of symbolic systems in primitive cultures. It is insufficient to demonstrate a contiguous logic that appears in myth, totemism and cross-cousin marriage. One must posit something more to the elementary structures of primitive society, and this is not done by Lévi-Strauss. This means drawing on the work of Jung (1959), Piaget (1971), MacLean (1973), Laughlin and d'Aquili (1974) and being concerned with an evolutionary structuralism which focuses on neurophysiological and cognitive structures (deep structures) whereby transformations in deep structure mediate the changes taking place in surface structures (Webber 1980:12).

In this manner an implicit convergence emerges between my interpretation of elementary structures, Jung's notion of the artificially induced individuation process, and the application of Buddhist meditation practices to the process of awakening. The links between each of these endeavours are more real than apparent. Thus while I maintain that elementary structures in primitive societies are systems of symbolic metaphor I also think that these systems have an intentionality analogous to Jung's concept of artificially induced individuation and the Buddhist use of meditation symbols. The end is the construction of coherence out of chaos in order to locate man firmly within his universe of potential experience, to complete the cosmic order. To achieve this "completion" requires that cognitive and neurophysiological modelling (deep organic structure) is "worked on" by symbol in order to release unconscious structures to the level of conscious awareness (McManus 1979).

This then brings me to a different understanding of myth, cave art, totemism etc. in primitive society. Humans in primitive society populated their immediate universe -- visual, aural, tactile -- with narratives, mandalas, totem poles, masks, art, etc. which were symbolic guides, reminders of parts of the collective unconscious that had been recorded by past masters and shamans. This constant surround is to engender an implicit awareness that specific ritual sequences then trigger into explicit, conscious awareness. Thus totemism, myth, art and narrative are part of a constant ongoing preparation for specific ritual stimuli to evoke elements of the unconscious in an ongoing process of reconstruction and healing. This is what I mean by the construction of coherence out of chaos. One wonders if, in principle, it is possible to work towards this position through alternative structures and vocabularies that do not limit our present conceptual grasp of symbolic worldviews. I do believe that oral and symbolic traditions can be created, patterns of resource exploitation can be changed, alternative structures that create a balance between nature and culture, conscious and unconscious can be devised and implemented. Total change requiring immense acts of human will is, in principle, possible. Whether or not it is probable is the final test of our humanity.

This is something that I believe Mao Tse Tung clearly understood and perhaps scholars interested in China may yet be prepared to see his Cultural Revolution, not just as a violent aberration, but as an attempt to restructure the entire symbolic basis of Chinese society.

Total change, however, and whether or not it is probable is the final acid test for humanity. This will provide the answer to Lévi-Strauss' question "What is Man?"

Conclusion

The direction taken in my criticism of Lévi-Strauss' logic disagrees with his contention that man has no further adaptive capacities, that we are on a downward trajectory which involves global entropy and eventual silence. While this conclusion is alarming, I submit that the act of civilization documented by Lévi-Strauss is not the ultimate stage in the drama of Man. By knowing, we are not necessarily caught in the trap of our own history. There is still the option of total change, a willingness to absorb different codes of meaning. Whether or not we take this option *is* the final acid test. I will, however, leave the last words of this essay with Lévi-Strauss. For without total change we are haunted by the last paragraph of *L'Homme Nu*. It is an involuted prose poem, an ambiguous play on the paradoxes of our culture by a man of our culture. As he tries to escape from the significance of elementary structures one sees that the "cold" hand of primitive wisdom fails to check his "hot" rush to entropy (Lévi-Strauss 1967). In his distinction between being and non-being Lévi-Strauss arrives at a meditation on nothingness, which at the same time is a metaphor for our humanity, a rebuke to our lack of consciousness:

"C'est a dire rien."

Acknowledgment

Critical comments from Bob Depew and Linda Rayner, graduate students at Carleton University stimulated the construction of this essay. I also drew a great deal from the eloquence of George Steiner's Plaunt Memorial lectures at Carleton in 1972. Colleagues at Carleton - John Cove, and Jacques Chevalier and the opportunity of discourse with gifted students such as Mark Webber provided the stimulus to complete the endeavour. I would like to acknowledge these debts while absolving all parties from the positions they could not persuade me to abandon! I am also grateful to Tarchin, Buddist monk, for his patience.

Notes

1. I am grateful to Bob Depew for his critical review of an earlier draft of this essay. He drew my attention to Rousseau and helped to clarify the main issues of this stage of the argument.

Bibliography

d'Aquili, E.G., C.D. Laughlin and J. McManus
1979 (eds.): The Spectrum of Ritual. N.Y.: Columbia University Press

Ardener, E.
1971 The New Anthropology and its Critics. Man 6, 3:449-467

Chang, G.C.
1963 Teachings of Tibetan Yoga. Secausus, New Jersey: Citadel Press

Eliade, M.
1964 Shamanism: Archaic Techniques of Ecstasy. Princeton: Princeton University Press

1969 Yoga: Immortality and Freedom (2nd edition). Princeton: Princeton University Press

Evans-Wentz, W.Y.
1958 Tibetan Yoga and Secret Doctrines. N.Y.: Oxford University Press

Govinda, A.
1960 Foundations of Tibetan Mysticism. N.Y.: Weiser

Jacobi, J.
1967 The Way of Individuation. N.Y.: New American Library

Jones, E.
1961 The Life and Work of Sigmund Freud. N.Y.: Basic Books

Jung, C.G.
1959 The Archetypes and the Collective Unconscious. The Collected Works of C.G. Jung, V.9. Princeton: Princeton University Press

Laughlin, C.D. and E.G. d'Aquili
1974 Biogenetic Structuralism. N.Y.: Columbia University Press

Laughlin, C.D., J. McManus and M. Webber
1979 Neurognosis, Individuation and Tibetan Arising Yoga Practise. Paper presented to Canadian Ethnological Society, Banff, Alberta.

Leach, E.
1979 Lévi-Strauss. London: Fontana

Leroi-Gourhan, E.
1963 Préhistoire de l'Art Occidental. Paris: Plon

Lévi-Strauss, C.
1958 L'Analyse Structurale des Mythes, In Anthropologie Structurale. Paris: Plon

1961 Tristes Tropiques (trans. by John Russell). N.Y.: Atheneum

1962 La Pensée Sauvage. Paris: Plon

1963 Structural Anthropology. N.Y.: Basic Books

1964 Mythologiques I: Le Cru et le Cuit. Paris: Plon

1966 Mythologiques II: Du Miel aux Cendres. Paris: Plon

1967 The Scope of Anthropology. London: Cape

1968 Mythologiques III: L'Origine des Manières de Table. Paris: Plon

1972 Mythologiques IV: L'Homme Nu. Paris: Plon

MacLean, P.D.
1973 A Triune Concept of the Brain and Behaviour. Toronto: University of Toronto Press

McManus, J.
1979 Ritual and Human Social Cognition. In d'Aquili, E.G., C.D. Laughlin and J. McManus (eds.): The Spectrum of Ritual. N.Y.: Columbia University Press

Piaget, J.
1971 Biology and Knowledge. Chicago: University of Chicago Press

Prattis, J.I.
1972 Science, Ideology and False Demons - a Commentary on Lévi-Strauss' Critiques. American Anthropologist, 74:1322-1325

Rossi, I.
1973 The Unconscious in the Anthropology of Claude Lévi-Strauss. American Anthropologist 75, 1973:20-48

Selby, H.
1969 Continuities and Prospects in Anthropological Studies. Bulletin of the American Anthropological Association. September, 1969

Steiner, G.
1972 Plaunt Memorial Lectures. Carleton University

Webber, M.
1980 Ritual: A Model of Symbol Penetration. M.A. Thesis, Carleton University

Weber, M.
1958 The Protestant Ethic and the Spirit of Capitalism. N.Y.: Charles Scribner's Sons

Chapter 2

Prelude to Parsifal and Semiotic Structuralism

Ivan Brady

Marking his poetic interests in this volume as a conflict of interpretations, Ian Prattis slips through the vines of art and science and returns us to the ambiguous problems of the subjective, the intentionality of meaning, and how interpretation might best proceed in certain circumstances. His contribution turns on different readings of the myth of Parsifal and the Quest for the Holy Grail, which Prattis learned as a child and in which he finds a linkage to a Celtic world he knows quite intuitively but thoroughly. The structuralist reading of Parsifal's "tale" in Claude Lévi-Strauss' "Mythologique" (i.e., as a symmetrical inversion of the Oedipus myth) is not convincing or complete to Prattis -- it is not something that he recognizes as authentic or that he agrees with analytically. He provides instead what he describes as a "mythopoetic" reading. The discrepancy between the two readings is the focus of this chapter.

Through the understanding of Carl Jung and the art of the German filmmaker Hans Jürgen Sybeberg, Prattis addresses what he considers to be a problem of existential universality in the Parsifal myth. He finds this great human drama to be about the male quest for "Christ Consciousness" in Western societies, access to which, he says, comes through experience that integrates the self with the symbolic complex of the feminine archetype Jung called *anima*. Where Lévi-Strauss' methodology "necessarily displaces the experience of both subject and object", Prattis demonstrates the centrality of the subject. In this treatment Parsifal is not simply a "problem" among the characters whose reality and concreteness are realized through the readers' own subjectivity. Part of all problems of communication, Prattis and Jung and Wagner would remind us, is that of "communication with the self". In Prattis' reading of Lévi-Strauss' reading of Parsifal, there is no such communication. What is missing, Prattis argues, is mythopoetic understanding, a reinstatement of the primacy of the subject in the study of language and culture, and a refocusing on historical action over structure, of *parole* over *langue* -- some things likely to be lost easily in certain kinds of structural inquiries.

Prattis sees in the variations of the eight-hundred year telling of the Parsifal myth an insistence that "we humans shift into a higher consciousness". Rather than feign satisfaction with a shallow "external view that finds the significance of the Parsifal myth in a structural inversion of relations", he suggest that "one both take an internal view that considers symbols as vehicles of personal transformation and an external view that places this phenomenon within a set of reference points". Echoing in this the spirit, if not the letter of Wilfred Cantwell Smith, Prattis would have us move to a deeper understanding of the integrity of critical self-consciousness, that is, a commitment to "knowledge which goes beyond the limitations of misplaced objectivity ... and mere subjectivity" (Coward and Royce 1981:129). Such humanistic and poetic claims to knowledge require two kinds of validation to be analytically (as opposed to just personally) satisfying; they "must be validated both by the persons directly involved and by external critical observers" (Coward and Royce 1981: 129). "A mythopoetic analysis requires an amalgam of such experience", Prattis says, plus "the facility to suspend disbelief sufficiently to enter into and comprehend phenomenologically someone else's symbolic system." Unsympathetic readings that substitute various forms of impersonal analysis for those judged to be more personally authentic only exacerbate the problem.

One of several conclusions that might be drawn from this effort is that a mythopoetic message requires a mythopoetic reading for proper interpretation. Aggressive "misreading" or naïve compression into abstract analytic forms, other language games, or exotic cultural costumes, insofar as those things can be known and controlled, are to be conscientiously avoided. And that requires a certain frame of mind for realization. It puts a premium on poetic form, media, and cultural preparation in an effort to preserve phenomenological integrity as much as possible; to speak the language of the object of inquiry, to hear its sounds, move its moves, and immerse self-consciously -- subjectively and poetically -- into its meanings. That puts a burden on comparative readings by other individuals, for their experiences are bound to be different. Deciding at *which* level(s) there might be subjective and comparative agreement is a matter of argument such as Prattis has made. Some impoverishing losses of translation will still be unavoidable, for analyzing a myth (or poem) from any perspective changes it, as does confining it to writing: under the gaze of the "science of reading ... like an animal long since captured and held in observation," Barthes (1977:166) has noted, myth becomes "a different object". As a contemporary vehicle, myth is discontinuous: where it is "no longer expressed in long fixed narratives but only in 'discourse'", contemporary myth becomes at most "a *phraseology*, a corpus of phrases (of stereotypes)". The myth disappears and leaves, "so much the more insidious -- the *mythical*" (1977:165).

Furthermore, the fact that we try to avoid unnecessary distortions of symbolically coded empirical reality in the study of myth is in this case doubly slippery: for the function of myth, Barthes says, "is to distort, not to make disappear." In that respect Barthes would agree with Prattis' ontological privileging of *parole* over *langue*, of the emphasis on the symbolic and historical action of discourse and performance over the synchronic structure of language. But he would also deny that Prattis' deep hermeneutic reading, especially for the discovery of "psychological" principles -- Prattis' effort to close the historical distance between the Lost and the Found, the Self and the Other in the "Christ Consciousness" of the Parsifal myth -- can be privileged necessarily over a concentration on surface structure. For Barthes, "myth hides nothing"; "surface is as telling as depth" (see Sontag 1982:xvii), although they say different things. There is room for at least three voices and a conjunction here: Lévi-Strauss, Prattis and Barthes, all centered on the long-run versions of Parsifal -- and this is to say nothing of the influence of our own voices as readers and critics of the meta-texts of each analyst. As in all interpretations of interpretations, the conjunction of these structures is quite evidently crowded. We can be equally sure that a strictly structuralist monologue fails to unlock the greatly polyphonic Parsifal on several counts. (See also Boon 1972, 1982; Detienne 1979, 1986; Izard and Smith 1982; Dundes 1984; LeRoy 1985.)

Bibliography

Barthes, R.
1977 Image, Music, Text (trans. by S. Heath). N.Y.: Hill and Wang

Boon
1972 From Symbolism to Structuralism: Lévi-Strauss in a Literary Tradition. N.Y.: Harper and Row

1982 Other Tribes, Other Scribes: Symbolic Anthropology in the Comparative Study of Cultures, Histories, Religions and Texts. Cambridge: Cambridge University Press

Coward, H.G. and J.R. Royce
1981 Toward an Epistemological Basis for Humanistic Psychology. In J.R. Royce and P. Leendert (eds.): Humanistic Psychology. N.Y.: Plenum

Detienne, M.

1979 Dionysus Slain. Baltimore: Johns Hopkins University Press

1986 The Creation of Mythology. Chicago: University of Chicago Press.

Dundes, A.

1984 Sacred Narrative: Readings in the Theory of Myth. Berkeley: University of California Press

Izard, M. and P. Smith

1982 Between Belief and Transgression: Structuralist Essays in Religion, History and Myth. Chicago: University of Chicago Press

LeRoy, J.

1985 Fabricated World: An Interpretation of Kewa Tales. Vancouver: University of British Columbia Press

Sontag, S.

1982 A Barthes Reader. N.Y.: Hill and Wang

Parsifal and Semiotic Structuralism

> Psychology as religion implies imagining all psychological events as effects of gods in the soul, and all activities to do with the soul, such as therapy, to be operations of ritual in relation to these gods ... It is not a question of religion turning to psychology -- no, psychology is simply going home.[1]
>
> (James Hillman, *Re-Visioning Psychology*)

The legend of Parsifal and the Quest for the Holy Grail has been one of my favourite stories since boyhood. The many versions I have encountered have never failed to fascinate and ignite the imagination. The long acquaintance with the story and the personal cultural tendrils that take me into the Celtic world are sufficient (and indeed necessary) to recognize an adequate treatment of the material when it is presented. Such a recognition was not forthcoming in my reading of Claude Lévi-Strauss' discourse on the myth (1985: 219-234). However, my respect for Lévi-Strauss' immense contribution to scholarship remains constant. It is the inspiration for this chapter. I would simply like to provide an alternative reading of this myth that is a more appropriate homology for the symbolic significance of Parsifal's wanderings.

In the first section of this chapter I outline the axioms inherent in Lévi-Strauss' structuralism and mark their inadequacy for a full treatment of myth and symbol. An alternative viewpoint is presented to introduce a phenomenological basis to interpret the transformative power of symbols described by myth. Then with two major assertions I place the Parsifal myth within the context of the male quest for Christ Consciousness in Western civilization; and I argue that access to this form of consciousness comes through experience with the symbolic complex of the feminine archetype. (A synopsis of the Parsifal myth is given in the appendix to this chapter.) A number of the ideas of Carl Jung are developed and then applied to the Parsifal story to demonstrate an eight-hundred year insistence, through the many variants of this legend, that we humans shift into a higher consciousness. The final threads of argument are drawn together by contrasting two different interpretations of Wagner's opera on Parsifal -- one by Lévi-Strauss and one of my own, drawing on Hans Jürgen Sybeberg's 1981 film of the opera for supporting evidence.

Lévi-Strauss and Parsifal

Lévi-Strauss proposes a universal model of "Parsifal"-type myths that he claims have an inverted symmetry with another universal model -- the "Oedipal" myths. Lévi-Strauss argues that:

> The Oedipal myths pose the problem of communication that is at first exceptionally effective (the solving of the riddle) but then leads to excess in the form of incest -- the sexual union of people who ought to be distant from one another -- and of plague, which ravages Thebes by accelerating and disrupting the great natural cycles. On the other hand, the Percevalian myths deal with communication interrupted in three ways: the answer offered to an unasked question (which is the opposite of a riddle); the chastity required of one or more heroes (contrary to incestuous behaviour); and the wasteland -- that is, the halting of the natural cycles that ensure the fertility of plants, animals and human beings (1985:231).

He later adds:

> These two types illustrate the two complementary solutions that human beings have devised for two problems of communication. One problem is excessive communication, too direct, too rapid and therefore fatally virulent; the other problem is an overly slow, if not interrupted communication, which causes inertia and sterility (1985:233).

These kinds of conclusions are to be expected once we understand the structure inherent in Lévi-Strauss' work. In the previous chapter on *Man and Metaphor* I outlined the premises that are axiomatic for structuralism. I would like to add that in the semiotic structuralist approach that Lévi-Strauss has developed, categories are identified in order to gain intellectual access to relations between phenomena, thence proceeding to an examination of relations between sets of relations (d'Aquili et al. 1979:388). Structuralism attributes meaning to signs and categories not in any absolute sense but in terms of relations and mutual dependence. In rejecting the primacy of the subject in language and by concentrating on *langue* at the expense of *parole*, structuralism has evolved to a preoccupation with, and identification of, states of the linguistic system. All signs are attributed to a closed system and their meaning is to be interpreted in terms of a system of relations that ignore whatever the sign may have initially referred to. Culler (1973:35) has pointed out that structuralism's point of departure is to locate meaning entirely within this notion of relation. Paul Ricoeur contends that structuralism "involves a view from without; it is not concerned with the relation of the subject to phenomena but only with the relations among phenomena themselves" (1967:801). For these reasons, Lévi-Strauss' interpretation of the Parsifal myth takes on a fairly predictable form. Although I think he is mistaken in his reading of it, my main objection has to do with the limited kinds of conclusions that his method of inquiry inevitably produces.

His decoding of the myth and proposed inversion to Oedipal-type myths relegates the symbolic richness of this story to the cutting-room floor and, in my opinion, totally misses the purpose of the myth. To understand the Parsifal story one has to explore the symbolic richness *within* each category and metaphor, as well as between categories, and recognize what this story has to say about and for our civilization. It is no accident that the Grail myth has inspired poets, iconographers, scientists, scholars, literati, opera and film makers since it was written by Chrétien de Troyes in the twelfth-century. Variants of the earlier text include Wagner's nineteenth-century opera, Sybeberg's twentieth-century film, and Wolfram von Eschenbach's elaborate medieval poem. Reference to any one of these reconstructions requires that one take both an internal view that considers symbols as vehicles of personal transformation and an external view that places this phenomenon within a set of reference points. In other words, eight-hundred years of attention to this story demand more than an external view that finds the significance of the Parsifal myth in a structural inversion of Oedipal relations.

Mythopoetics and Parsifal

My starting point in presenting an alternative view is the unconscious, not from a Lévi-Straussian source, but through the development of a number of ideas on symbolism inherent in the work of Carl Jung[2] and also through my personal experience of the transformative power of symbols.[3] This latter consideration is difficult to communicate precisely but does lie in the domain of what Husserl meant by "bracketing" (1960, 1970:291ff). Bracketing assumes first of all the recognition that there is a reciprocal feedback relationship between cognition and perception (Merleau-Ponty 1962); furthermore, it assumes that the events/texts/realities that a scholar engages with are perceived within the framework of that scholar's particular state of conscious awareness (Tart 1975); and, finally, it assumes that an understanding of perceived reality requires a "suspension of disbelief" so that one may bracket one's self from the phenomena under consideration and - insofar as it is possible - prevent one's own conditioning from interpreting the reality in axioms that may well be inappropriate. This phenomenological dimension is an attempt to determine the significance of phenomena from within and accepts Husserl's idea of intentionality, which defines the subject as a "bearer of intentionality, giving him not a Nature but placing him as a maker of meaning" (Ricoeur 1963:600). This is particularly important in any analytical discourse in the domain of myth and symbol.

I have noted elsewhere (1985:274) that:

> At a simple level there is the notion that if anthropologists study someone else's symbolic language and do not attempt to put it in a comparable symbolic language of their own then the sense perceptions of the sensuality, colour, pathos and tragedy of field observations are deleted and the necessary "clicks" of comprehension are not there. What is actually communicated can be an arid and erroneous reckoning of reality.

What this amounts to is an argument that conceptual clarity in reading and analyzing texts calls for the scholar to be able to code and understand symbolic transformation phenomenologically. This provides a clarity that permits the scholar to see through the false intellectualism of analytic formulas that have little or nothing to do with the direct experience of the scholar as subject or his or her experience of the observed as object. A mythopoetic analysis requires an amalgam of such experience and the facility to suspend disbelief sufficiently to enter into and comprehend phenomenologically someone else's symbolic system (Laughlin, McManus and Shearer 1982). So that the reader may directly anticipate my argument and then respond critically to the direction I am proposing, let me state in two blocks of assertions what I think the Grail myth is fundamentally about. I will then proceed to provide conceptual support for these assertions.

(1) The Grail symbolizes a transcendental consciousness (Ring 1974) that can be translated into a culturally and historically specific concern with Christ Consciousness, specifically that of twelfth-century Europe. The term Christ Consciousness does, in the twentieth-century, carry a value-laden reaction that must simply be anticipated in this chapter. From the perspective taken in this work both transcendental and Christ Consciousness are to be regarded as energy forms. Furthermore, I assert that particular symbols (or complexes of symbols) provide entry gates to the experience of these energy forms. Finally, encounters through symbols with the energy form carry with them incipient transformative experiences for individuals. These assertions are basic to a mythopoetic unravelling of what the Parsifal story is all about. In other words, the experience of Christ Consciousness is a state of perception and cognition that can be

arrived at by integrating the self with particular symbols. Archetypes, meditation mandalas, and initiation rites all provide symbolic gateways to a differing state of perception and cognition once self and symbol achieve integration. This can occur spontaneously and also be intentionally induced (Stephen 1986:14). The significance of symbols and their integration through experience is that unconscious structures can be penetrated and brought up to conscious awareness (Prattis 1984; Webber 1980; d'Aquili et al. 1979).

The particular symbolic complex used will of course vary from culture to culture, but I must emphasize that there is much more to it than Geertz would advocate with his thesis of cognitive coherence of a perceived system of meanings (see Geertz 1973; Stephen 1986:40). There is a common process whereby integration between self and symbol produces a coherence between unconscious truths, which are universal, and ritual procedures, which are culturally specific (see Bourguignon 1968; Hilgard 1977; Peters and Price-Williams 1983; Eliade 1964; Govinda 1960). The complex cognitive process that obtains between ritual procedures and unconscious imagery brings us to a different understanding of symbolic systems in both primitive and modern society. This is what I refer to as "the construction of coherence out of chaos" (1984:201). Kracke's (1986) work on the dialectics between self and cultural symbols among the Kagwahiv and Tedlock's (1986) views on cultural symbolism and dreaming have latent similarities with this approach.

(2) The Parsifal story speaks not only to a particular time/space conjunction but to trajectories and evolutions beyond it. The significance of this theme will be elaborated later. The reader is alerted at the moment to the insight that Chrétien de Troyes' work anticipated by eight-hundred years the holistic teachings of Jung and postmodern philosophy.

The story establishes that for the male in Western civilization the most important initial gateway to Christ Consciousness is through the feminine archetype (Jung 1959), which can be symbolized in many different ways and was referred to by Jung as the anima. This is what the Parsifal story is about -- the male quest for Christ Consciousness through encountering and integrating with different levels of the feminine archetype. There are many manifestations of this symbolic complex in the various Parsifal stories -- Blanche Fleur, maiden who laughs, female chalice bearer, damsels in distress, the old hag, the seducing maidens, Kundry, and so on. For the sake of brevity and clarity, I will deal extensively with only one manifestation of the female archetypal complex in this story -- that of Blanche Fleur, who is relegated to several lines in Lévi-Strauss' treatment of the myth:

> ...he rescues the lady of a manor who is being besieged, delivers her from her enemies, and forms a tender bond with her... He puts off his marriage plans (1985:222).

> ...a wild goose that has been wounded by a falcon lets three drops of its blood fall upon the snow. This contrast reminds Percival of the fair complexion and vermilion lips of his beloved (1985: 223).

As will become clear, the significance of these sentences is not something that can be fully drawn out by Lévi-Strauss' conceptual preferences because his methodology necessarily displaces the experience of both subject and object. This is part of my contention that Lévi-Strauss has misread the myth. His method of semiotic structuralism takes him past the keystones inherent in the story.

Jung and Symbol

Before I examine the myth, let me introduce some strategic concepts from Carl Jung's work. Jung assumed that the human psyche was androgynous, being composed of both masculine and feminine elements. He distinguished three major levels of the human psyche: (1) conscious awareness; (2) the personal unconscious; and (3) the collective unconscious, and one major process -- that of individuation. Individuation encourages the emergence of a balanced psyche through an ever-increasing dialogue between conscious awareness and the personal and collective unconscious (1959:283-342). The personal unconscious according to Jung:

> consists firstly of all those contacts that become unconscious either because they lost their intensity and were forgotten or because consciousness was withdrawn from them (repression), and secondly of contacts, some of them sense impressions, which never had sufficient

> intensity to reach consciousness but have somehow entered the psyche (1959:283-342).

The personal unconscious thus refers to the domain of repressed, conditioned material that is culturally specific (see Prattis 1984:198). Of particular importance in this domain is a culture's definition of sex categories and the assertion made by Jung about the androgynous nature of the human psyche. It provides a clue as to why Parsifal in the Holy Grail myth is so thick, such an unaware clod, and as such represents the state of male awareness in Western consciousness. Let me elaborate on this.

Every culture, including our own, subjects its members to specifics of sex role education that then become entrenched through social mores and cultural conditioning. To conform to these constraints and to develop the appropriate social mask -- the persona -- males are usually required to repress the female energy within their psyche and females the male energy within theirs. Given Jung's assumption that the psyche is composed of both male and female structures and energies, social and cultural conditioning produces a repression that has to be reversed if individuation is to produce a healthy and balanced psyche. Also given that the feminine element relates to intuition and feeling while the male element is referred to in terms of logos, individual males in their development of a socially appropriate persona repress and relegate aspects of intuition and feeling that constrain their transformation to a more conscious awareness. In other words they are severely restrained in integrating the separate parts of their androgynous psyche, simply because the properties required for such integration have been repressed. Jung felt that the point of individuation was to bring about an increasing dialogue between conscious awareness and the full potential of being human, through an incorporation of ever-increasing amounts of the repressed unconscious into the domain of conscious awareness. For the male this implies an incorporation of those feminine elements repressed in the personal unconscious and furthermore with that complex of feminine symbols to be found in the collective unconscious -- the anima.

The collective unconscious according to Jung (1971) is, "the ancestral heritage of possibilities of representation...it is not individual but common to all men...and it is the true basis of the individual psyche." He goes on to state that:

> The collective unconscious -- so far as we can say anything about it at all -- appears to consist of mythological motifs or primordial images, for which reason the myths of all nations are its real exponents. In fact the whole of mythology could be taken as a projection of the collective unconscious (Jung 1971:39).

A further discussion of Jung's ideas on archetypal experience and symbols, and his distinction between "natural" and "artificially induced" individuation, is contained in Chapter 1, *Man and Metaphor*. In this previous chapter I show how the individuation process is designed to heal potentially dangerous splits in the psyche. In my opinion the most dangerous of all the potential splits is the separation of male and female energies. And here lies the significance of myth, particularly the one that sustains the writing of this chapter. In the genesis and telling of myths there is a process of natural individuation. Myths are spontaneous presentations from the unconscious of psychological and spiritual truths, rich sources of psychological insight, and a special kind of literature (Johnson 1977:2). While myth-making clearly belongs to the domain of "natural" individuation, the understanding and communication of the inner meaning of a myth belongs to the category of "accelerated" individuation, whereby we learn the lessons of the myth and the directions indicated and incorporate these lessons and directions within our everyday lives, so that our conscious awareness grasps and acts upon the deeply unconscious spiritual questions of life.

Blanche Fleur, Christ Consciousness, and Parsifal

Recall my assertion that the Parsifal story is about the male quest for Christ Consciousness in Western civilization and that the path for this lies through integrating conscious awareness with the feminine archetype. The Grail outlines how individuation takes place in a man's psyche and the important emphasis throughout is that the emergence or transformation of the male occurs through the struggle to integrate consciously with his inner femininity -- the complex of symbols in the archetypal pattern labelled as anima by Jung. An integral part of this pattern in the myth is occupied by the figure of Blanche Fleur, and here I deal with the same passages referred to by Lévi-Strauss (1985:222- 223) in an attempt to demonstrate what can be seen through a mythopoetic lens rather than "The View from Afar" - Lévi-Strauss' semiotic structuralist focus (1985).

Parsifal encounters Blanche Fleur in the story when her castle is besieged and she appeals to him for succour. He responds, defeats her enemies and provides her with freedom. He then spends the night with her in a chaste union. Chrétien de Troyes portrays a touching gentleness in how they lay in an embrace head to head,shoulder to shoulder, hip to hip, knee to knee, and toe to toe (Johnson 1977:29). This gentleness is a guide for maleness -- a direction that access to the inner feminine is through the Parsifal nature in a man, the naïve foolishness that is manifested through gentleness and tenderness. These characteristics are a prerequisite for the inner encounter with this part of the female archetype and provide the most important narrative in the entire myth. It is also a most difficult lesson and therefore very easily and conveniently forgotten. The forgetting, however, prevents an integration between the masculine and feminine elements in the male psyche. Carol Pearson (1986:90) has pointed out that, "Men appropriately have asserted their own truths in the world, but the suppression of the female voice leaves the culture dangerously lopsided". The overemphasis on the male principle and the neglect of the female prevents individuation, which is the process whereby the recognition of the androgynous nature of the human psyche is secured by being brought to conscious awareness. This permits clarity, balance, and further transformation (Pearson 1986:144).

The Parsifal story illuminates this clearly as Parsifal forgets about Blanche Fleur and descends into a grimness that prevents him from finding his path to the Grail. His access to the Grail is through the feminine and this he abandons as he roams the countryside doing what knights in armor are socially and culturally constrained to do. He is basically stupid, a clod in terms of awareness of his task. He has forgotten entirely about Blanche Fleur, and his Parsifal nature -- gentle naïveté -- until a falcon attacks three geese in the air and wounds one of them. Three drops of blood fall from the wounded goose onto the snow and put Parsifal into a trance of reverie as he remembers his encounter with Blanche Fleur. He is released from his trance when two of the drops of blood melt in the snow, and one remains He can now function again and is hailed as a hero at King Arthur's court for his deeds in battle; but once again he loses touch with and forgets the significance of his encounter with Blanche Fleur.

The anima when neglected turns ugly. It was insistent through Blanche Fleur that Parsifal lift the siege to her castle, break the constraints and conventions of life's conditioning, and approach his inner femininity through his gentle, naïve, and foolish nature. He did this once and was then on track for the Grail, but he lost it by being unaware of the significance of his encounter with Blanche Fleur. At King Arthur's court, where he is being lionized for his deeds in battle, the dreadful old hag riding a crippled mule -- a darker manifestation of the anima complex -- harangues him in front of the court about his misdeeds, his stupidity, cruelty, lack of awareness of his actions, and the neglect of his quest for the Grail. The hag sends all the knights of the Round Table, including Parsifal, out once more to quest the Grail -- to experience Christ Consciousness. But once more Parsifal and the other knights lose it, alienated from the encounter with their internal femininity.

Emma Jung and Marie-Louise von Franz (1960) refer to the multi-level meaning of Parsifal's encounter with Blanche Fleur. Blanche Fleur personified the "oppressed beauty in need of deliverance", specifically a "man's own individual femininity, the anima" (1960:64). The ability to integrate with this symbolic reminder of the internal feminine is not highly developed in the male and this is what the story repeatedly alludes to. Emma Jung is quite insistent that the anima for males is the designated mediator between conscious awareness and the unconscious (E. Jung 1957:56). Parsifal forgets the significance of his anima encounter, remains in unawareness, and loses sight of his quest for the Holy Grail until he is set on track again by the anima turned ugly -- the hideous hag on the crippled mule.

Jung and von Franz (1960:183) note of Parsifal's leaving Blanche Fleur that:

> he did not realize the emotional suffering that he was thereby imposing both on her and on himself. His real offense lay in the primitive unambiguousness of his behaviour, which arose from unawareness of the inner problem of the opposites. *It was not what he did but that he was not capable of assessing what he did.* His one-sided attitude accords with an identification with the masculine logos principle, whereby the emotional and feeling side of the anima, the conflict and suffering which result from such an attitude are not given sufficient consideration.

The authors interpret the wounded goose and the drops of blood in the snow as the image of the suffering anima and this is what brings Blanche Fleur back to Parsifal's memory. But since he does not recognize the significance of his encounter with her, preferring to be lionized by King Arthur's court for his adeptness in violence, the suffering anima turns ugly at his neglect and unawareness and appears to him as the hideous hag who confronts him with all his failures.

Despite the hag's strictures and directions, Parisfal wanders for years in a fog of disarray until close to the end of the myth when he once more remembers Blanche Fleur and the Grail and receives absolution from a hermit who provides direction to the Grail castle. And here the poem by Chrétien de Troyes stops, possibly because there was nothing more to be said at that time (Johnson 1977:72). Now there is much more to communicate. This myth contains a directive for our civilization of logos and masculine structures: access to Christ Consciousness is through the integration of male selfhood with the feminine archetype. But we may be no further toward this achievement than when the Parsifal myth first appeared as a text in the twelfth-century.

If we wish to examine the inner meaning of this myth from the perspective of accelerated individuation, the lesson is to understand our Parsifal nature, the gentle naïve fool within males, as this is the only avenue that may engage with the symbolic complex of inner femininity. This is the theme explicitly explored in the Parsifal myth. The chaste union between Parsifal and Blanche Fleur is a reminder that the human psyche is androgynous, composed of male and female structures and energies. Transformation of the individual is through a progressive process of individuation that integrates male and female energy in the psyche and then provides access through the feminine gateway (archetype) to the Grail -- Christ Consciousness.

This twelfth-century poem still provides us with a story for our times. We no longer talk about Holy Grails and castles but we are concerned with consciousness and the madness inherent in many of the structures that encase our world. Perhaps it is a male madness that requires a Blanche Fleur and allied representatives of the feminine archetype to tutor it, but the story clearly indicates that such a tutoring requires a particular aspect of maleness to come to the fore -- gentleness, naïveté and foolishness.

In this way the Parsifal myth anticipates by eight-hundred years an insistence that the species evolve. The transformation of masculine energy and the fine tuning of feminine energy to this transformation is what the story is about. It could just have easily been written by a contemporary radical scholar - Bohm (1980) in physics, Sheldrake (1981) in chemistry, Toulmin (1982) in theology, or Hillman (1975) in psychology - anticipating that relationships for the new era require that masculine and feminine not be regarded as antagonistic and separated energies but as complementary facets of the same unity.

Lévi-Strauss and Parsifal - A Drawing Together of Threads

Lévi-Strauss' interpretation of the Parsifal myth as a symmetrical inversion of the Oedipus myth is, from this perspective, unconvincing and incomplete. It is the only interpretation, however, that his methodological and conceptual preferences allow. The semiotic structuralism of Lévi-Strauss provides only a partial explanation for the meaning of symbolic systems, particularly of myths. One cannot understand the anima with intellect and logos alone. It is insufficient to demonstrate a contiguous logic in myth, totemism, and cross-cousin marriage in order to identify common characteristics of elementary structures. The semiotic structure of the unconscious, which is where Lévi-Strauss starts and ends, excludes the possibility that symbolic metaphor has an intentionality; it excludes the possibility that the creativity of modelling located in the unconscious accepts coherence and completeness as the natural ordering of things rather than the entropic future portrayed in Lévi-Strauss' *L'Homme Nu* (see Prattis 1984:191ff).[4]

In other words, the generating base of duality -- the binary oppositions fundamental to Lévi-Strauss' thought -- can be thought of as the separation of the conscious from the unconscious. Mythology, especially the example used in this essay, provides key guidelines for the reintegration of conscious and unconscious domains in order that dangerous splits in the psyche can be healed. Once we decide that coherence and integration of the human psyche lies in a dialectical link between these parts of the mind, and that mythology provides an effective guide for such integration, then we may be discovering something enormously significant with respect to our own civilization.[5]

In Lévi-Strauss' treatment of the Parsifal myth, it is clear that something crucial is missing: it is the exploration of the symbolic richness *within* categories as well as a different conceptualization about the significance of relations *between* categories. The male awareness (ego) - anima (archetype) relationship and its transformation permits comprehension of an evolving state of affairs and a credible reading of the Parsifal myth. The ongoing dialectic in sexual symbolism found in myth, ritual, and symbolism everywhere directs our attention to a separation of masculine and feminine components in conscious and unconscious domains respectively. Jung's concepts of the collective unconscious and individuation permit us to address a constant cross-cultural process that Lévi-Strauss' conceptual preferences do not. As Culler (1973:61) points out, "if structural analysis is to make sense as an intellectual enterprise it must specify clearly what are the facts about human experience which it attempts to explicate. Such a sense involves coming to grips with the experience of the Other -- myth-maker, native informant -- and transmuting that experience with the phenomenology of self so that a credible text of interpretation may emerge."

Wagner

In his analysis of the Parsifal myth, Lévi-Strauss devotes a great deal of attention to Richard Wagner's treatment of the legend in his opera *Parsifal*. It is only proper that I do the same -- to work with the same material but to provide a more credible interpretation. My source of inspiration is, however, different. The source I draw on, as mentioned previously, is that remarkable interpreter of German myth-making, Hans Jürgen Sybeberg. I introduce Sybeberg's film of Richard Wagner's opera partly because Lévi-Strauss makes so much of Wagner's exegesis of the Parsifal myth but mostly because Sybeberg is able to interpret the German myth motifs used by Wagner from the inside, both as subject and object -- a privilege that Lévi-Strauss' semiotic preferences does not permit.

Lévi-Strauss alludes to Wagner's interpretation of the Parsifal story in laudatory terms: "His solution to the problems posed by the mythology of the Grail is powerfully original...Wagner had intuitively grasped a scheme that he rethought, reorganized and transformed in the course of time" (1985:255). Lévi-Strauss presents Wagner's motif as follows:

> Communication is assured or re-established not by intellectual operation but by an emotional identification. Parsifal does not *understand* the riddle of the Grail and remains unable to solve it until he *relives* the catastrophe at its source. This catastrophe was a rupture; and because the hero feels it in his flesh, the rupture is located no longer only between the natural and supernatural worlds, but now between the emotions and the intelligence, between suffering humanity and other forms of life, between earthly and spiritual values (1985:231).

This concern with communication axioms is confused and misplaced. Lévi-Strauss' analysis does refer to the phenomenological resolutions of Parsifal as object -- Parsifal "*relives*", "*feels it in his flesh*". But this concern with experience is at odds with his own axioms. An alternative reading of Wagner's opera is therefore necessary.

Sybeberg directed a film of Wagner's *Parsifal* in 1981 and added yet more richness to an already overloaded symbolic feast. One of his major innovations was to have two Parsifals -- one masculine (Parsifal I) played by Michael Kutter, and one feminine (Parsifal II) played by Karin Krick. Neither performer was an opera singer or an actor and, moreover, each knew very little about Wagner. Sybeberg met them at a dinner party at the home of some friends in Switzerland and promptly engaged them to play the role of Parsifal. The East German heldentenor, Reiner Goldberg, sings both their roles to dramatic effect.

In the second act, the female Parsifal (II) first appears at a most critical juncture in terms of my reading of this opera. The male Parsifal (I) has resisted the temptations of the seducing flower maidens. He is stopped by Kundry's voice calling him by his name, Parsifal. This is the first time he recognizes his own name and identity. Kundry embraces him and is then thrust away by Parsifal. Her kiss brings him to self knowledge and it is at this point that he understands everything; the mysteries he has witnessed and the sense of his mission to quest the Grail. At this point of realization the Parsifal played by Karin Krick, looking like a young Joan of Arc, walks up behind the young innocent boy Parsifal (Michael Kutter). They are both singing but it is one voice that comes through, the heldentenor of Reiner Goldberg. Karin Krick steps in front of Michael Kutter and his Parsifal slowly steps back and fades out of the film.

Karin Krick's Parsifal then holds sway for the remainder of this remarkable production. She demonstrates that it is the resistance to seduction, the turning away of violence (Klingsor's Sacred Lance), and the presentation of the male Parsifal's nature through self knowledge, that permits the inner feminine to be accessed. The inner feminine can only be reached through a gentleness hitherto not portrayed by the male Parsifal (I). The anima complex has been released to conscious awareness once the male ego/anima relationship is chaste, gentle, and tender. Sybeberg makes this point brilliantly in the film by introducing Karin Krick's Parsifal to replace Michael Kutter's. The male Parsifal reappears briefly and follows the female Parsifal at the end of Act II as she bring Kundry back from the underworld -- a Kundry who became humanized once she acknowledged the feminine in the Parsifal role, and saw her own transformed role as service to the Grail.

In the long third and final act of the opera, Sybeberg has the female Parsifal in sole possession of the Parsifal role. She sings with a male voice (the heldentenor of Reiner Goldberg) and it becomes explicitly apparent that access to the Grail is through her. When the male Parsifal joins his female counterpart at the very end of the film, Sybeberg has them first of all singing sequentially with the same voice, then brings them side by side singing together but with one voice: a male voice influenced by, tutored by, and integrated with the feminine experience of Parsifal II. As they sing together, the mountainside that conceals the path to the Grail sepulchre opens, giving out great bursts of light. The two Parsifals enter the mountain, embrace chastely and gently, and the film ends with the promise and expectation of access to and experience of the Grail.

This remarkable film by Sybeberg and his explicit use of two Parsifals -- male and female -- is consistent with the interpretation of the Parsifal myth offered in this chapter. He demonstrates transformation in masculine energy and an adjustment of feminine energy to it, showing in convincing detail that these energies are not separate in individual human beings -- male or female -- but are different facets of a single, undifferentiated consciousness and energy. His film thus makes the novel statement that the sense of separation between that which is defined as "masculine" and that which is defined as "feminine" has to be replaced by a complementary expression. The alternative is a grim wasteland. The messages from the twelfth-century to the present day have all been the same in the many variants of this myth -- "transform or perish". It is evident that Sybeberg has enhanced the richness of the Parsifal myth with his employment of the two Parsifals, whereas Lévi-Strauss' communication axioms, the necessary end product of a semiotic structuralist approach, reduce and lose the symbolic richness of this myth and fail to deliver the message.

To Wagner, Parsifal was not an opera like any other. It was a "*Buhnenweihfestpiel*" -- a sacred scenic action akin to a liturgy. In *Religion and Art*, Wagner defines what is at stake in Parsifal: "One might say that where Religion becomes artificial, it is reserved for Art to save the spirit of religion by recognizing the figurative value of mythic symbols which the former would have us believe in their literal sense and revealing their deep and hidden truth through an ideal presentation" (1966:213). Semiotic structuralism and inverted symmetries are clearly inadequate tools for the task of understanding the significance of the Parsifal myth. The mythopoetic genesis implicit in Wagner's conception of Parsifal can only be understood through an analogous mythopoetic analysis, and in navigating a fine line between orthodox distinctions between science and art I trust I have provided the basis for a different level of understanding.

Appendix 1: Synopsis of the Grail Legend According to Chrétien de Troyes[6]

The Holy Grail, the chalice of the Last Supper, is kept within a castle. The king of the castle has been severely wounded and suffers continuously because his wound will not heal. The entire country and its people are in desolation.

The king had been wounded early in his adolescence. While wandering in a forest, he had reached a camp that was empty except for a spit on which a salmon was roasting. He was hungry, so he took a bit of the salmon. He burned his fingers horribly. To assuage the pain, he put his fingers into his mouth and tasted a bit of the salmon. He is called the Fisher King because he was wounded by a fish. He was also wounded in the thighs, so he is no longer productive, and his whole land is no longer productive. The Fisher King lies on a litter and must be carried everywhere, but he is sometimes able to fish, and only then is he happy.

The Fisher King presides over the castle where the Grail is kept, but he cannot touch the Grail or be healed by it. The court fool has prophesied that the Fisher King will be healed when a wholly innocent fool arrives in the court.

In an isolated country a boy lives with his widowed mother, whose name is Heart Sorrow. At first the boy does not seem to have a name; much later he learns that his name is Parsifal. His father was killed while rescuing a fair maiden, and his two brothers were also killed as knights. His mother took him to this faraway country and raised him in primitive circumstances. He wears homespun clothes, has no schooling, and asks no questions. He is a simple, naïve youth.

Early in his adolescence, he sees five knights riding by on horseback. He is dazzled by the knights, their scarlet and gold trappings, their armor, and all their accoutrements. He dashes home to tell his mother that he has seen five gods and wants to leave home to go with them.

His mother weeps. She had hoped that he would not suffer the fate of his father and his brothers But she gives him her blessing and three instructions: He must respect all fair maidens; he is to go daily to church where he will receive all the food he needs; and he is not to ask any questions.

Parsifal goes off to find the knights. He never finds the same five knights, but he has all kinds of adventures. One day he comes to a tent. He has only known a simple hut, so he thinks this is the church his mother had told him about. He sees a fair damsel wearing a ring on her hand, so he obeys his mother's instructions by embracing the damsel, taking her ring, and putting it on his own hand. He sees a table set for a banquet and, thinking it is the food his mother had told him he would find in church, he eats it, not realizing it is prepared for the damsel's beloved knight. The damsel begs Parsifal to leave, because if the knight finds him there he will kill him.

Parsifal goes on his way and soon finds a devastated convent and monastery. He cannot restore them, but he vows to return and raise the spell when he is stronger.

Then he meets a Red Knight who has come from King Arthur's Court. Parsifal is dazzled by the knight and tells him that he too wants to be a knight. The Red Knight tells him to go to Arthur's court, which he does. In this court is a damsel who has not smiled or laughed for six years. A legend says that when the best knight in the world comes along, she will smile and laugh again. When she sees Parsifal, she bursts into laughter. The court is impressed. Arthur knights Parsifal, gives him a page, and tells him that he may have the horse and armor of the Red Knight if he can get it.

Parsifal finds the Red Knight, kills him, and takes his armor and puts it on over his homespun clothing. He finds his way to the castle of Gournamond, who trains him to be a knight. Gournamond gives him two instructions: He must never seduce or be seduced by a woman, and when he reaches the Grail castle he must ask, "Whom does the Grail serve?"

Parsifal goes off and tries to find his mother and help her, but he finds that she died of a broken heart. Then he meets Blanche Fleur. From this time on, everything he does is in her service. She asks him to conquer the army besieging her castle, which he does, and then he spends the night with her.

After travelling all of the next day, he meets two men in a boat. One of them, who is fishing, invites Parsifal to stay at his house for the night. When Parsifal reaches the house, he finds himself in a great castle, where he is royally welcomed. He learns that the fisherman is the Fisher King. He sees a ceremony in which a youth carries a sword that drips blood constantly and in which a maiden carries the Grail. At a banquet the Grail is passed about and everyone drinks from it. The Fisher King's niece brings a sword, and the King straps it to Parsifal's waist. But Parsifal fails to ask the question Gournamond had told him to ask. The next morning Parsifal finds that all the people of the castle have vanished. Then the castle itself disappears.

He goes on and finds a sorrowful maiden. He learns that her knight had been killed by the jealous knight of the maiden of the tent, so the death was really his fault. When she learns that he has been in the Grail castle, she berates him for all his sins and tells him that the land and its people will continue to be desolate because he failed to ask the right question.

Later he again finds the maiden of the tent. She reiterates all his misdeeds and tells him that the sword he had been given will break the first time is it used in battle, that it can only be mended by the smith who made it, and after that it will never break again.

In the course of his journeys, Parsifal has subdued many knights and sent them back to King Arthur's Court. When he was there before, they had not realized who he was. Arthur sets forth to search for Parsifal so the court can honor him. Parsifal happens to be camping nearby. A falcon attacks three geese and wounds one of them. Its blood on the snow reminds Parsifal of Blanche Fleur, and he falls into a trance. Two of Arthur's men see him and try to persuade him to return to the court, but he unhorses them. A third knight, Gawain, gently persuades him to go to the court with him. Parsifal is received in triumph at the court.

But the rejoicing ends when a hideous damsel on a decrepit mule enters and recites all of Parsifal's sins. Then she points a finger at him and says, "It is all your fault." She assigns tasks to all the knights. She tells Parsifal to search for the Grail castle again and this time to ask the right question.

Parsifal goes on through many episodes. Some versions say that he travels for five years; other say twenty years. He grows bitter and disillusioned. He does many heroic deeds, but he forgets the church, Blanche Fleur, and the Grail castle.

Then one day he meets some pilgrims who ask him why he is armed on Good Friday. He suddenly remembers what he had forgotten. Remorsefully he goes with the pilgrims to a hermit for confession. The hermit absolves him and tells him to go immediately to the Grail castle.

Notes

1. This quotation is not an original find. It was used by Carol Pearson (1986) to introduce her fascinating book on archetypes, *The Hero Within.* Hopefully, it will set the stage for this work as it did for her compelling reading of unconscious structures.

2. It is interesting to note that Lévi-Strauss' commentary on psychoanalysis (1985:220) invokes only Freudian notions -- the bleeding lance as phallic symbol, the Grail as female sexual symbol, and so on. My development of Jung's ideas in this reading may not be so readily cast aside.

3. I have for the past decade engaged in a process of artificially induced (i.e., accelerated) individuation, so that symbols have more than intellectual allure; they are part of my own phenomenology.

4. Jung's notion of individuation and the evolutionary structuralism of Piaget (1971), MacLean (1973), and Laughlin and d'Aquili (1974) address the processual qualities of human potential emerging from the dialectic between consciousness and the deep-rooted symbolic patterns of both the personal and the collective unconscious.

5. To put a Jungian angle on Lévi-Strauss' motifs, myth can be viewed as a homology generated by the unconscious for the conscious to integrate with and thereby be effectively changed, that is, individuated. This means making an analogy between Nature as both concrete model and generating base and the notion of the unconscious as the anchor of truth and awareness.

   (Nature : Culture) : : (Unconscious : Conscious)

   There is of course a deeper level yet:

   (Nature : Culture) : : (Brain : Mind)

   which invites the evolutionary structuralists to the table with their developmental and neurophysiological concerns (Count 1974; MacLean 1973; Piaget 1971; Laughlin and d'Aquili 1974; McManus 1979).

6. This synopsis of the Grail legend is taken from Johnson (1977).

Bibliography

d'Aquili, E.G., C.D. Laughlin and J. McManus
1979 (eds.): The Spectrum of Ritual. N.Y.: Columbia University Press

Bohm, D.
1980 Wholeness and the Implicate Order. London: Routledge and Kegan Paul

Bourguignon, E.
1968 World Distribution and Patterns of Possession States. In Prince R. (ed.): Trance and Possession States. Montreal: R.M. Bucke Memorial Society

Count, E.M.
1973 Being and Becoming Human. N.Y.: Van Nostrand Reinhold

Culler, J.
1973 Phenomenology and Structuralism. The Human Context, V. 5:34-42

Eliade, M.
1964 Shamanism: Archaic Techniques of Ecstasy. Princeton: Princeton University Press

Geertz, C.
1973 Religion as a Cultural System. In Geertz, C.: The Interpretation of Cultures:87-125. London: Hutchinson

Govinda, A.
1960 Foundations of Tibetan Mysticism. N.Y.: Weiser

Hilgard, E.R.
1977 Divided Consciousness: Multiple Controls in Human Thought and Action. N.Y.: John Wiley and Sons

Hillman, J.
1975 Re-Visioning Psychology. N.Y.: Harper Colophon Books

Husserl, E.
1960 Cartesian Meditations. The Hague: Nijhoff

1970 The Crisis of European Sciences and Transcendental Phenomenology (trans. by David Carr). Evanston: Northwestern University Press

Johnson, R.A.
1977 He, Understanding Masculine Psychology. N.Y.: Harper and Row

Jung, C.G.
1959 The Archetypes and the Collective Unconscious. The Collected Works of C.G. Jung, V.9. Princeton: Princeton University Press

1971 The Portable Jung. N.Y.: The Viking Press

Jung, E.
1957 Animus and Anima. N.Y.: Analytical Psychology Club of New York

Jung, E. and M.L. von Franz
1960 The Grail Legend. A C.G. Jung Foundation Book. N.Y.: G.P. Putman

Kracke, W.
1986 Dream, Myth, Thought and Image: An Amazonian Contribution to the Psychoanalytic Theory of Primary Process. In Tedlock, B. (ed.): Dreaming, the Anthropology and Psychology of the Imaginal. Alberquerque: University of New Mexico Press

Laughlin, C.D. and E.G. d'Aquili
1974 Biogenetic Structuralism. N.Y.: Columbia University Press

Laughlin, C.D., J. McManus and J. Shearer
1982 Dreams, Trance and Visions: What a Transpersonal Anthropology Might Look Like. The Journal of Transpersonal Anthropology 7, 1/2:141-59

Lévi-Strauss, C.
1972 Mythologiques IV: L'Homme Nu. Paris: Plon

1985 The View From Afar. Chapter 17, From Chrétien de Troyes to Richard Wagner. N.Y.: Basic Books

MacLean, P.D.
1973 A Triune Concept of the Brain and Behaviour. Toronto: University of Toronto Press

McManus, J.
1979 Ritual and Human Social Cognition. In d'Aquili, E.G., C.D. Laughlin and J. McManus (eds.): The Spectrum of Ritual. N.Y.: Columbia University Press

Merleau-Ponty
1962 Phenomenology of Perception. London: Routledge and Kegan Paul

Pearson, C.S.
1986 The Hero Within - Six Archetypes We Live By. San Francisco: Harper and Row

Peters, L.G. and D. Price Williams
1983 A Phenomenological Overview of Trance. Transcultural Psychiatric Research Review 20:5-39

Piaget, J.
1971 Biology and Knowledge. Chicago: University of Chicago Press

Prattis, J.I.
1984 Man and Metaphor: An Exploration in Entropy and Coherence. Communication and Cognition, V.17, No. 2/3:187-204

1985 (ed.): Reflections, the Anthropological Muse. Washington, D.C.: American Anthropological Association

Ricoeur, P.
1963 Structure et Herméneutique. Esprit, V.30.

1967 La Structure, le Mot, l'Evénement. Esprit, V.35.

Ring, K.
1974 A Transpersonal View of Consciousness: A Mapping of Further Regions of Human Space. Journal of Transpersonal Psychology, 6, 2:125-155

Sheldrake, R.
1981 A New Science of Life. London: Blond and Briggs

Stephen, M.
1986 Culture, the Self and the Autonomous Imagination. Paper presented to the American Anthropological Association, Philadelphia, December

Tart, C.
1975 States of Consciousness. N.Y.: Dutton

Tedlock, B.
1986 (ed.): Dreaming: The Anthropology and Psychology of the Imaginal. Albuquerque: University of New Mexico Press

Toulmin, S.E.
1982 Return to Cosmology: Post Modern Science and the Theology of Nature. Berkeley: University of California Press

Wagner, R.
1966 Religion and Art. In Richard Wagner's Prose Works. (trans. by W.A. Ellis). V. VI. N.Y.: Broude Brothers. Reprinted in the 1987 London edition, Routledge and Kegan Paul.

Webber, M.
1980 Ritual: A Model of Symbol Penetration. M.A. Thesis, Carleton University

Chapter 3

Dialectics and Experience in Fieldwork: The Poetic Dimension

There is a crucial epistemological gap in anthropological field reporting. Most anthropologists are aware of the cultural and professional constraints that restrict and colour their perceptions of events in other cultures. They may be less readily aware of similar epistemological constraints that restrict what the cultural other transmits across the observer/other divide in the form of information that eventually constitutes field data. Anthropology tends to handle this paradox in the theory of knowledge with an orthodox strategy that divides the phenomena of field observation into emic and etic categories (or something akin to them). This ignores an unreported dialectic between observer and cultural other and, furthermore, obscures the collision of cultural assumptions that provides much of the raw material of the discipline.

The process of observation does, I believe, require a participation that must be self-aware. As epistemology lies within the field of self-reference (Bronowski 1966:9), this implies that the dialectics of participation by the observer with the cultural other requires an expression that does not rely on emic/etic disjunctions. What is needed is a language that reflects the dialectics of experience, subsumes emic and etic distinctions, and moves both to a new language of experience. This is the missing component in anthropology. In this essay and volume (see also Prattis 1985), I advocate poetry as a language form that closes the epistemological gap between observer and cultural other. For me, poetry functions as a missing component in anthropological field reporting. It is a new signifying process that alters the observer's perception of self and cultural other in such a way that the observer's *own* perception of society is influenced and changed. Poetry as an expressive vehicle for field reporting makes it possible to comprehend another culture in a way that moves beyond that distinct culture, and in the process removes fieldwork from the hierarchical legacy of our anthropological forebears (Rose 1983:354). But why poetry? Before I can persuade the reader to join me in this perspective I must provide some building blocks before returning with conviction, to these themes in the conclusion.

What possible relevance could poetry have for anthropology? Can the discipline be informed by it, or develop because of it? Anthropologists have written and published poetry, but this endeavour did not provide any guidelines or direction to anthropology. Anthropologists who commit themselves to poetry move between the domain of literary criticism and the writing of poetry to express parts of their anthropological experiences. The common thread lies in their use of poetry as a novel form of ethnographic account. Perhaps I should first try to unravel the poetic process and examine its critical relevance to anthropology in the latter part of the twentieth-century. There are a number of critical themes to explore. Marcoux points out that one tradition in poetry -- the fascination with the strange and the exotic -- can lead the anthropologist to an awareness of the strange within our own culture, and by doing so provide a method of radical reflection that critiques some key elements of anthropological practice (Marcoux 1977, 1982, 1983). It will be argued that, with poetry, anthropology can come to terms with certain deficiencies in its own practice of fieldwork, with its own epistemology and sensitivity and just perhaps with its own reason for being. In other words the poetic dimension in anthropology is not just an expressive mode but a crucial part of the developing methodology of the discipline (Marcoux 1977:2). If anthropology *is* to move it must be informed not just by the culture bearers painstakingly examined in the field, but by some of the discipline's professionals who are trying to say something about the process of recording and communicating field experience with a startling and new candour. This new direction draws its inspiration from the poetic domain.

As anthropologists we move between worlds, a clutch of words hovering to regroup themselves before the set of our astonished eyes. With words we create our images, polish the projections of reason and emotion. Without that connection (of words) there is no world (Ridington 1982). Ridington adds that, "The physical information now upon us calls for a language rich and suggestive enough to make the ancient mythic connections between the state of nature and the state of mind" (Ridington 1982:3).

I believe that our standard language system is not equal to the problem raised by Ridington. As scholars we often fail to be self-conscious about our use of language as a professional tool. The heterogeneity and multiple phases of consciousness within the domain of anthropological discourse need, within the discourse's repertoire, a different kind of symbolic language to develop the necessary connections between observer/observed and also to develop a methodology of understanding. Poetry as a technical tool, in the hands of anthropologists, provides such an instrument, as I will try to argue more cogently below. It is an instrument designed to alleviate some of the epistemological difficulties inherent in fieldwork. Bronowski, in discussing literature, alluded to its component of self-reference and noted a tension between watching our own minds from the inside and someone else's from the outside (Bronowski 1966:11). He goes on to state that:

> The force and meaning of literature is to present the lives of others to us in such a way that we recognize ourselves in them and live them from the outside and from the inside together....Literature and art...come alive in the sense of our own self stretching into the action and disasters of someone else's self, and thereby mapping the human self as a whole (Bronowski 1966:12).

It is my hope that in a similar fashion anthropology through poetry may also come alive.

One of the major issues raised by Marcoux's work (1977, 1982) is that in poetry there is a search for truth and a deeper knowing, a compulsion to write and communicate the event of going beyond oneself to others who may or may not be prepared to listen. Poetry contains a rhythm whereby words are used for sound as well as sense, and experience is expressed in a symbolic cluster of meaning, brevity, and intensity. There is almost a ritualistic aspect to poetry embodying the idea of language as revelation, as pure symbol, the language of something deeper than surface reality. A poet is simultaneously estranged from life as the observer but also involved in subjection to its patterns and rhythms. Rather than seeing oneself walking, the poet sees the ground moving beneath one's feet. The task for the poet is to try and take the phenomenon experienced, grasp its very significance, and then transform it to a meaningful form. Poetry operates as a symbolic code that expresses an engagement, or interiority of experience, which moves beyond the poet and the experience, taking them both into a new space/dimension/accounting of events. Poetry offers a codified system of action which we take as informing us about such depths and interiority.

The contrast with the field situation is that the anthropologist is constrained by his or her career dictates to suppress a great deal of the phenomena of experience, and interpret and communicate in preprogrammed ways that can leave the culture and self devoid of meaning. The point I wish to build here is that vital aspects of what is known from the field experience are rarely communicated in the monographs and articles that result from it. I believe this situation results from the lack of an appropriate language by which to communicate the significance of the anthropologist engaging with the cultural other and expressing the dialectic of transformation that takes place during fieldwork.

If one wishes to be honest about fieldwork the least that can be said is that it is not easy, often impossible. There is a collision of cultural assumptions that anthropological reporting obscures and overrides because the quality of control is not a measure of good methodology, rather an indicator of a power relation that most often remains implicit. Understanding, on the other hand, requires a comprehension of the collision (and often merging) of unfamiliar cultural assumptions and their expression. The latter rarely finds a place in anthropological texts or monographs. It does, however, appear in the poetry that anthropologists write about fieldwork. This is why poetry should not just remain within the confines of comparative literature, particularly as it can become a powerful transforming medium for present anthropological practice.

The opening to a new vitality that poetry offers anthropology has already been touched upon within the discourse of literary criticism. Critical formalism would limit poetry to a harmless dead end, an instrument that simply extends and perpetuates in a self-serving way the status quo of literature. A poetics of literature informed by anthropology claims for poetry the function of revealing what has been suppressed and ignored. Thus Kristeva's notion of poetry underlining the limits of socially useful discourse leads one to examine the moments when the wider society permits a different signifying process under its practices (Kristeva 1974:14). A poetic anthropology offers similar benefits to our discipline, and I do believe that the critical conditions for such a change in emphasis are upon us right now.

The past decade in anthropology (1975-1985) has been remarkable in that a reflexive pause in the discipline has taken place, a pause for re-evaluation that may permit the introduction of a new signifying process as a necessary supplement to present anthropological practice. Anthropological poetics expresses the collision of cultural assumptions in a signifying process that uses a different structure and attaches a new set of meanings to the terms used to communicate the results of fieldwork. Part of the reflexive pause has also encouraged uncertainty and has introduced a cynicism where professional apathy and career entrenchment are too often the watchwords of the day. Anthropological poetics then becomes far more crucial for the discipline than we perhaps care to realize. This is because it becomes the still silence of consciousness whereby anthropologists use a symbolic system that becomes a necessary form of knowledge for their own discipline and culture. The problem of observation for both the poet and the anthropologist is that they are not bound by the one dimensionality of the everyday world. Marcoux points out that, "the poet is a listener, as well as a speaker, paralleling again the researcher, where both are careful observers who by their attentiveness and involvement go beyond masks and social roles" (Marcoux 1977:6).

Here perhaps is a distinct gap between poetry and anthropology. The exegesis of poetry is the collision of assumptions, points of contact and confrontation, a breaking out of "everydayness" and a thrust to comprehend and express in poetic form (Marcoux 1977:2-6). In anthropology, on the contrary, the collision of cultural assumptions encountered in *every* field situation is suppressed in terms of approved and accepted communication structures within the discipline. This difference then marks less a logical distinction than a gap to be crossed. Poetics provides access to a vital sphere of reality for anthropology that remains largely unexplored and insignificant, despite the fact that this reality influences what is written and communicated within the discipline.

Much has been made of the anthropologist as a stranger in other cultures. We need to be aware, as Marcoux has argued (1977), of the fact that strangeness is a major component of critical consciousness. The strangeness of what is "other" does not lie *out there*, in other cultures, but is incorporated within ourselves. But if the otherness is within us we must ask just where is the "field" for anthropology (a point I will deal with below). It is essential to identify the source of strangeness in our own existence in order to enhance further evolution for the discipline. Indeed, some have argued that poetry itself has foundered due to the neglect of strangeness within existence. Robert Graves maintains that poetry has been on a downward trend since the Celtic bards of the thirteenth-century lost the ability to imbue poetry with a magical language (Graves 1968:9), and he dismisses many poems, particularly those of the contemporary era, as being without poetry, that is, lacking that mystical and magical connection between the author, his honesty, and the Muse -- the "White Goddess." Poetry to Graves is a particularly honest form of communication, and by implication much of poetry and anthropology does not touch the basal level of truth. I would not presume to castigate contemporary poets and anthropologists as dishonest. That implies an intent. I see the situation in terms of poets and anthropologists needing to develop an awareness to avoid the situation of being locked into a limited rationality.

Many poets do not engage with the essence of poetry, merely recording a darting thought that reflects back from the surface image (Marcoux 1977:6). If we regard other cultures as a mirror, or surface image for our discipline, there are then many dimensions to the notion of "Reflection" that are vital for considering the present epistemological status of anthropology. First of all there is the notion of the other culture simply reflecting back the presuppositions, intents, and personal epistemology of the observer. Much of the acrimonious debate concerning Margaret Mead's first contribution to the discipline can be rendered redundant if we consider that some of her work clearly lies in this particular category, as does the work of her critics! Her early work in fact tells us a great deal about the cultural and conceptual preferences of Margaret Mead and less about the reality-as-experienced by the culture bearers examined. Anthropology thus has a great potential for delusion in that fieldworkers record and communicate only what they wish to have reflected back to them. The particular epistemology of the observer and his or her self-interests provide a form of tunnel vision that perhaps indicates that the first recordings of data in a fieldwork situation should always be critically re-examined. Such a scrutiny would indicate an adjustment, an acknowledgment that the observer is dealing with a different reality.

There is also a second level of "Reflection" that has a myriad number of dimensions and forms. This is the process of standing back and reflecting upon the endeavour of fieldwork -- reflecting upon fieldwork experience/its relevance for the everyday life of the observer/the effects of everyday life upon the fieldwork experience/an awareness of one's own life cycle that leads to particular field interests and not others/the reflections of others about the myriad influences that bear upon the field situation (Leeds 1982). Other factors are the personality, emotional, and epistemic state of the observer/the political and social commitments of the knower/the field experience and its reshaping of the anthropologist/and the notion that after a time all personal poetry becomes ethnographic poetry. There are many more such threads, but this level of "Reflection" embraces the idea of the anthropologist coming to terms with self, the field situation, and the discipline. The importance of this stream of awareness, variously expressed in poetry, is that it provides a "focus on what the anthropologist, poetizing, illuminates about ethnography that his *not* writing poetry omits" (Leeds 1982).

There is of course yet another level, one difficult to grasp but containing within it a dynamism for evolution. This level goes beyond cultural relativity, which renders standard orthodoxies of objectivity as highly problematic. "The observer moves toward the observed, and draws, in turn, the observed closer to the observer, suspending both in a new space, somewhere not wholly here and not wholly there" (Rose 1983:353). The anthropologist at this level achieves an "interiority" that includes self and other culture and moves beyond it to a new form of expression, in that the experience in and of a different culture draws that culture and the observer to a different consciousness that will have its effect within Western civilization. Here I refer to a dialectic between the observer and the cultural other that takes as its raw material the collision of cultural assumptions mentioned earlier, expressing it in a higher order linguistic usage -- that of anthropological poetics. In poetry concerning the field, the anthropologist expresses the dialectic between self and field experience but moves it on. So he or she is not simply reporting on his or her own analytic model or using emic and etic distinctions to get at the material of observation. The anthropologist has engaged with the cultural other and taken it one step further by expressing this engagement in the symbolic language of poetry. The total field report becomes more complete because anthropological poetics, particularly at the level of "interiority," is a distinctive kind of ethnographic account that the accepted discourse in anthropological monographs and articles does not convey. It is the vantage point that permits the collective experience of other cultures to influence and humanize the observer's own civilization.

But before this long-range consideration becomes too contentious I must return to the caprice of the field situation.

to be without words
a rock dry and still
in other people's river

(Flores 1982:17)

The field sequence of observing/recording/communicating is a phenomenological exercise whereby one code of meaning is transferred to other codes. The code of meaning that is most acceptable to the profession of anthropology often bears an uneasy correlation with the code of meaning felt/sensed/initially observed. The many dilemmas concerning the lack of fit among the different levels that anthropologists use are handled (though not necessarily resolved) if poetry can be regarded as an intermediary code between levels of meaning. In other words, poetry becomes a field device that functions as a homology or myth -- a coded set of information that deals with contradictions -- and necessarily leads to different kinds of investigations.

In her article "Field Poetry" (1982), Toni Flores charts the numerous ways in which poetry functions as a code between levels of meaning. Poetry about one's self in the field turns the subjective "I" into an objective "me" and puts the observer into the same framework as the "objects" of anthropological observation (Flores 1982:18). The "straw man" of scientific objectivity in both natural and social sciences has to a certain extent been replaced by the development of a self-conscious awareness about the nature of the human observer's capacities to be a scientific agent. Rose points out that:

> anthropologists have been engaged in establishing privileged positions from which to view other humans. One such privileged position is "objectivity," which is nothing less than that effort to remove oneself morally, intellectually and emotionally from the people being studied. (Rose 1983:352)

Whether we do this by emic/etic distinctions or oscillate between mundane local detail and global structure (Geertz 1979:239; Rose 1983:354), we still fall short of expressing the significance to anthropology of being periodically in and out of participating in native life (Rose 1983:352).

The emic/etic distinction certainly serves a purpose in terms of mapping phenomena, but it does not communicate the significance of engaging with the cultural other and being changed by it. We are still concerned with the dividing line between "their" model and "our" model, and our ethnographies will remain incomplete until the interface between the two models can be expressed. A great deal of knowledge is suppressed because everyday discourse within the discipline of anthropology does not have the linguistic qualities to express what we know and experience of the interface between models. We can and do convey a great deal of information in our analyses and ethnographies, but certain details of interface, collision of cultural assumption, etc. need a richer semantic field. The "interior" position that can be found in anthropological poetics does, I feel, have a rich enough semantic field to fill this linguistic gap. Otherwise the reification of objectivity eliminates the sensitivity and awareness of the knower, whereas such sensitivity is the central methodological issue of contemporary anthropology.

The language we use to describe events imposes both the form and the limitations of the accounts we give. Everyday language and scientific discourse omits and suppresses a significant part of what we experience and know of other cultures. Thus our communication of cultural experience takes place within a rationally preprogrammed format that deletes so much of the very bases of knowledge. The language form that is intended to help us understand and express the human condition alienates itself from that which it tries to know (Leeds 1983:2). It is from this viewpoint that poetry may provide an answer. Poetic language is almost an "otherness" of language, distinct from everyday forms of communication. As Roudiez points out:

> it is the language of materiality as opposed to transparency (where the word is forgotten for the sake of the object designated), a language in which the writer's effort is less to deal rationally with those objects or concepts words seem to encase than to work, consciously or not with the sounds and rhythms of words in transrational fashion (Roudiez 1980:5).

As a code for expressing multiple levels of meaning, and an evocation of the entire range of sensory experience, what is reaped from the poetic domain is a reconstruction of knowledge which provides the context for our knowing -- scientific or otherwise. Poetry provides a vehicle for the doubts, dilemmas, experiences, and interiority that are often suppressed by the discipline and ignored by literature, and as such it can be regarded as a tool for fieldwork.

At a simple level there is the notion that if anthropologists study someone else's symbolic language and do not attempt to put in a comparable symbolic language of their own then the sense perceptions of the sensuality, colour, pathos, and tragedy of field observations are deleted and the necessary "clicks" of comprehension are not there. What is actually communicated can be an arid and erroneous reckoning of reality. The working through of puzzlement and incomprehension can be posed in poetry and surrounding metaphors, so bit by bit the puzzles that eluded the observer come to the surface through repetition in different forms. Poetry becomes as myth, containing dilemmas and contradictions that come to the understanding of the observer by being set in rich semantic fields that ordinary fieldnotes and everyday language do not contain. Here there reappears in diminished form the theme that Graves exaggerated in "The White Goddess", poetry as a mystical and codified language.

Poetry for the anthropologist not only expresses but codifies, abstracts, and then decodes vital aspects of self-realization and field experience, ultimately turning it into self-awareness. Perhaps at this point the logic of this chapter suddenly makes the writing of it redundant, because if we pose poetry as myth, revealing the paradoxes of the discipline, the field situation and the individual, then those anthropologists who commit themselves to poetry in order to say something about field experience are the tricksters and shamans of the discipline. They transform elements of natural language to a poetry that has the status of a distinct expressive code -- a homology between levels of interpretation that tells us something *different* and something *more* about ethnography than the natural everyday language used in anthropological reporting. The myth makers are using language forms that act as triggers into comprehension and consciousness. The unknowing keepers of a "secret," a suppressed part of anthropological endeavour that must now be revealed to a wider audience -- the body politic of anthropology. Herein lies the dilemma or contradiction of this volume (Prattis 1985). It makes public, expressions that have remained private and silent, and one wonders if the demystification will destroy the genesis of the endeavour. That is the risk openly taken.

We are unfolding an additional dimension of the "field" of anthropology. The excursion to other cultures is part of a career trajectory. The revelations of self and other acquired from it lead to the field that lies within *us*, the professional community. The anthropologist as scholar and fieldworker is often not part of the continuing unfolding of the client community but they are part of him or her. They visit, observe, then leave and if a well-cultivated rapport holds up, returns are made on occasions that grow more infrequent with the passing years. Yet field experiences continue to work within each scholar as part of his or her own personal evolution, in that the field situation becomes internalized to an extent that one may not be readily aware of. Kakar comments on this theme and the notion of strangeness in a highly imaginative manner:

> A degree of alienation from one's culture, a deep exposure to other worldviews and even a temporary period of living "as others" may indeed be necessary for heightening one's perceptions about the culture and society one is born into (Kakar 1982:9).

He also alludes to Merleau-Ponty's (1962) discussion of knowing oneself "only in ambiguity" to indicate that anthropologists through their fieldwork in other cultures are equipped perhaps not so much for the study of other societies but for a critical examination of their own society. These factors, taken together with the way in which the anthropologist relates to his or her own life cycle, contribute to the equation the anthropologist-as-poet brings to bear on the circumstances of the moment.

The otherness within the fieldworker and the alienation of ambiguous self-knowledge take a critical form in such cases as moments of culture shock. The client community and the professional community alike may then seem distant or irrelevant. Flores, for example, has pointed out that poetry about culture shock in the field, and upon returning from it, is a public naming of a private experience that condenses and diminishes potentially disastrous effects on the fieldworker (Flores 1982:17). Wengle compares anthropological fieldwork with the liminal phase of a *rite de passage*, a phase that can lead to a sense of renewal and revitalization within the practitioner (Wengle 1983;9). His psychoanalytic framework views fieldwork as a process that stimulates conscious awareness of repressed material within the anthropologist's own unconscious, thereby producing a sense of coherence, creativity, and well-being (Wengle 1983). Poetry about fieldwork is one way of achieving this cohesion. The therapeutic and self-revealing aspects of field poetry, and their contribution to a process of completion and personal unfolding will come as no surprise, but there is much more involved than an oblique form of self-completion.

Self-revelation through poetry adds a dimension to the study of our own methods because, as I alluded to above, the subjective "I" has, through poetry, become an objective "me" and this induces a discourse that does not draw upon the reification of an unattainable objectivity. Poetry also expresses the sensual, the colour and smells, the postures of human beings at leisure and when tensed to kill; paints a landscape; reveals the total vulnerability of the fieldworker, yet leads to something other/beyond the self. "The poems never stop at the particular and personal but begin with it and then press on, skipping from the cultural and social to meditations on our common humanity" (Flores 1982:19). There is a movement from self-therapy and revelation to a consciousness that incorporates the cultural other. This consciousness may then be taken back to our own civilization in terms of a humanism that can counter the angst of alienation in our own society. This is one possible outcome of the dialectic between observer and cultural other. Its expression in anthropological poetics moves both to a new domain, and implies that the process of observation is not simply that of recording what one thinks one sees -- there is a sense of engagement, taking the cultural other and self beyond the existing state of observation and finding an expression for the dialectic experienced whereby an increased awareness and perception is created. This opens up some very exciting domains in anthropology about multiple levels of coding and their significance for our *own* society.

The task for anthropology, at least a significant part of it, lies in transmuting the field experience within ourselves so that something constructive in the way of personal growth and consciousness that incorporates the cultural other is brought back to our own civilization. Poetry once again serves as one intermediary code between these levels of experience. It permits an awareness, attention, and understanding that would not be there without it and leads steadily and ultimately to a change in anthropological practice. I started this essay with the epistemological difficulties inherent in field observation. I then moved to poetry as a solution to these difficulties as it has the properties of a signifying process that can record the dialectic of participation between the observer and other. The final step is to suggest that the experience of the cultural other, and its expression, may well provide for a radicalization of the discipline. My argument is that the collective experience of other cultures sharpens the perceptions of the observer to the extent that a more encompassing humanism may permeate the observer's own civilization.

Conclusion

The poetic dimension in anthropology is real, a code for understanding, a metaphor for truth, a myth about anthropology-as-practiced, revealing the paradoxes of that discipline. Where, then does *Reflections: The Anthropological Muse* lead us? What are the implications of realizing that there are whole areas of anthropological field experiences that have never been communicated in monographs and journal articles? Does a resolution of paradox, of the myths created by anthropologists, require the leaving of anthropology and university departments and an active engagement in praxis rather than an armchair documentation of consciousness raising? Is there to be an inversion between a practical endeavour that is non-praxis in outlook?

It is true that a reflexive, self-aware anthropology and the radicalness of poetic expression put anthropology into question, but therein lies the basis of evolution into a different kind of anthropology. This is important as it becomes more and more difficult to justify fieldwork, particularly for professionals alienated from their *own* society and discipline. There is, however, a more important consideration. If the field lies to a great extent within us, then just what is anthropology doing in other people's cultures? Rarely are anthropologists invited to a particular field locale by the cultural groups living there. Their own presuppositions and career dictates lead to a global selection, which is then rationalized and justified to university departments and funding bodies. It is an obvious fact that the discipline and culture of the anthropologist is located firmly within the social and ideological context of which it is a part. Anthropologists, therefore, require a critical awareness of their relationship to the ideology of their *own* society and must take care that they do not unthinkingly aid in the reproduction of those conditions that in fact frame their object of study. The major part of anthropological practice has dealt with traditional and modernizing societies and anthropologists are often identified with the ideological dimension of a dependency that has already been defined in economic and political terms.

Much of the reaction to and ambivalence toward anthropologists on the part of native groups is in terms of their implicit awareness that the anthropologist is part of the process that defines their present situation. Furthermore, they realize that the anthropologist needs them far more than they need the anthropologist. Without a critical awareness it is unfortunately the case that, despite the best intentions of the anthropologist, his or her presence in another culture is often part of an ongoing process that weakens and eventually destroys the culture chosen. Lévi-Strauss is exceedingly bitter about the role of anthropology as the harbinger of destruction (1972) because an anthropology geared to the exigencies of professionalism is the vanguard of a destructive process that seems unrelenting. I want a different kind of anthropology, one that will engage dialectically with the cultural other and express it in a way that is ultimately useful for the other culture *and* my own society.

Edmund Carpenter's introduction to Stephen Williams' *In the Middle: The Inuit Today* (1983) speaks eloquently to this issue of destruction. He describes how "the newcomers could not see the patterns of Inuit life; they smashed into them almost as innocently as men walk through cobwebs" (Carpenter 1983:2). Professionalism, whether by anthropologists, explorers, or art experts, resulted in a devastation that Carpenter alludes to as a faith being lost, an art replaced:

> We emptied graves, moved sacred objects from secret caves to public vaults, transferred songs to tapes, stored myths on dusty shelves. Reverential became referential; private became public; theirs became ours (1983:10).

And later,

> When Inuit history got classified as loot, the past was rewritten to justify the present. We re-invented the Inuit, then hired them to act out this

> action on film. We even re-invented their art, then taught them how to make it (1983:10).

Carpenter's anger is directed at the way in which scholars use their "tribe" for self-promotion, for movement along a professional career trajectory that bears little relation to those communities that hosted their initial intrusion -- a double and devastating alienation. It must be pointed out, however, that anthropologists have increasingly moved into new venues -- large urban areas of their own and other cultures, hospitals, factories, ghettoes, and unemployment lines. The potential for unwitting damage is less obvious, but one wonders if the ideological component of a hierarchical methodology is just as dangerous in these situations.

Does all this necessarily lead us into the streets, missions, and revolutions of this world *or* is it possible for anthropology to find an additional documentation of observation that will heighten perception about cultural others then diffuse to the civilization surrounding us? Both options are readily open, just as are the different methods of dealing with alienation for self and society, praxis or a gathering of the forces that may overcome alienation. This is where I wish to ground my argument about anthropological poetics. My contention is that something crucial is missing from fieldwork reporting. The collision of cultural assumptions that is the raw material of the discipline is usually expressed in emic/etic distinctions, whereas I am proposing that a dialectic that subsumes both emic and etic considerations and moves both to a new language of experience is the missing component in anthropology. It can be expressed in various ways -- art, narrative, theatre; anthropological poetics is simply the medium I have chosen to write about. What I am referring to is a process of incorporation that is coded in a symbolic way that then alters the professional anthropologist's perception of self and cultural other, which *then* makes a different kind of impact on the professional's own society. The experience of other cultures by anthropologists should have diffused a greater humanism into Western consciousness. By and large this has not happened because as professionals we have not found the means to represent accurately the dialectic engaged with in the field. It is my conviction that anthropological poetics is one way of completing the anthropological endeavour, thereby changing it. This is one of the major challenges facing the discipline in the closing era of the twentieth-century. This latter theme has been elucidated in a highly instructive form in Stanley Diamond's poetry volume *Totems* (1982), which brings me to a final statement.

Stanley Diamond, in an interview with Dan Rose, charted his evolution as a poet with the attendant circumstances that displaced the poetic impulse and lead him to anthropology (Rose 1983). He emerged with a marvellous line to the effect that he chose anthropology because it was the next best thing to poetry. Diamond's original contribution to anthropological poetics demonstrates how the sensibilities of self and the cultural other can be fused (1983:346). Poetry in its own right is a powerful and moving mosaic of experience, but for anthropology in its present state of evolution it is so much more. It is a vital spark, a new signifying process for a discipline that is rethinking its own foundations and methodology. By methodology I refer specifically to the context of observer effects and follow Rose in treating poetry as poetic observation (1983:351). His comments are a critique particular to Stanley Diamond's *Totems*. Diamond (1982) achieves the interiority I have referred to earlier. It is not so crucial for me that he is superb poet, it is that he has taken ethnography into a new domain, beyond the emic/etic distinction that shackles the discipline to methodological stasis. Diamond's ethnographic account in his poetry mirrors that which is not yet communicated within the discipline but it speaks directly to his *own* society rather than simply reporting on the state of the cultural other or Diamond himself. This is why I wish to take Rose's comments and move them to the general as his observations about Diamond (Rose 1983) provide possible guidelines for the further development of anthropological poetics.

Rose has described poetic observation as a vantage point:

> where the poet resides in relation to his experience and to the poem, where the subjects of the poem exist in relation to the poet and where the reader stands in relation to subjects, author (observer) and text (1983:351).

This set of connections succinctly exposes the dilemmas of interpretation and communication found in *every* field situation. The argument is that anthropological poetics as methodology permits another culture and comprehension of it to be expressed and interpreted in a way that moves beyond it (1983:354). In this way one refers not just to interpretation but to a different way of "relating to meanings inherent in another cultural system" (1983:354). Rose argues further that:

> The accepted fieldwork device of plunging from the global to the local and rising from the local to the global preserves an older hierarchical methodology -- a legacy of our anthropological forebears (1983:354).

He invites us to compare this hierarchical legacy with the establishment of a new dimension between the anthropologist and native that involves different ways of perceiving the relation between cultural others and ourselves.

Anthropological poetics -- poetry as observation -- thus has a crucial transforming role that should not be confined to the literary outlets of the day, but placed within the mainstream of anthropology as an evocation of a new consciousness for the discipline and the society of which it is a part. It is an ethnographic statement that is presently missing from the discipline, wherein the anthropologist uses a rich linguistic code and different structures to express certain crucial areas of field experience that have not been communicated in professional monographs and articles. In addition, the evocation of a critical self-awareness within the discipline underlines the argument that a significant part of the field for anthropology lies within its professional practitioners. Fieldwork therefore belongs to *us* and our own civilization. The cultural other is a crucial part of our developing self-awareness and as such contributes to the transformation of the discipline. The anthropologist-as-poet using field experience as part of his or her raw material has chosen a form to convey the experience of the cultural other so that a different kind of text is available to members of the discipline. The resulting combination of internal and external transformation is a textual experiment that brings into being not so much a new body of knowledge but a different dimension of understanding, "a new surface of emergence" (Rose 1985:8). Anthropological poetics seeks new realities and audiences, new relationships with the cultural other, and new definitions for the discipline of anthropology. If it can move the listener, the reader, and the unconvinced (Rose 1983:354), it may also change the manner in which anthropology is justified and perhaps practiced.

Bibliography

Bronowski, J.
1966 The Logic of the Mind. American Scientist 54, 1:1-14.

Carpenter, E.
1983 Introduction. In S.G. Williams (ed.): In the Middle - The Inuit Today. Don Mills, Toronto: Fitzhenry and Whiteside

Diamond, S.,
1982 Totems. Barrytown, N.Y.: Open Book/Station Hill

Geertz, C.
1979 From the Native's Point of View. In P. Rabinow and W.M. Sullivan (eds.): Interpretative Social Science. Berkeley: University of California Press

Graves, R.
1968 The White Goddess. London: Faber and Faber

Kakar, S.
1982 Shamans, Mystics, and Doctors. N.Y.: Knopf

Kristeva, J.
1974 La Révolution du Langage Poetique. Paris: Seuil

Leeds, A.
1982 Personal Communication. Lecture Notes for Poetry Colloquium at Boston University

1983 Being Human: Epistemology, Poetry and Anthropology. Comment for Conference on Poetry and Anthropology. New School for Social Research, New York

Lévi-Strauss, C.
1972 Mythologiques IV: L'homme Nu. Paris: Plon

Marcoux, M.
1977 The Relationship between Poetry, Philosophy, and the Anthropological Imagination. Paper presented to the N.E.A.A. March

1982 Cursillo: Anatomy of a Movement - The Experience of Spiritual Renewal. N.Y.: Lambeth Press

1983 Personal Communication. The Poet's Work (1980), Creativity (1978)

Merleau-Ponty, M.
1962 The Primacy of Perception. Evanston: Northwestern University Press.

Prattis, J.I.
1985 (ed.): Reflections: The Anthropological Muse. Washington, D.C.: American Anthropological Association

Ridington, R.
1982 Personal Communication. Images of Creation (1981)

Rose, D.
1983 In Search of Experience. The Anthropological Poetics of Stanley Diamond. American Anthropologist 85:345-360

1985 Experimental Writing and the Dispersion of Ethnographic Methods and Genres (ms.)

Roudiez, L.S.
1980 Introduction. In J. Kristeva (ed.): Desire in Language: A Semiotic Approach to Literature and Art. N.Y.: Columbia University Press

Wengle, J.
1983 Fieldwork, Sunsets, and Death. Anthropology and Humanism Quarterly 8,2:2-12

Chapter 4

"Reflections" as Myth

The overall context for *Reflections: The Anthropological Muse* is part of my general concern about the exploitative nature of anthropological endeavours. In a previous work co-authored with Derek Blair we suggested a solution to such exploitation by drawing on discursive strategies from the field of anthropological poetics (Blair and Prattis 1994). This discourse was pioneered by Stanley Diamond at the New School of Social Research and has produced a number of landmarks in the attempt to change the nature of anthropological science (Prattis 1985; Brady 1991b). A new ethnography has emerged that begins with a renewed focus on the relationship between subject and object, anthropologist and cultural other (Clifford and Marcus 1986; Dwyer 1982; Friedrich 1986). Our intention, however, is not to review this emerging ethnography, but rather to simply note it and focus on *Reflections* in particular and the strategy of anthropological poetics it evokes (Prattis 1985, 1988; Brady 1991b).

Reflections: The Anthropological Muse is *not* primarily a volume of poetry. It is a statement about anthropology, language, and civilization that uses the poetic and artistic voice of colleagues, fieldworkers, and cultural others in order to address fundamental issues in anthropological practice. This assertion requires elaboration as it locates anthropological poetics at a critical juncture in the re-thinking of anthropology, particularly as it seeks an appropriate epistemological basis for anthropological conduct in the field. Anthropological poetics has a foundation within the anthropology of myth. I understand mythology as a sacred narrative, drawing upon deep unconscious structures of archetypal imagery. These structures, deep in the human mind, are species-specific, not culturally specific, and this accounts for the similar forms and imprints found in mythology irrespective of particular cultural traditions. In different ways, the works of Claude Lévi-Strauss and Joseph Campbell bear eloquent testimony to the remarkable similarities found in culturally separate mythologies (Campbell 1949, 1960, 1962, 1968, 1974, 1988; Lévi-Strauss 1969, 1973, 1978).

My understanding and experience of mythology is that its symbolic sequences activate deep unconscious structures. The world's mythologies, that is, the protohistories of its religions, are highly complex forms that have kept alive the realities of creation and the manner in which light and life came to humankind. They also provide graphic insights into the way that light and life are being lost. In a highly coded way, these accounts throughout time and space document the placement of humankind within the universe and on the globe. The accounts are coded and multi-levelled so that directions for the integration of awareness with the unconscious slip through the barriers imposed on the human individual. In so-called primitive societies studied by anthropologists, the shamans and seers believe they have been called to be intermediaries between the earth and the universe. Their task is to maintain a balance between the multi-dimensional levels of reality known to them by ensuring that these levels can be experienced and honoured. The rich field of effective ritual through which this is done operates with precision. It includes particular rites to effect and alter the physical and spiritual conditions of those who seek healing or initiation.

All myths are rich in symbolic metaphors. Particular symbolic sequences are woven into the narrative to take the adventurer, one step at a time, into further self-knowledge. The encounters and battles with strange entities, demons and dragons spotlight the debris placed by ourselves in our own lives. By recognizing the significance of these encounters and being willing to come through with new awareness, our patterns of violence, insensitivity, denial, and shame can be abandoned (Prattis 1996). Mythology provides fertile ground for this drama. It prepares the field of insight for a new dimension of knowing. At the same time, it deflects the awesome power of archetypal experiences. Conscious awareness could be damaged and overwhelmed by a direct encounter with such experiences. Mythology filters them so that they can be progressively encountered and eventually integrated with conscious awareness. In other words, the symbolic structures in a mythological narrative are created from the deepest structure of the unconscious -- the archetypal -- yet at the same time they are placed in a metaphoric form which mediates the potentially devastating effect of archetypal material on conscious awareness (Prattis 1996). The mediating function of mythological narrative thus allows one to avoid being overwhelmed by archetypal material, and one can experience the release of deeply-held unconscious structures.

In culture after culture the constancy with which these sacred stories narrate the lessons of being, creation, and transformation provides overwhelming evidence that the distinctive style of these accounts is no haphazard accident. Through ritual sequences they make it possible to know more deeply the universal structures contained in the unconscious. Anthropological poetics takes as its object of study this crucial process. Poetry, in our civilized world, resists the order of reason and, consequently, is often dismissed from "serious" discourse. It should not be forgotten that poetry continues the mythic voice and the central power of ritual. This now brings me back to *Reflections* as myth.

Ivan Brady has pointed out how this volume has opened the discipline to new methods and writing genres in anthropology, "to more creative interpretations on all fronts..." (Brady 1991b:205, 263). Remarking on Romanucci-Ross' work, he also observes "that we have no option but to grow up poetically now that we know the difference between an artificially selfless and an inescapably self-grounded system (Brady 1991b:47, 48). Toni Flores argues that *Reflections* is an exploration of the archetypal imagery she calls *Goddess consciousness* (Flores 1991:137-158). These asides bring me to a statement about the appropriate reading of *Reflections* as myth. Regarded incorrectly only as a volume of poetry, the reader could dip into *Reflections* at random. This would likely miss the purpose of the construction of the volume. To read *Reflections* as myth, one starts at the beginning with the frontpiece by John Cove that stylistically captures the dilemmas and paradox of subject-object relationships in the fieldwork enterprise, and then proceeds sequentially through each section. Following a brief foreword by Dell Hymes, there are nine sections:

I. BEGINNINGS
II. THE ETHNOGRAPHIC OTHER
III. CULTURAL IDIOMS: THEIRS AND OURS
IV. THE ANTHROPOLOGIST'S VISION QUEST
V. THE FIELD WITHIN
VI. TO SEE OURSELVES
VII. AS OTHERS SEE US
VIII. REQUIEM
IX FINALE

The transition from BEGINNINGS to FINALE is a deepening journey of awareness into the dilemmas that face the anthropologist and the cultural other in the fieldwork endeavour. Each section has a variety of poetic and artistic voices that plays out variations on the particular theme of the section and then one moves into the next, and more complex, stage of thematic expression. The progression is made possible by the many different voices in the volume that represent anthropologists, cultural others, and the fieldwork enterprise. Each voice is respected for what it has to say, and there emerges a compelling statement about our discipline, the cultural other, and the language that can be used to represent both.

The previous essay on "*Dialectics and Experience in Fieldwork*" (Chapter 3) brings the mythic journey provided by *Reflections* back into the concrete realm of anthropological conduct and method. In it I point out the epistemological constraints inherent in modern ethnographic practice (Prattis 1985:266), and argue further that the raw material of fieldwork, the collision of cultural assumptions of subject and object, is ignored and has the status of an unreported dialectic. To recognize the dialectic and close the gap between subject and object requires a different approach to language and communication. Anthropological poetics, the art of making the interior life of persons on one side of a cultural barrier available to those on the other, provides this. It calls on a sense of respect in the relationship of other and observer, and entails a hermeneutic process whereby whatever becomes data in a field setting is expressed in a language that more accurately portrays the unrecognized space created by the interaction between researcher and consultant, out of which the field data arise. The mapping and expression of this interactive space through the vehicle of poetics alters the observer's perception of self and cultural other, since a language is being used that reflects something other than surface reality. It expresses an interiority of experience which moves beyond the observer and observed into a new ethnographic accounting of events.

The power relation between the observer's cultural assumptions and those of the cultural other often results in fieldworkers recording and communicating only what they wish to have reflected back to them. So the collision of cultural assumptions, the interactional and negotiating premises that exist in every field situation, are frequently not examined or represented, whereas they are all integral to the approach of anthropological poetics. The reflective process of standing back and examining the constraints on perception and the production of knowledge involves coming to terms with what one brings into the field situation and recognizing (and respecting) what is already there in terms of the other. What is observed is rarely the other acting in isolation without constraints. It is often a result of "anthropologist-other" interaction, so both the anthropologist and the other are always co-determinants of any resulting event that is recorded by the anthropologist. The cultural relativity in this can be extreme, with a resulting disquiet about identifying any patterns that would have cross-cultural comparability. This factor has instigated much of the reflective process inherent in the new ethnography (Myerhoff 1978; Rabinow 1977; Taussig 1980). Yet underlying the disquiet and confusion in the new ethnography is a standpoint of necessary respect for both subject and object. This provides the foundation for a hermeneutic exercise that Rose describes as follows:

"The observer moves towards the observed, and draws, in turn the observed closer to the observer, suspending both in a new space, somewhere not wholly here and not wholly there" (Rose 1991).

I elaborate on Rose and describe this state as an "interiority" that incudes self and other culture and moves beyond it to a new form of expression (Prattis 1985:279). One manifestation of this new form is anthropological poetics. It describes the dialectic between observer and cultural other and draws explicitly on the collision of cultural assumptions mentioned earlier, thus telling us something *different* and something *more* about ethnography that is missed when one uses the language of everyday scientific discourse. The methodology involved requires treating poetry as poetic observation which I elaborated on in Chapter 3.

The advantage of anthropological poetics is that its grounding in interiority permits another culture to be expressed in a way that relates to that culture's inherent meanings, while at the same time the awareness and sensitivity of the anthropologist/ observer is not discarded. The latter is part of the hermeneutic process that produces a different kind of text, a different dimension of understanding. Brady comments that "there is more than one way to say anthropology...that some things said poetically about anthropological experience can't be said with equal effectiveness any other way" (Brady 1991a:5). This particular thrust forces anthropology into being a voice, and a very important voice, in the postmodern dialogue. Without poetics it is highly doubtful if anthropology would have a credible foundation to be in the vanguard of postmodernist debate; it would remain in the modernist mode. For instance, in judging the poetry competition held by the Society for Humanistic Anthropology in 1988, I stated that:

> The final selection was an experimental construction that emerged from interaction between the contributions and from the implicit architecture inherent in the words and images that lead to certain selections and juxtapositions (and not to others) that no pre-set mental design of my own could have achieved. The sequence of the selection demanded its own implicate order...and this progression enabled me to present a particular statement about how I feel about anthropology, society and language, that I could not make in any other way...

> This selection presented itself to me as a whole, engaging with my preconceptions and preferences and moving beyond them so that there is movement to a singular statement that neither I alone nor the contributors alone would make. The hermeneutic exercise that produced the selection of prize-winning poems is also inherent in how I believe the subject matter of anthropology may best be approached (Prattis 1988:67-91).

In this selection process, the prize-winning poems constituted the object, as poetry judge I was the subject, and the open space of subject-object interaction provided a forum for all the basic issues of epistemology in the field to be expressed. The poems created a highly articulate balance concerning the problematic of self/other alienation, entertained a lyricism to combine personal growth with collective expression, introduced shamanic type chants that took the reader to other realities and reflections on continuity through time and space, and eventually reminded us of our fallibility as scientists (Prattis 1988:69). A new mode thus emerges for the exploration of other cultures and self that rests on non-exploitative relations between subject and object (Rose 1991). It is essential to deconstruct the subject so that the observer's perceptions can be understood. The object then must be reconstructed so that a basis of respect is accorded to the cultural other. A new two-way relationship between subject and object can be created and has as its necessary core the sense of anthropological poetics itself. It places tremendous demands of reflexivity on the subject's self-awareness, but it is this awareness that drives the conduct of inquiry, moving positivistic reifications into the possibility of an interactive discourse.

Bibliography

Blair, D. and J.I. Prattis
1994 Exploitation in the Field. Anthropology and Humanism, V.19, 1:36-39

Brady, I.
1991a Harmony and Argument: Bringing Forth the Artful Science. In I. Brady (ed.): Anthropological Poetics: 3-30. Savage, Maryland: Rowman and Littlefield

1991b (ed.): Anthropological Poetics. Savage, Maryland: Rowman and Littlefield

Campbell, J.
1949 The Hero with a Thousand Faces. Princeton: Princeton University Press

1960 The Masks of God I: Primitive Mythology. London: Secker and Warburg

1962 The Masks of God II: Oriental Mythology. N.Y.: The Viking Press

1968 The Masks of God IV: Creative Mythology. N.Y.: The Viking Press

1974 The Mythic Image. Princeton: Princeton University Press

1988 The Power of Myth. N.Y.: Doubleday

Clifford, J. and G. Marcus
1986 (eds.): Writing Culture: The Poetics and Politics of Ethnography. Berkeley: University of California Press

Dwyer, K.
1982 Moroccan Dialogues. Baltimore: John Hopkins University Press

Flores, T.
1991 The Goddess as Muse. In I. Brady (ed.): Anthropological Poetics:137-158. Savage, Maryland: Rowman and Littlefield

Friedrich, P.
1986 The Princes of Naranja: An Essay in Anthrohistorical Method. Austin: University of Texas Press

Lévi-Strauss, C.
1969 The Raw and the Cooked (trans. John and Doreen Weightman.) N.Y.: Harper and Row

1973 From Honey to Ashes (trans. John and Doreen Weightman.) N.Y.: Harper and Row

1978 The Origin of Table Manners (trans. John and Doreen Weightman.) London: Jonathan Cape Ltd.

Myerhoff, B.
1978 Number Our Days. N.Y.: Simon and Schuster

Prattis, J.I.
1985 (ed.): Reflections: The Anthropological Muse. Washington, D.C.: American Anthropological Association

1988 Prelude. Anthropology and Humanism Quarterly. V.13, 3:67-71

1996 Living Breath. Forthcoming

Rabinow, P.
1977 Reflections on Fieldwork in Morocco. Berkeley: University of California Press

Rose, D.
1991 [1983] In Search of Experience: The Anthropological Poetics of Stanley Diamond. In I. Brady (ed.): Anthropological Poetics, 219-233. Savage, Maryland: Rowman and Littlefield

Taussig, M.
1980 The Devil and Commodity Fetishism in South America. Chapel Hill: University of North Carolina Press

Chapter 5

Reflexive Anthropology

Epimenides the Cretan and Groucho Marx provide an exceptional entry point to Reflexive Anthropology. The Cretan paradox was created by Epimenides when he said "All Cretans are liars." This paradox and ambiguity lives on in Groucho Marx's famous comment that he would not think of belonging to a club that would consider having him for a member (Bronowski 1966)!

In these instances language and metaphor are used to refer to themselves in a relativistic sense and inevitably a process of reflexivity enters in, which is capable of creating an infinite hall of mirrors. This is because of the relativity, ambiguity and paradox that are built in to every language. This applies to all languages -- mathematical, literate and symbolic. The full significance of this process of built-in reflexivity was not recognized in anthropology until relatively recently, though our distant cousins in mathematics attacked this problem with great vigour in the 1930's. Scholars such as Gödel (1931), Turing (1937) and Tarski (1956) provided an internal critique of positivism by demonstrating that mathematics and numbers are a language system with tendencies of ambiguity; they concluded that there cannot be an account of reality in a single, closed, consistent language. As Bronowski (1966) points out, any language the mind uses -- speech, poetry, rhetoric or formalized mathematics -- has self-reference and therefore built-in paradoxes and ambiguities that prevent the logical closure that the axiomatic system demands.

I do not regard the paradox of ambiguity as a negative event, however, because it is the mainspring of creativity and insight in physics, art, literature and anthropology. Bronowski (1966) points out that science tries to untangle the ambiguities, whereas literature permits the ambiguities to work their way through to our consciousness -- hence the supreme importance of myth and poetry (Prattis 1988). The full force of Gödel's and Tarski's work undermines the axiomatic conception in science and furthermore implies that self-reference and reflexivity underlies the social sciences everywhere. This requires of our model builders and theorists a radically different kind of intellectual effort.

In anthropology there has been a reflexive component ever since anthropologists raised questions about the validity of their data, the authenticity of their endeavours, and why they were in someone else's cultural backyard. But these concerns remained largely implicit and were reflected in a periodic re-examination of anthropological theory and methodology. When the issues of reflexivity became explicit over the past two decades, the discipline of anthropology was forced to take a very hard look not just at theory and methodology, but at ethics, truth and epistemology and to look anew at the question of anthropology's exploitation of the cultural other.

It is no accident that the reflexive pause in the discipline coincides with the development of new ethnographic accounts (Clifford and Marcus 1986) and postmodern perspectives (Tyler 1984, 1987; Rosenau 1992) and is about re-evaluating what we do as anthropologists. It has lead to a re-examination of the entire epistemological basis of what we know, how we communicate it, and how do we know if it is valid. Epistemology lies within the field of self-reference (Prattis 1985:266) and here lies the basis of much confusion, because the infinite regress of reflexivity can take one into a never ending hall of mirrors. Our various methodologies are devices to stop the hall of mirrors from spinning us off into an extreme cultural relativity as they allow the investigator to observe patterns, correlations and transformations and thus make translations across cultural and personal boundaries. Without this kind of pragmatism social science would be impossible or irrelevant; for the hall of mirrors would not allow us to make sensible statements about any cultural or social situation. We would be left with the postmodernist package, expressed by Carlos Fuentes, of "nothing matters, anything goes" (Fokkema 1984:45). This misunderstands the significance of different levels of reflexivity and is a recipe for poor scholarship.

The implications of reflexivity are very important and far reaching. The first thing to do is to take the notion of reflexivity apart and see exactly what it means and implies. My starting place is science where new conceptual cutting edges explored by Bohm (astronomy), Wheeler and Zurek (physics), Sheldrake (biology) and Capra (new science) -- have in common the notion that science cannot evolve further until it determines if scientists have the capacity to be reflexive and self-aware. Our present scientific paradigm inherited from Descartes, refined through Newton, and implemented through the Vienna school of positivism, prevents this issue of reflexivity from being fully explored. This oversight was pointed out as long ago as 1938 when the atomic physicist Niels Bohr addressed the International Congress of Anthropological Sciences at Elsinore, Denmark. In the setting for Shakespeare's *Hamlet* he raised the question of what kind of knowledge we are producing when our descriptions of atoms, nature and social behaviour are inherently connected to the properties of the observer (1938); in other words to the biases, conditioning and perceptual blinkers of the observer, and the measuring instruments used by that blinkered observer. Anthropology, at that time, did not have an answer to Niels Bohr. Now more than fifty years later I feel it does.

In Chapter 3 I pointed out that an essential starting point is the language used to describe events as this places limitations on the accounts we give. Furthermore, that a significant part of what we experience and know of ourselves and others is deleted and supressed because our standard language system is often not equal to the problem of communication across cultural and personal boundaries. I referred to this problem in the final chapter of *Reflections: The Anthropological Muse* (1985:274) - Chapter 3 of this volume - before identifying three levels of reflexivity, which I would like to explicate further in this essay.

First is the exploitative level: the other culture simply reflects back the biases, presuppositions, interests and personal epistemology of the observer. In an examination of biographical, ethnographic and in-cultural field scenarios (Blair and Prattis 1994) we suggest that there is an inherently exploitative aspect in the relationship between anthropological researcher and field consultant. The process of interviewing, for instance, is anchored in a unidirectional "giving relationship" from the field consultant to the observer. The exploitative nature of this relationship is even more severe when the resulting monograph is rendered inaccessible to the people who provided the information, as they have very little say about what conveyed information will find its way to the finished monograph. There is a direct power relation here: the anthropologist has the power to hear, write, and produce whatever information serves his/her research interests. This is the power to exploit and is an inappropriate relationship, because it is often the anthropologist who is the student in the field situation.

In the cross-cultural ethnographic field relationship the anthropologist as researcher brings to the field personal factors of educational and anthropological training, conditioning, culture and ideology which provide perceptual screens that distort observation. These factors do not become invisible once the fieldwork coat is put on by the anthropologist, and blatant misrepresentations of a people may result until observer effects and the "stranger factor" are taken into account. With this and all the biases we pack into our travel bags is it possible to conduct honest and truthful fieldwork that is non-exploitative?

The "in-cultural" field situation is one where the researcher is a member of the culture under examination yet approaches the research relationship from the perspective of a special interest group (e.g. aboriginal rights, feminism, class etc.). Thus the information extracted from any research participant is interpreted in terms of the interest of the researcher's personal reference group -- even when the participant is *not* a member of that interest group. These field scenarios at the first level of reflexivity depict in different ways the power relation between the observer's cultural assumptions and those of the cultural other. At this level of reflexivity fieldworkers tend to record and communicate only what they wish to have reflected back to them. This poses a dilemma for fieldwork as it seems increasingly difficulty to justify an endeavour so exploitative of the cultural other, the raw material used by the anthropologist to garner kudos in the arena of academic achievement. This dilemma is not new in anthropology and has preoccupied generations of scholars well before Project Camelot startled the discipline into a necessary, and overdue, review of ethics in inquiry.

The second level of reflexivity is the process of standing back and examining the constraints on perception and knowledge production -- one's own and the other's. This involves coming to terms with what one brings into the field situation and recognizing what is already there in terms of the "other". The result of this second level of reflexivity is a reassessment of the entire anthropological endeavour. As I have mentioned before, what is observed is rarely the "other" acting in isolation without constraints. There is a two-way intersubjectivity between the anthropologist and the "other" which shapes the data recorded by the anthropologist. Although the cultural relativity in this can be extreme, this problematic has been a catalyst for the new ethnography (Myerhoff 1978; Rabinow 1977; Taussig 1980).

Without this second level of reflexivity, of standing back and examining the constraints on perception and knowledge production, we would simply project our own biases and preferences onto the behaviour and accounts of the cultural other, and remain stuck in the first level of reflexivity -- the *exploitative* realm. In this second level of reflexivity we find the work of the Rice University group (Clifford and Marcus 1986; Marcus and Fisher 1986), the postmoderism of Stephen Tyler (1984, 1987), the new ethnography mentioned above and the dialogical hermeneutics of Michrina and Richards (1995).

There is a third level of reflexivity which is difficult to pin down, though it has been consistently expressed in anthropological poetics (Prattis 1985; Brady 1991). This level goes beyond cultural relativity, assumes a marked respect between the researcher and the field person; and engages in a slippery hermeneutic exercise that Dan Rose (1983) and I (Prattis 1985) have tried to explicate. I discuss this exercise as producing an "interiority" that states the dialectic between observer and cultural other, and provides the foundation for a different ethnographic format and language of reporting.

Here the anthropologist is not simply reporting on his or her own analytic model or using emic and etic distinctions to get at the material of observation. The anthropologist has engaged with the cultural other and taken it one step further by expressing this engagement in the symbolic language of poetry. The total field report becomes more complete because anthropological poetics, particularly at the level of "interiority", is a distinctive ethnographic account that the accepted discourse in anthropological monographs and articles rarely conveys. By treating anthropological research as poetic observation, a new surface of emergence is created for the exploration of other cultures and the self (Rose 1993), one that rests on candour and overtly engineered non-exploitative relations between researcher and field community. Derek Blair and I have referred to this as a focus on "universal similarism" (1994). At this level of reflexivity field scenarios are seen as richly symbolic encounters and we assume that there exists at a deep level an aspect of global existence that is unhampered and unhamperable by conditioning. It is a step towards what Buddhists would describe as mindfulness.

I pointed out in the previous chapter that one advantage of poetics is that its basis of interiority permits comprehension of another culture to be expressed in a way that relates not only to that culture's inherent meanings, but also to the awareness and sensitivity of the anthropologist as observer. This kind of hermeneutic engagement produces a different kind of text as it taps into a different dimension of understanding. As Dove point out, poetics is simply the art of making the interior life of one individual available to others (1994). At this level of reflexivity cultural differences between field person and researcher are a matter of mere surface reality. This leads to an anthropology based on selves, as it proposes that the understanding of one's own self is through the building of a relationship by the other self and vice versa. This is the dialectic of the researcher/field person encounter.

It leads to a strategy that begins with a renewed focus on the relationship between subject and object, anthropologist and cultural other. To restate the obvious -- first of all it is essential to deconstruct the subject (the anthropologist as observer) so that bias and distortion in the anthropologist's perceptions are understood. Secondly, the object must be reconstructed in order that a basis of respect is accorded to the cultural other. This creates a new two-way relationship between subject and object and this relationship is what reflexive anthropology explores. It is found in the ongoing discourse on postmoderism, the methods of dialogical hermeneutics, the new ethnography, and is most graphically demonstrated in anthropological poetics. These endeavours place tremendous demands on the anthropologist's capacity to be self-aware and self-reflexive, yet these qualities also undermine positivistic reifications and move anthropological enquiry and the conduct of science into a hermeneutic framework.

Anthropology is a science of experience; a science of understanding. Acknowledging this in turn calls for the recognition that understanding the field that we see outside entails an understanding of the field within. It is evident that the practice of science and scholarship cannot be divorced from the person of the scholar, or that scholar's reflexive self-awareness. The openness and clarity that enables science and scholarship to evolve requires a reflexive knowledge of self and how that self relates to the phenomena being examined.

Bibliography

Blair, D. and J.I. Prattis
1994 Exploitation in the Field. Anthropology and Humanism, V.19, 1:36-39.

Bohm, D.
1980 Wholeness and the Implicate Order. London: Routledge and Kegan Paul

Bohr, N.
1938 Natural Philosophy and Human Cultures. Nature V. 143:268-272

Brady, I.
1991 (ed.): Anthropological Poetics. Savage, Maryland: Rowman and Littlefield

Bronowski, J.
1966 The Logic of the Mind. American Scientist 54, 1:1-14

Capra, F.
1974 The Tao of Physics. Boston: Shambhala

Clifford, J. and G. Marcus
1986 (eds.): Writing Culture: The Poetics and Politics of Ethnography. Berkeley: University of California Press

Dove, R.
1994 What Does Poetry Do For Us? University of Virginia Alumni News, Jan-Feb:22-27.

Fokkema, D.
1984 Literary History, Modernism and Post Modernism. Philadelphia: John Benjamins

Gödel, K.
1931 Über Formal Unentscheidbare Sätze der Principia Mathematica und Verwandter Systeme. Monatshefte für Mathematik und Physik 38:173-198.

Marcus, G. and M. Fisher
1986 (eds.): Anthropology as Cultural Critique. Chicago: University of Chicago Press

Michrina, B. and C.A. Richards
1995 Person to Person: Fieldwork, Dialogue and the Hermeneutic Method. Albany: S.U.N.Y. Press

Myerhoff, B.
1978 Number Our Days. N.Y.: Simon and Schuster

Prattis, J.I.
1985 (ed.): Reflections: The Anthropological Muse. Washington, D.C.: American Anthropological Association

1988 Prelude. Anthropology and Humanism Quarterly. V.13, 3:67-71

Rabinow, P.
1977 Reflections on Fieldwork in Morocco. Berkeley: University of California Press

Rose, D.
1983 In Search of Experience. The Anthropological Poetics of Stanley Diamond. American Anthropologist, V. 85:345-360.

Rosenau, P.
1992 Post-Modernism and the Social Sciences. Princeton: Princeton University Press

Sheldrake, R.
1981 A New Science of Life. London: Blond and Briggs

Tarski, A.
1956 Logic, Semantics, Metamathematics. Oxford: Oxford University Press

Taussig, M.
1980 The Devil and Commodity Fetishism in South America. Chapel Hill: University of North Carolina Press

Turing, A.M.
1936 On Computable Numbers with an Application to the Entscheidungsproblem. Proceedings of the London Mathematical Society, 2nd ser 42 (1936):230-265 and 43 (1937):544-546

Tyler, S.
1984 The Poetic Turn in Postmodern Anthropology. American Anthropologist 86, 2:328-336.

1987 The Unspeakable: Discourse, Dialogue and Rhetoric in the Postmodern World. Wisconsin: University of Wisconsin Press

Wheeler J.A. and W.H. Zurek
1983 Quantum Theory and Measurement. Princeton: Princeton University Press

Chapter 6

Opening Ourselves up to the Voyage of Anthropological Practice

"You could say I lost my faith in science..."

- Sting -

Introduction

This essay navigates the shoals, reefs, and cross-currents of rationality, experience, epistemology and knowledge production. In it we encounter the good ships of "-ism" and "-ive" and meet the anthropological fleets from Positivism, Postmodernism, Reflexive, and Interpretive that compete for berths at the ports of Logos, Eros, Mythos, Boundary, and Fuzzy. There are many brilliant mariners that have gone before us and they are unusual companions because despite their differences they all ask surprisingly similar questions. "Is my knowledge rational?" "If experience is not rational, what is science?" "What is reality?" "Who am I in the process of enquiry?" Plato,

Descartes, Habermas and Calvino have tested the waters. Lévi-Strauss, Bastian, Campbell, Grof, and Jung have been there; also Einstein, Bohr, von Kekule, and Ricoeur.

"What and where is the field of study?" "Is there a conflict between my scientific reason and my humanity?" "What happens if we open ourselves to other reasonings?" So ask later explorers such as Turner, Diamond, Laughlin, Dwyer, Young, Goulet, Rodman, and Brady.

- all voyaging in a search for truth -

Truth and Rationality are an Odd Pair...

Truth and rationality are an odd pair, or rather are they a pair at odds? The recent debates surrounding epistemology, ethnography, and issues of "truth", have grappled with this dilemma, and one might question whether anthropology needs another discussion about such issues. We feel, however, that we have something more and different to say, especially in light of recent edited compilations in the area (Brady and Turner 1994; Borofsky 1994; Young and Goulet 1994). These works relocate the epistemological endeavour by removing it solely from the rational realm and finding a new home for it in the realm of experience. Experience is coincident with the erocentric realm, though we are careful not to dichotomize and pit this at one end of the epistemological spectrum and logocentrism at the other. If this were our agenda, then we would have certainly fallen victim to "rationalization" which serves to construct dichotomies and which, by itself proves to be incompatible with ethnographic examinations, as we will show. What these works and others have done is to persuade us that logos and eros are, in fact, quite inseparable. Understanding this is a necessary step in enhancing the explanatory power of anthropology. Enlightenment rationalism and Cartesian "science" have provided an epistemology based on rational truth and reason (logos). Labouvie-Vief would submit that this was far from a revelation, since Platonism gave us the same message; that although logos is certainly a more recent phenomenon, it is certainly far superior to the arcane mythos (1994).

Drawing on Plato, Labouvie-Vief sees logos and mythos as the two primary modes of knowing; logos being the realm of logic and objectivity, and mythos being organic, private, and emotional -- the realm of feelings (1994:1). What is notable is that modern conceptualizations of logos have themselves been subject to rationalization, and even in Plato's work the distinction between logos and mythos is not consistently clear and definitive. Recently, Roy Rappaport has discussed modern conceptions of logos and rightly points out that in its more archaic form, it is not merely an intellectual phenomenon: "one grasps it by becoming part of it" (1994:158). At times Plato does present logos as a mode of knowing superior to mythos, as Friedlander reads in *Republic*: "The mind of the god, in his journey through the heavens, sees justice itself, sees measure, sees truth; and after it has seen the world of true being and has nourished itself, it returns home" (1973:14). Following this trajectory we are thus brought to Plato's point that thinking is the "eye of the soul" (1973:15). Furthermore, in *Phaedo*, Plato presents mythos in opposition to logos. However, Socrates' indication that *Republic* is both mythical and logical in construction raises the point that myth is in itself a kind of logos (Friedlander 1973:368). In Plato's *Censorship of Literature for School Use* it is quite directly stated that mythology is fiction mixed with truth (and therefore logos). Based on his reading of Plato, Friedlander sees mythos as somewhat akin to logos: "the myth -- like the *Logos* -- not invented, but discovered, has -- again like the *Logos* --- its own structure. And mythology makes sense only if it can be shown that the myth carries forward the lines of argument set by the *Logos*" (1973:189).

What this demonstrates is that although Plato's position was that "both divine inspiration and mathematical science lead upward" and that "geometry leads to God" (Friedlander 1973:78) when discussing mythos, logos did become a necessary consideration. This elaboration on the Platonic mythos/logos dichotomy serves the purpose of demonstrating first that this dichotomy was not always clear, and second that traditional science served to solidify distinctions between logos and mythos. For us "logos" refers to the rationalized, objective realm which has its basis in the rigors of the modern scientific method. But whereas the distinction for Plato was between mythos and logos, we believe that a more apt characterization is achieved by distinguishing between logos and eros.

For our purposes, "eros" is a concept which contains all aspects of the mythos, but it connotes a greater amount of emotiveness, affectivity, and consequently relatedness. Certainly for Plato, eros or "the erotic" was meant to connote more than the merely sexual, as he and Socrates saw it as relatedness -- "an original and living experience which brings two people together" (Friedlander 1973:45-50). For Plato, Eros was not a god but a demonic mediator between the human and the divine worlds. Friedlander further points out that it is this demonic element which keeps the Platonic logos from being a strictly rational pursuit (1973:36). As for ourselves, we draw our conception of eros from psychiatrist William J. Perry, who characterized "the living mythological symbol as an *affect image*" (Campbell 1973:89). Logos, as it has come to be known in the modern sense, is incompatible with the erocentrically laden affect images. These latter images are "felt" experiences as opposed to "thought of" rationalizations, and are often represented in symbols. Our use of the term eros is to be seen in this light, as affective, emotive, and experiential; non-rationally inspired or verified, it is beyond the present reach of the scientific and empirical logos.

Postmodernisms have emphasized that logos is not the ultimate mode of knowing and have launched an attack on scientific rationalism, all the while themselves remaining rational and thus questionable. Lyotard (1984), for example, points out that "Scientific knowledge does not represent the totality of knowledge; it has always existed in addition to and in competition with, another kind of knowledge, which I will call narrative in the interests of simplicity" (In Sassower 1993:431). Lyotard argues further that scientific knowledge should not be seen as the basis by which all other modes of knowing are constructed and judged, and he argues that "the game of science" should be "put on par with others" (1993:431). As for ourselves, we find utility in scientific truth, and see that it is not at all at odds with the future plans of anthropology although science is no longer what it was, so we heed Robin Fox's warning not to throw out the "scientific baby with the scientific bathwater" (1994:15; see also Rappaport 1994; and Smith-Doody 1992).

Anthropology is no longer the formalized endeavour which sought to decode the cultural other and provide interpretations on exclusively scientific grounds. What anthropologists are beginning to realize is that though our discourse continues as science, what constitutes "science" is, at best, in question. We see anthropology as a science of experience; a science of understanding (see also Fox 1994). Further, with the emergence of reflexive and interpretive movements, and with the onslaught of postmodernism, the place of "the field" in the ethnographic enterprise has certainly been put into question. Does the field, as anthropological poetics has told us, not have a justified place within the interior realms of anthropologist and cultural counterpart? With this, can we be honest and justified in asking if anthropology is self-understanding as opposed to the understanding of selves?

Recently (1990) Maggie Ross wrote a wonderful story entitled *Seasons of Death and Life: A Wilderness Memoir* and what she has to say rings true. About the "truth" of her account, she states:

> Hunter is a real place, as are the animals and humans who populate this book, though I have changed their names and locations as I have Hunter's.... All the same, I hesitate to say this book is nonfiction. Indeed I begin to wonder if we rightly label any book nonfiction, because perception and memory, the filters of living and dying, pain and joy, hurting and healing, all conspire to make liars out of those rash enough to write about their experiences (1990:1).

With this, Ross captures the dilemma of the anthropologist who has been "changed by the cross-cultural encounter". Has truth, then, become relative to such a degree that it causes fuzziness about the boundaries between fiction and nonfiction? It is becoming more and more apparent that perhaps truth is not contingent on fiction or nonfiction. Habermas, in his essay *Philosophy and Science as Literature?* (1992), cites Italo Calvino, who argues that "literature does not recognize Reality as such, but only *levels*" (1992:215). Habermas explains that it is Calvino's goal to make it apparent that the border between fiction and reality is a mere perceptual appearance which is generated by the text itself (ibid.). In this sense, Calvino's text (and all texts for that matter) are "recognizable as a fragment of [what he calls] a *universal* text, a primordial text, which knows no limits of possible delimitations, space and time..." (1992:214-215). So in a sense, the literary and imaginative creation is something which is "real" in that it has a universal nature which lies beyond the spatio-temporal realm. Referring to Calvino's *If On a Winter's Night a Traveller* (1981), Habermas points out Calvino's success in persuading the reader "to take the arguments that are stated in it by fictional characters seriously *as arguments*" (1992:220). Jerome Bruner discusses these issues of fuzzy boundaries as he distinguishes between two modes of knowing, the logico-scientific and the poetic or novelistic mode (Brady 1991b:15, 27). The logico-scientific mode pursues truth in the vein of "good science". It "deals in general causes, and in their establishment, and makes use of procedures to assure verifiable reference and to test empirical truth. Its language is regulated by requirements of consistency and noncontradiction" (1991b:15). The poetic or novelistic mode, on the other hand, has been considered questionable regarding any level of truth, because it cannot stand up to the rigors of a scientific method. Bruner as Brady tells us, was careful not to deny the truth message of either the logico-empirical sciences, or the experiential sciences where the former assesses truth by way of well formed arguments, and the latter by way of lifelikeness (1991b:15). Thus, the "true to conceivable experience" and the "truth of fiction" (Bruner in Brady 1991b:27) cannot be compared hierarchically, but rather, can be compared only.

Certainly, one would expect that the experiences described by Goulet and Turner (discussed later) respectively in Young and Goulet's *Being Changed by Cross-Cultural Encounters* (1994) could not withstand verification in the logico-empirical realm. Regardless, the truth of these experiences can neither be dismissed nor denied. On this note, Grof points out that some of the most logical science has come from the least logico-empirical of circumstances (Grof 1993:168-170). Take for example Friedrich August von Kekule, who envisioned the chemical formula for benzene while lost in a trance, "gazing into his fireplace coals", or Mendeleev who "envisioned his famous periodic table of the elements while he was lying in bed exhausted after a long struggle to categorize these elements according to their atomic weight". Other examples include Einstein, whose theory of relativity came to him "in the form of kinaesthetic sensations in his muscles", and Niels Bohr's discovery of the model of the atom, and Heisenberg's preliminary work in the area of quantum physics. Certainly these are far from anthropological encounters, but they do say something about the fuzziness of boundaries between "modern scientific" conceptions of the reasonable and unreasonable, rational and irrational, truth and untruth. Perhaps this fuzziness is best exemplified by the experience of Descartes, as Grof describes:

> The paradox is that Rene Descartes' *Discourse on Method*, the book that reformed the entire structure of Western knowledge and that provided the foundations for modern science, came to its author in three visionary dreams and a dream within a dream, which provided the key for interpreting the larger dream. What an irony it is that the entire edifice of rational, reductionist, positivist science, which today rejects "subjective knowledge" was originally inspired by a revelation in a non-ordinary state of consciousness! (Grof 1993:170).

Jean-Guy Goulet tells a fascinating story of how he gained rational knowledge in a situation that traditional science would consider the least rational of circumstances while conducting fieldwork with the Dene Tha. While sitting with the elders about a fire in a teepee, smoke began to sting his eyes. Wondering what to do about this, he suddenly envisioned a rather detailed life-size image of himself, fanning the flames with his hat. Soon after this vision, a non-Native arose and started blowing on the fire. At this point, an elder immediately spoke and told him not to blow into the fire since "such an action would offend spiritual entities and induce a violent windstorm in the camp". The elder suggested using a hat or some other object to fan the fire instead (Goulet 1994:30). In this example, Goulet discovered the proper way to fan a fire through a vision of himself doing simply that. Edith Turner, too, tells a story of an unusual experience which she had while conducting fieldwork in Zambia in 1985 (Turner 1994). In this case, Turner was asked to take part as a doctor in an Ihamba curing session among the Ndembu. While doing this, she was eyewitness to the emergence from the body of the victim, Meru, of the Ihamba (tooth) spirit, which she described as a large, opaque, gray blob (1994:83). Anyone less open to the world of Ndembu might have considered such an extraction as "shamanic trickery", but Turner's care to take the world of the informant seriously left the door for extraordinary experience "unlocked" (1994:93).

Science, as Fox has recently discussed (1994:16), reaffirmed by Lyotard (1984:7,40,42), is simply one mode of knowing. It has become overly rationalized and preoccupied with logos. It should not be viewed as the sole concern of physics, chemistry, or biology, nor should it necessarily involve quantifications and statistics (Fox 1994:16). On rationality, Goulet quotes Rappaport's well-known *Ecology, Meaning, and Religion* (1979); "the empirical and logical rationality that defines knowledge as knowledge of fact" is one defiant of "the insights of art, religion, fantasy, or dream" (1994:18). The problem becomes one of competing epistemologies, conflicting ways of knowing.

We have previously defined our use of the term *logos* to designate the reasonable, rationalized mode of knowing based in empiricism, logic, and most explicitly, the scientific method. *Eros* on the other hand, designates the realm of affect, of experience, of interiority. Here is the realm of art, poetry, dreams, myths and symbols. If anthropology is to make room for experience, and the truth that accompanies it, it must then make room for eros. Goulet and Young remind us that experience provides a great deal of the essential data which could not be obtained by any other means (1994:315). They do not suggest dumping logos altogether, this would be absurd. Rather, they imply an acknowledgement of a third space, where logos and eros become vivid components of the research process. Thus, just as allowing ourselves to be changed by the cross-cultural encounter necessitates a world to be changed in, eros, an *episteme* based in experience, requires logos, through which it can be addressed and realized. Goulet and Young conclude that it is no longer practical to think that one can "go native" since one thing will always set us apart from our cultural counterparts: we must come back (1994:309).

A Lesson in Rationality

Recently, Blair discussed some of the ideas presented here with a group of doctoral candidates in Sociology. (Admittedly, he was met with a great deal of skepticism!) Our recent short piece *Exploitation in the Field* (1994) came under discussion, as did the entire collection of articles with which it appeared. We had begun this work with a wonderful piece of poetry by Miles Richardson, the first line of which was "If the anthropologist doesn't tell the human myth, then who will?" Almost immediately, one colleague had circled the line, commenting something along the lines of "Quite a large task, don't you think?" "I was hoping that you would read the entire piece first, and then comment on the piece as a whole" Blair replied. "It's poetry" he continued, "it isn't meant to be diced up into little parts and its components examined. It's meant to be read as a whole." Blair explained that such a logocentric examination of an affective document such as poetry, was akin to examining a Pablo Picasso snippet by snippet, not acknowledging how it is that the parts are connected, neglecting to examine the statement made by the relations between all components of the piece.

Recall what Ivan Brady had to say about poetry, "It is personal experience, however, and sometimes it takes lessons from elsewhere" (Brady 1991c:215). Stanley Diamond who became a poet first, and an anthropologist later, told Dan Rose that he turned to anthropology "because it was the next best thing to poetry" (Rose 1991:223). Joseph Campbell, too, had something to say about poetry, which as he demonstrates, is an affect image. Referring to psychiatrist William J. Perry, Campbell states:

> It is image that hits one where it counts. It is not addressed first to the brain, to be there interpreted and appreciated. On the contrary, if that is where it has to be read, the symbol is already dead. An "affect image" talks directly to the feeling system and immediately elicits a response, after which the brain may come along with its interesting comments (Campbell 1988:89).

Poetry is no different from art, dreams, or mythology in that it is erocentrically based and experiential. A strictly logocentric reading would drain the message contained therein, the meaning of which must be "felt" and discovered, not simply pointed to or pointed out. Poetic "meaning" does not reside in the text, but rather comes alive when the reader chooses to be reflexive and see himself and his own life in relation to the poem (see also Bronowski 1966). In that poetry is experiential, what is one to make of Diamond's assertion that poetry is not science and does not aspire to be science (Brady 1991c:215)? Is experience not justified as part of the scientific project as discussed above? (Dan Rose believes that poetry is poetic observation, and in Chapter 3 I refer to the way in which he demonstrates how the poetic enterprise exposes the communication paradoxes of the field situation.)

The point here is not to engage in a discussion about poetry. Rather, it is to acknowledge its status as experience. With this, we can take Campbell seriously when he implies that affective experience cannot be addressed with a strict logocentrism. What is becoming apparent is that the teleology of erocentrism and affective experience is such that it can only be realized through a logocentric episteme. To put it simply, what good is experience if you cannot apply it beneficially through conscious, rational awareness? Given the status of poetry as poetic observation and experience, what about its status as science? Young and Goulet quite aptly demonstrate that experience can provide data that we would not, could not, attain by any other means, thus it becomes quite empirical.

We like what anthropological poetics has to say. Brady describes the task of anthropological "poets":

> They seek an anthropology that, rather than equate its own narrow idealities with reality, as is common practice today, opens itself instead to more creative interpretations on all fronts -- in the poetics of the observed and observer, of self and other, from ivy hall to cross-cultural frontier -- and does so with an eye on the transformative processes of mind and culture that connect these things in the daily rounds and the deeper histories of human experience (Brady 1991b:6)

Poetics is asking us to be aware of our cultural boundedness and constructions, to cast aside total reliance on logocentric rationalism, and to make room for erocentric experience. After all, it is only through an erocentric episteme that we can truly "know" that culturally diverse peoples are merely different aspects of the same essence. That is to say, Jung's collective unconscious or Lévi-Strauss' deep structure can best be demonstrated by the likes of dreams, visions, and mythologies, all of which are affective dimensions of reality -- of nonempirical origin and therefore less rational according to the premises of conventional science.

Edward Bruner discusses the separation between the ethnographic self and the personal self in the modern condition, and cites Brady (1991c), as he clarifies that this also translated into "a split between anthropology and poetics" (Bruner 1993:4). The acknowledgment that the ethnographic document tells us a great deal about the anthropologist, despite the most rigorous of methods, has allowed for the realization that the ethnographer's voice must always be heard. So when Bruner, commenting on essays by Ridington and Turner, asks "do we learn more about the Eskimo and the Omaha than we do about Turner and Ridington?" we can rephrase the question at a more general level: "In the cross-cultural encounter, does the anthropologist learn more about himself/herself or the cultural other?" We feel that the dialogism such as that suggested by Young and Goulet allows for a middle ground in answering this question (see Goulet 1994; Goulet and Young 1994), as their entire volume provides a commentary on Bruner's point that it is the anthropologist who is changed by the encounter, not the other (1993:20). Rodman might, however, disagree.

In William Rodman's essay "*When Questions Are Answers: The Message of Anthropology According to the People of Ambae*" (1993), he tells an almost mythical story about how a peoples' "interpretation of the message of anthropology had played a crucial role in changing their way of life" (1993:173). He describes the account as "true fiction" since it is based on his own personal experience. Several years prior to Rodman's third term of fieldwork in Aoba in 1982, a certain anthropologist had made a visit to the island where he asked questions concerning sand drawings, magic, supernatural power, and the likes. These can be considered as part of the local *kastom*, which translates into "traditional cultural ways". Apparently nothing became of these discussions, and for this reason it was suspected that they meant little, if anything, to the anthropologist. But this was far from the case with the local people. Andrew, who appears to be the key informant in the story, discovered the implicit meanings behind the questions asked -- they were a form of *qaltavalu*, meaning literally, "hidden talk". Traditionally, one of the main uses of *qaltavalu* was in the transmission of *kastom* from one generation to the next. In this sense, it might be defined as a "form of communication based on a system of implicit meanings" (Rodman 1993:184). "Teachers on

Ambae seldom state the obvious. Instead, they teach by parable, by indirection raised to the level of fine art" (ibid.). For Andrew, this anthropologist became a teacher who brought a message about the great value of traditional culture, of *kastom*. For Rodman, this became the message of anthropology. On this learning experience, he states. "Quite possibly, he had a larger purpose, an aim rather more important than teaching an anthropologist the meaning of anthropology" (1993:188).

This short account presents us with a scenario in which the cultural other certainly benefitted from the cross-cultural encounter. Rodman, himself, shared a true dialogism with his cultural counterparts and by opening himself up to experience, he was changed by it. This is what Goulet and Young might describe as participant-comprehension as opposed to participant-observation. Participant-comprehension, as Laughlin subsequently described it, requires "leaving oneself open to whatever experiences arise as a consequence of performing ritual and symbolic practices, and recording what happens using whatever symbolic media are available" (Laughlin 1994:102; Goulet and Young 1994:312). Of course, this definition is limiting, since comprehension does not necessarily come about only through explicit immersion into such symbolic systems. Comprehensibility can be quite spontaneous, as Goulet's experience of seeing himself fanning the fire, as previously discussed, reveals.

In Rodman's case, the experience of the anthropologist was made possible only by the desire of the cultural other to share their insights and wisdom. On a similar note, recall Dwyer's conversation with Faqir Mbarek while on fieldwork in Morocco:

A: Could you explain to me what you think I'm doing here?

P: My thoughts about that are what you've told me yourself, that's what I've put into my thoughts. What you write down is what you understand, and you try to understand a lot, so you can make the others understand, those whom you teach. This is as far as my thoughts go.

A: Well, I ask you a lot of things. To your mind, what is the most important subject that we talk about? You know, for some subjects you might say to yourself, "What is the sense of talking for so long about such a thing?" Or on the other hand, you might think, "Oh that's really interesting".

P: As for me, I know that I'm not concerned with a single one of your questions. I know that these questions serve your purposes, not mine. I think about the questions, whether they are small questions or large ones, and I think about them because they serve your purposes, not mine (Dwyer 1977:144).

Anthropologists have certainly benefitted by the generosity of our cultural counterparts. Without this generous gift of "a willingness to participate", it is questionable whether anthropology could be possible at all. This willingness is a result of good rapport and a carefully cultivated field relationship. In fact, as cross-cultural agents, we are there as learning subjects and therefore objects of knowledge production. In this sense, we have become the students of those we have gone to study, and have come to respect. And our efforts have been met with the best of wishes, even when a reciprocity -- a return of the gift, is not an anticipated outcome of the field encounter.

Barry Michrina, whose recent ethnographic depiction of Pennsylvanian coal miners (1993), demonstrates not only a carefully cultivated and genuine rapport with the people from whom he learned, but also a collegial approach to the entire fieldwork endeavour. Not only did he share his preliminary drafts with several of his informants, but he took advice from them regarding the creation of the monograph -- all of this with the hopes that his final creation would be genuinely a part of them, as well as a part of him. This dialogism is partially reflected in the remarks of one of his informants, prior to having corrected Michrina on some misunderstandings evident in the draft: "I'm really going to enjoy reading this. I feel like I'm a part of it now" (1993:172). The result of this shared dialogism between an anthropologist and his cultural counterpart is summed up by one informant's statement which most certainly touched Michrina's heart, "We hope something comes of this for you" (1993:173). Another draft reader humorously commented, "A woman was here to buy carpets, and I was telling her about your book. I'm selling so many books for you! I should be your agent" (1993:172). To leave the field scenario with the best wishes and blessing of our cultural counterparts is what we, as anthropologists have striven for. Perhaps this is the natural result when our cultural counterparts are seen not as objects of study, but as colleagues with whom we share insights, dialogue, wisdom, and research.

Of course, there are several ways to "do" ethnography, and what is becoming evident as anthropology becomes more interpretive, experiential, and reflexive, is that deriving standard methods regarding field relationships is a difficult project. We like what Michrina has accomplished. But what about the question of replicability of data? We are taught that the method of proper science is such that replicability of data ensures the validity of our investigation. What the works being discussed presently reveal is that replicability is quite a problematic means of assessing quality of data. At the symbolic-experiential level, experiences such as those documented by Turner and Goulet tell us that opening ourselves to the worldview of those we study means "taking their world seriously". By this, Goulet and Young mean that we must suspend disbelief and accept the worldview of the cultural other, and their descriptions and recollections of it, as "truthful" accounts. By doing this, we not only recognize the rational boundedness of our commonsense world, but we also recognize "the limits of scientific investigation" (Goulet and Young 1994:329). This leaves us open to an experiential anthropology which has its basis in reflexivity, thus experiences which are hardly empirically verifiable, let alone replicable and testable, become valid data as well as elicit it. What Michrina and Rodman show us is a model based less in symbolic penetration, more in what might be termed "epistemological permeability". Here, the openness of these anthropologists to the message and worldview brought by the cultural other, and their willingness to assume a collegial position with those they wished to learn from and understand, resulted in great reflexive experiences. Rodman learned the true meaning of anthropology, and Michrina discovered that he could, in fact, understand the message of his informants, despite differences in enculteration, by reflecting on his own cultural experiences and worldview (Michrina 1993:167).

This type of reflexive anthropology acknowledges a certain fuzziness of conventional epistemological boundaries which have been erected by modern rationality. First is the dissolution of the dichotomy between anthropologist and informant, where it is acknowledged that the field experience can only be cultivated through a dialogism between the colleagues involved. Self and other are atoned, as there is the recognition that the beings of the anthropologist and her/his cultural counterpart are two aspects of the same essence. Thus, when we look at our cultural counterparts, we are staring into another aspect of ourselves. When we open ourselves up to the experience of the cultural other, we are simply opening up to the experience of ourselves. For Rose, these are a reflection of "deep links, whether broken or unbroken..., among ourselves, our forbears, and our diverse contemporaries as we variously conceive of and use the palpable world" (Rose 1994:95). We have also attempted to invoke a discussion about a second, perhaps just as obvious, fuzziness -- this one between logico-empirical and erocentric-experiential epistemes. The suggestion was not to do away with science, but to recognize its practical limitations. Richardson entreats us to do away with the dichotomy between art and science (Richardson 1994:83). Of course, art here is a metaphor for the affectual dimensions of science which have evaded rationality -- as have poetics and experience. Rationality and empiricism are about recognizing limits; they have yet to identify limits of their own. Coming to terms with the "reality" of the ethnographic scenario requires an awareness of scientism's insistence on dichotomizing between the real and the non-real. Rachelle Smith-Doody, seeing science as "a convenient label for the sorting-out process by which sense is separated from non-sense", points out the scientific preoccupation with the "real", and thus "useful", at the expense of the non-real (Smith-Doody 1992:222), which is judged by notions of objectivity, replicability, and the ability to withstand the rigors of empiricism. It is doubtful whether the experiential anthropology presently discussed could withstand any of these, but what this essay hopes to demonstrate is that experience does provide valid data nevertheless.

Relocating the "Field" in Fieldwork

The recent critical debates surrounding anthropological practice include poetics and reflexive anthropology (Benson, Brady, Prattis, Young and Goulet), hermeneutics and interpretivism (Geertz, Ricoeur, Michrina), and postmodern critique (Tyler, Clifford, Denzin). They have all been harshly criticized, yet their discourse has been surprisingly successful and provocative, moving us to think more seriously about anthropology. Of course, we recognize that this has been half of the project of anthropology since its conception, the other half being ethnographic examination. Thus, recent anthropology has benefitted from its ability to be self-critical and reflexive, regardless of the outcomes of the debates and the plausibility of postmodernism. (The question of comprehension of levels has been discussed in Chapters 3 and 5 of this volume. In Chapter 3, *Dialectics and Experience in Fieldwork*, the epistemology of language and understanding is discussed. In Chapter 5, *Reflexive Anthropology,* there is an elaboration on levels of reflexivity in anthropological discourse and a re-evaluation of subject-object relationships.)

At one level, anthropology has always been about experience, but the scope of modern anthropological study has allowed room mostly for a filtered understanding of the experience of the cultural other. To say that the anthropologist had any gain whatsoever, for that matter, might have been considered blasphemous and exploitative. So modernist anthropology was caught between two poles. At the emic extreme, we attempted to "get into the heads" of the other and experience their world as they did by participating in their culture. Going native was cool. At the etic extreme, we believed that we could stand back and, with rigorous empiricism, grasp the "native's point of view" through mere "unobtrusive observation" (Goulet and Young 1994:312). The third level of reflection discussed by Prattis (see Chapter 5, *Reflexive Anthropology*) reveals that when we engage in a hermeneutic dialogism with the cultural other, we necessarily engage with an aspect of ourselves. More than this, we gain self-understanding from reflecting upon this engagement, and we use this to enhance our awareness in our own cultural circumstances. Michael Taussig has recently raised these issues in *Mimesis and Alterity* (1993), where he documents how the concepts of mimesis (imitation) and alterity (otherness) play off one another in maintaining and strengthening cultural solidarities and identity. He chooses the Kuna Indians as his example. Among the Kuna, the Self is understood through an examination of its Alter. Thus, Kuna ritual and mythological incorporations of European characters and characteristics have the purpose of strengthening their identity at a personal and collective level. What Taussig is telling us is that understanding and experiencing what appears at a surface level to be "foreign" can inevitably lead us home. In short, human beings understand through interactional experience, whether this experience is in the form of reading books, being in the world, or interacting in foreign locales under specific circumstances. Anthropologists are in the awkward predicament of attempting to juggle with all three. Therefore if we do not make sense of our cross-cultural encounters by using what we do already know, we are simply not recognizing our humanness.

Recently, Lynn Hirschkind has written a piece entitled "*Redefining the 'Field' in Fieldwork*" (1991), and she advocates the use of a model somewhat akin to full participant observation. Her suggestion is "that anthropologists drop academic auspices and take on locally defined roles having relevance to their research topics. The advantage of this approach is that it situates the ethnographer as plainly and concisely as possible within the social structure and culture in question, which in turn gives an unambiguous perspective from which to proceed in research" (1991:237). In Michrina's case, he might have taken on work as a miner, in Hirschkind's case, the role was that of a farmer. Might such a suggestion have been a plausible one for Napoleon Chagnon or Colin Turnbull? How easy might it have been for them to undertake roles as local aboriginals? Certainly, characteristics ranging from their academic training to their status as white Americans would have hampered any efforts to undertake "locally defined roles". Furthermore, how much role-playing time is sufficient in order that one be acknowledged locally as being a role-player? We believe that what Hirschkind is suggesting, which is no more than an emic role, simplifies the complex issues surrounding fieldwork to an extreme. For her, the position of fieldworker is a "nebulous" one in which he/she is in jeopardy of "*not* being taken seriously" (1991:248, emphasis ours). The project presently proposed takes care to ensure that it is *the informants* who are taken seriously.

Hirschkind argues that by "having a stake in local affairs", the anthropologist "cannot back out of involvement, or claim exemption from the exigencies of local mores, expectations, and routines... integration into the community is assured" (1991:248). Once again, the problem is more complex than this, and the simple assuming of a local role does not ensure better data by any means. This is not to deny that what Hirschkind is suggesting might be beneficial to the anthropological project, it is merely to say that full immersion, as she implies, is idealistic. "Going native" is no longer an option. We have different ideas when it comes to the place of "the field" in anthropology.

Grant me self-delusion,
it is my proof that I exist.
Let me put on my self-made mask
before we peer into the mirror,
and I will show you to your satisfaction
that Self exists.
(The secret, which I'll let you guess yourself,
is that the mirror has twice the magic of the mask.)

Grant me the mask.
Take for granted the Mirror.
And we can pretend
to the act of recognition.
We can perform
the act of knowing.

These words are Wilson Duff's (1985:160-161) and they appear in *Reflections: The Anthropological Muse* under the section entitled "*The Field Within*". They capture the dialogical self-construction involved in the field encounter and they suggest that anthropology might be more than the "understanding of selves". We believe that anthropology can be considered as self-understanding. Human beings share a collective existence and this has been well established by Lévi-Strauss's work on "deep structure", Bastian's "elementary ideas", and Lévy-Bruhl's "representations collectives". Of course these reflect in their distinct ways, what Jung has termed a "collective unconscious", which he demonstrated through the existence of archetypes that manifest themselves through primordial images. In fact, the recent work of Grof has demonstrated that there is a consciousness beyond even what has come to be known as humanity -- a "cosmic consciousness" that most sages and seers find unsurprising! Grof's findings have demonstrated that in altered states of consciousness, humans can experience the essence of plants, animals, and elements (Grof 1993). What this demonstrates is that the anthropologist and the cultural other do share a collective existence at a particular level. This is "the field within"; the realm of interiority. We are not suggesting that anthropology have as its focus this field alone, but rather, we would like to suggest that it be acknowledged as a valid field locale.

Certainly there will always exist a field "out there", but with the realization that humans share an internal field scenario, it no longer seems outrageous to suggest that anthropology might be better accomplished if it accepts a dialogism between these two. It is in this sense that anthropology might be self-understanding. By the term "self" we are referring to the realm of humanity as suggested by Jung -- the ordering and unifying aspects of our universal psyches (see Edinger 1972; Jung 1959a, 1959b). These all provide support for the contention that when anthropologists attempt to gain understanding about the cultural other, they necessarily gain self-understanding, since they are two aspects of the same reality. This is what we mean by universal similarism -- "seeing the Self in the Other".

So anthropologists do stand to gain from the anthropological enterprise, and reflexivity provides a feasible way of understanding what transpires in the field. Thus we suggest seeing "the field" as a dual entity with both an external and an internal component. The two share such a relationship that one cannot exist without the other. Just as previously, where we stated that the teleology of eros is that it can only be realized via logos, so the teleology of the internal field is such that it can only be realized via the external field. The same relationship holds for the ego-Self distinction in Jungian psychology. The Self in and of itself is essentially useless unless there is a conscious existence to which an understanding of it may be applied. Young and Goulet are correct; anthropologists can be changed by cross-cultural encounters -- if they open themselves to the experience of the cultural other. This requires suspending disbelief, and acknowledging the limits of Newtonian-Cartesian scientific notions which perpetuate a rationalism which is too often seen as incompatible with the affectual experiences such as those presented earlier in this chapter. So what might appear extraordinary to us, such as waking visions of spirits, become the most human and ordinary of events. "In other words, from our perspective, what we have called an extraordinary experience probably is not the result of experiencing something from another dimension, but an experience which occurs when one opens one's self to aspects of experience that previously have been ignored or repressed" (Young and Goulet 1994:9).

So Our Discussion Has Come Around Full Circle...

So our discussion has come around full circle, and the central question again emerges: "What happens when we open ourselves to others, specifically to those who are at home in a world that to us seems strange?" Rab Wilkie asks this question, and gives us a lesson in reality, as he takes us through a four round discussion in which eight persons pondered the question above. As Vera (one of the discussants) tells us, we are obviously "changed by 'opening ourselves' to a new experience" (Wilkie 1994:158). What makes the round of discussions even more fascinating than the insights they provide is the fact that it is fictitious, or as Wilkie admits "It did take place, but only within the author's imagination" (1994:162). He tells the reader this only after presenting a transcript of the talks. By doing this, he is giving us insights to our narrow-minded epistemological constructions of "the real". Initially addressing the account as factual causes the reader to address the essay "with a different level of interest and receptivity than he or she would if the proceedings were known beforehand to be imaginary" (1994:162). Wilkie points out that after we discover that the account is neither factual nor empirically verifiable, a rereading would be met with a differing perception.

The present essay has made use of the more recent literature in the area of anthropology and epistemology to suggest that the place of ethnographic examination includes the fields of both interiority and exteriority. This allows for a dialogism between self and other culture, and posits a merging trajectory by which both are atoned in a new form of expression. This describes the dialectic between observer and cultural other and sees differing cultural assumptions not only as colliding, but also as meeting at a center. All of this has transpired with the intent of telling anthropology something *different* and something *more* about ethnography -- something that is missed when approached with the notions of everyday, rational, scientific discourse (Prattis 1985a). Often, our most informative data comes from personal experiences which cannot be subjected to any forms of empiricism, verification, or replicability. What this tells us is that experience counts. Turner's witness to the presence of the Ihamba spirit, Goulet's vision of himself, and Wilkie's experiment with the reader are only a few of the examples which demonstrate that data is far from a strictly logico-empirical phenomenon.

Opening up to an experiential anthropology means opening up to anthropological humanism. It also means opening up to the world of the cultural other which is not as foreign as it might first appear. Rab Wilkie found that when working with Native shamans, he "could not begin to understand their worldview and experiences without giving more attention to [his] own" (Wilkie 1994:163). This is a valid point, for, how can we be expected to understand "foreign" worlds when we are uncertain as to our own internal complexities? To approach ethnographic field scenarios as has been suggested, from the perspective of experience, allows us to engage in a respectful dialogism not only with the cultural other, but also with a deeper aspect of ourselves. Respecting ourselves necessitates respecting the other humans with whom we share a fundamental existence. Knowing our cultural counterparts, and getting to know ourselves along the way, this is what the anthropological project means to us.

- It is a lesson in kastom -

Conclusion

We must leave our images in mid-air
to get closer to our transfigurations
and converse with them at the edge of the whiteness
with no letter for witness.

(Juarroz 1988:149; in Brady 1991:341)

Our navigational voyage is certainly not over. The questions of boundary and fuzziness are unresolved and in our view must remain so. For without ambiguity and paradox to excite and stimulate curiosity, the intellectual endeavour would stagnate. We have listened to the voices of many mariners -- some clearly stranded, others shipwrecked -- and take careful note of those who navigate the shoals and reefs with careful elan. To discard logos at the expense of eros is worse than ignoring eros altogether. We need both as we stretch science beyond its present limitations. As we move from participant-observation to participant-comprehension and emphasize the sheer necessity of a hermeneutic sensitivity we progress from blind voyaging to the triangular system of navigation. It is not spot on in terms of a particular location, yet it does provide parameters and guidance for the next stage of the voyage.

Bibliography

Blair, D. and J. I. Prattis
1994 Exploitation in the Field. Anthropology and Humanism, V.19, 1:36-39

Borofsky, R.
1994 (ed.): Assessing Cultural Anthropology. N.Y.: McGraw-Hill, Inc.

Brady, I.
1991a (ed.): Anthropological Poetics. Savage, Maryland: Rowman and Littlefield

1991b Harmony and Argument: Bringing Forth the Artful Science. In I. Brady (ed.): Anthropological Poetics:3-30. Savage, Maryland: Rowman and Littlefield

1991c Prelude to Chapter Ten. In I. Brady (ed.): Anthropological Poetics:215-218. Savage, Maryland: Rowman and Littlefield

Brady, I. and E. Turner
1994 (eds.): Anthropology and Humanism. Special Issue: Humanism and Anthropology V.19, 1

Bronowski, J.
1966 The Logic of the Mind. American Scientist 54,1:1-14

Bruner, E.M.
1993 Introduction: The Ethnographic Self and the Personal Self. In P. Benson (ed.): Anthropology and Literature:1-26. Urbana: University of Illinois Press

Campbell, J.
1988 [1972] Myths to Live By. N.Y.: Bantam Books

Clifford, J. and G. Marcus
1986 (eds.): Writing Culture: The Poetics and Politics of Ethnography. Berkeley: University of California Press

Duff, W.
1985 Come Seem With Me. In J.I. Prattis (ed.): Reflections: The Anthropological Muse:160-161. Washington, D.C.: American Anthropological Association

Dwyer, K.
1977 On the Dialogic of Fieldwork. Dialectical Anthropology 2:143-151

Edinger, E.F.
1972 Ego and Archetype. N.Y.: G.P. Putnam's Sons

Fox, R.
1994 Scientific Humanism and Humanistic Science: A Personal View. Anthropology and Humanism 19, 1:15-19

Goulet, J.G.
1994 Dreams and Visions in Other Lifeworlds. In D. Young and J.G. Goulet (eds.): Being Changed by Cross-Cultural Encounters:16-38. Peterborough: Broadview Press

Goulet, J.G. and D. Young
1994 Theoretical and Methodological Issues. In D. Young and J.G. Goulet (eds.): Being Changed by Cross-Cultural Encounters:298-336. Peterborough: Broadview Press

Grof, S.
1993 The Holotropic Mind: The Three Levels of Human Consciousness and How They Shape Our Lives. San Francisco: Harper San Francisco

Habermas, J.
1992 Postmetaphysical Thinking: Philosophical Essays (trans. W.M. Hohengarten). Cambridge: MIT Press

Hirschkind, L.
1991 Redefining the "Field" in Fieldwork. Ethnology. 30, 3:237-250

Jung, C.G.
1959a The Archetypes and the Collective Unconscious. The Collected Works of C.G. Jung, V.9, 1. Princeton: Princeton University Press

1959b [1951] Aion. The Collected Works of C.G. Jung, V.9, 2. Princeton: Princeton University Press

Labouvie-Vief, G.
1994 Psyche and Eros: Mind and Gender in the Life Course. Cambridge: Cambridge University Press

Laughlin, C.D.
1994 Psychic Energy and Transpersonal Experience: A biogenetic structural account of the Tibetan Dumo Yoga Practice. In D. Young and J.G. Goulet (eds.): Being Changed by Cross-Cultural Encounters:99-134. Peterborough: Broadview Press

Lyotard, J.F.
1984 Postmodern Condition: A Report on Knowledge. Minneapolis: University of Minnesota Press

Marcus, G. and M. Fischer
1986 (eds.): Anthropology as Cultural Critique. Chicago: University of Chicago Press

Mascia-Lees, F.E., P. Sharpe and C.B. Cohen
1993 [1989] The Postmodernist Turn in Anthropology: Cautions from a Feminist Perspective. In P. Benson (ed.): Anthropology and Literature:225-248. Urbana: University of Illinois Press

Michrina, B.
1993 Pennsylvania Mining Families: The Search for Dignity in the Coalfields. Lexington: University of Kentucky Press

Michrina, B. and C.A. Richards
1995 Person to Person: Fieldwork, Dialogue and the Hermeneutic Method. Albany: S.U.N.Y. Press

Myerhoff, B.
1978 Number Our Days. N.Y.: Simon and Schuster

Prattis, J.I.
1985a (ed.): Reflections: The Anthropological Muse. Washington, D.C.: American Anthropological Association

1985b Dialectics and Experience in Fieldwork: The Poetic Dimension. In J.I. Prattis (ed.): Reflections: The Anthropological Muse:266-281. Washington, D.C.: American Anthropological Association

Rabinow, P.
1977 Reflections on Fieldwork in Morocco. Berkeley: University of California Press

Rappaport, R.
1994 Humanity's Evolution and Anthropology's Future. In R. Borofsky (ed.): Assessing Cultural Anthropology:153-177. N.Y.: McGraw-Hill, Inc.

Richardson, M.
1994 Writing Poetry and Doing Ethnography: Aesthetics and Observation on the Page and in the Field. Anthropology and Humanism 19,1:77-87

Rodman, W.L.
1993 When Questions Are Answers: The Message of Anthropology According to the People of Ambae. In P. Benson (ed.): Anthropology and Literature:173-191. Urbana: University of Illinois Press

Rose, D.
1991 In Search of Experience: The Anthropological Poetics of Stanley Diamond. In I. Brady (ed.): Anthropological Poetics:219-232. Savage, Maryland: Rowman and Littlefield

1994 The Evolution of Intervention. Anthropology and Humanism 19,1:88-103

Ross, M.
1990 Seasons of Death and Life: A Wilderness Memoir. San Francisco: Harper San Francisco

Sassower, R.
1993 Postmodernism and Philosophy of Science: a Critical Engagement. Philosophy of the Social Sciences 23,4:426-445

Smith-Doody, R.
1992 Sense and Non-Sense: Dissemination and Empiricism in Practice. Ethos. 20,2:220-229

Taussig, M.
1980 The Devil and Commodity Fetishism in South America. Chapel Hill: University of North Carolina Press

1993 Mimesis and Alterity. N.Y.: Routledge

Turner, E.
1994 A Visible Spirit Form in Zambia. In D. Young and J.G. Goulet (eds.): Being Changed by Cross-Cultural Encounters:71-95. Peterborough: Broadview Press

Tyler, S.
1984 The Poetic Turn in Postmodern Anthropology. American Anthropologist 86,2:328-336

1987 The Unspeakable: Discourse, Dialogue and Rhetoric in the Postmodern World. University of Wisconsin Press

Wilkie, R.
1994 Spirited Imagination: Ways of Approaching the Shaman's World. In D. Young and J.G. Goulet (eds.): Being Changed by Cross-Cultural Encounters:135-165. Peterborough: Broadview Press

Young, D. and J.G. Goulet
1994 (eds.): Being Changed by Cross-Cultural Encounters: The Anthropology of Extraordinary Experience. Peterborough: Broadview Press

Chapter 7

Celtic Festivals and Bilingualism Policy: The Barra "*Feis*"

This chapter examines the Barra *Feis*, a summer festival and year-round commitment to the performing Gaelic arts made by the population on the island of Barra, in Scotland's Western Isles. My contention is that such events emerge only after certain preconditions about minority language maintenance, biculturalism and education have been met. In order to set the stage for a discussion of the Barra *Feis* and its cultural significance it is necessary to have a prior theoretical discussion about the general conditions of minority language bilingualism and the specific bilingualism practices adopted by *Comhairle nan Eilean*, the regional council for the Western Isles. This is to permit the reader to understand more fully the emergence of the Barra *Feis* and its consequences for cultural and community solidarity.

Minority Language Bilingualism

It is true to say that minority languages spoken by populations in the peripheral areas of modern nation states are under severe pressure, and the fears that these languages may soon diminish beyond the point of no return are more real than apparent. Gaelic within the Western Isles is no exception. The location of this region within the wider political economy of the U.K. defines a situation of unequal power relations which has placed Gaelic culture in a position of dependency vis-a-vis the wider society (Hunter 1977; Withers 1985; Prattis 1977, 1979; Hechter 1975). One way in which the dominant character of external political and economic linkages is reflected at the local community level is in terms of an erosion of mother tongue linguistic usage and often a passive acceptance of mass culture.

Previous work (Prattis and Chartrand 1985) has pointed to the fact that the survival of minority languages and cultures under these conditions ultimately depends on two factors:

(1) the grassroots commitment by the minority population to the native language, and their political will to argue for comprehensive policies designed to protect their language (Fennell 1981:32);

(2) the willingness and active intervention by the state, at its different levels, to implement such policies.

A major instrument for intervention is bilingualism policy and its meaning can be summarized in terms of preparing minority culture bearers to have access, through English, to the metropolitan world, while at the same time retaining a dynamic link with their natal community in terms of a social and linguistic world of solidarity, locality and self confidence.

The inevitability of modernization and socio-economic change is certainly not a factor that communities in the Western Isles are unprepared for. A major result of these factors has been the expansion and extensive use of English in mass communication structures. This expansion, however, should not obscure the distinct advantages to be derived from effective bilingualism in the minority culture situation:

> It is axiomatic that the best medium for teaching a child is his mother tongue. Psychologically, it is the system of meaningful signs that in his mind works automatically for expression and understanding. Sociologically it is a means of identification among the members of the community to which he belongs. Educationally he learns more quickly through it than through an unfamiliar linguistic medium. (U.N.E.S.C.O. 1953:7).

The advantages of bilingualism operate at several levels of a social system. Psychological benefits from mother tongue usage in school derive from the fact that a young child does not embrace schooling with apprehension and fear. Instead self confidence is enhanced by a continued use of a familiar language. Effective bilingualism, from a base point of security for the child, then increases the scope of flexibility and creativity of thought (Lambert 1969; Torrance et al. 1970; Balkan 1970; Ben-Zeev 1972; Scott 1973). The numerous studies by Lambert and his colleagues (Dubé and Herbert 1975a, 1975b; Lambert, Giles and Picard 1975; Lambert, Giles and Albert 1974) demonstrated that, contrary to popular expectations, English facility of bilingual school children, educated in a language other than English, was superior to that of comparable monolingual English speakers. This indicates that effective English usage is not discriminated against in a minority culture bilingual situation -- it is in fact enhanced.

It is very unlikely that adults in Western Isles communities are opposed to having their children speak English, since they recognize that effective English is required in today's modern world. The fact that bilingualism equips children at a psychological level to deal on more balanced terms with the requirements of English usage in today's world while not alienating themselves from their own linguistic and cultural community, leads to broader benefits at a social level. Here Barth's (1969) concern with the mechanisms and institutions relevant for cultural boundary maintenance is salient. If a minority culture has a grassroots commitment to the survival of its language, then minority language maintenance will be the crucial mechanism for social solidarity and community cohesion (Reitz 1980;

Prattis and Chartrand 1985). However, work by Mitchell (1979) and Prattis (1980b) points out that ethnic (minorities') categories of difference from the mass culture (e.g. the desire for language retention) must have structural realizations at the concrete societal level if these categories are to persist.

In other words the implementation of bilingualism policy must provide visible and practical feedback to minority culture bearers of the utility of their language on a day to day basis. We must grasp these major considerations in order to understand the situation of Gaelic cultural decline in the Western Isles. There are two major considerations to come to grips with. One concerns history, and the other involves State policy. First of all one must recognize historically that Gaelic cultural decline is a product of a situation of dependency and unequal power relations (Withers 1985; Prattis 1977, 1979). Second, that the state at its different levels is the main institution with the capacity to effectively counter the present conditions of socio-cultural erosion (Prattis 1980a; Prattis and Chartrand 1990). This is why the domain of policy is a necessary starting point for us to understand the significance of a cultural festival such as the Barra *Feis*. In particular we must examine the formulation of bilingualism policy at the local government level and the support received from institutions and ministries located at higher levels of the state apparatus.

The point I would like to establish at this juncture is that bilingualism is a systemic issue. It is not simply a matter of the medium of instruction in schools. Bilingualism thus has to be considered at all levels of a social system and must be placed not just within the educational context of school curricula but within broader community programs of adult education and biculturalism. In light of this brief overview on the multi-level benefits and implications of bilingualism, it may be that a necessary prerequisite at the policy level for successful bilingualism is a vigorous biculturalism and broad based community education programs. These considerations informed previous work which addressed the minimum preconditions for an effective bilingualism policy for the Inuit in Northern Canada (Prattis and Chartrand 1985). My co-worker and I were not concerned with arresting social change or preserving traditional cultures. Our arguments formed the basis of a blueprint for the adaptation and evolution of small scale communities. This blueprint would enable ongoing constructive modification from within communities, rather than an erosion of community solidarity arising from destructive changes that are imposed from external sources.

The blueprint is contained in Appendix A and presents the minimum requirements for an effective bilingualism/biculturalism policy so that a minority cultural group secures sufficient feedback from everyday experiences to retain its distinctive cultural identity. A major implication of this blueprint in previous arguments (Prattis and Chartrand 1985) was that once bilingualism is effective then a climate is established whereby other things can then happen on a voluntary, cultural basis that result in a self sustaining modality for communities rather than the ethic of total dependency and all that such dependency entails. Enter at last the Barra *Feis*, but from the wings. The reader, however, is cautioned to delay anticipation as the stage and props are not quite ready. Before the *Feis* can be brought centre stage, we must examine bilingualism policy in the Western Isles.

Bilingualism Policy in the Western Isles, Scotland

The Western Isles Island Council is an "all purpose" local government authority that came into existence after the 1974-1975 reorganization of local government in the United Kingdom. The islands - Lewis, Harris, Uists, Benbecula, Barra and Vatersay - shared a common background, culture and history of neglect (Hunter 1977; Prattis 1977, 1979) and were the main repository of a population that retained Gaelic linguistic usage. A major priority of the new body which adopted the Gaelic name *Comhairle nan Eilean*, was to produce a bilingualism policy and implement it where practical in a broad spectrum of council based activities, but particularly in schools. The population of the region is approximately 30,000 and over 80% of this number are bilingual. The use of the two languages is asymmetric: Gaelic usage is generally confined to everyday life situations whereas English is the language of wider "official" communication. However, the penetration of English usage into everyday situations (McKinnon 1977; Prattis 1981) has been of such a nature that an effective ongoing bilingualism was called for to change the precarious position of Gaelic language.

The particular problem facing the new council was clear evidence of decline in Gaelic language functions and a general extension of English usage in local community domains. The council, shortly after its inception, initiated a bilingual project in twenty selected primary schools. Supported by the Scottish Education Department the aim of the project:

> ... was to produce Gaelic/English bilinguals with a mastery of the skills of understanding, speaking, reading and writing in both languages together with an appreciation of the nuances, emotional overtones and cultural dimensions of the two languages ... (Murray and Morrison 1984; Gaarder 1967).

The project ran as a pilot-scheme between 1975-1978 with a second phase running from 1978-81. The Bilingual Education project was often confused with bilingualism policy, partly because it was the most visible Council effort but also because the project team's Director played a part in formulating a comprehensive bilingualism policy for *Comhairle nan Eilean* (Murray and Morrison 1984:73). The general aim of the Council's policy is that the Western Isles should be a fundamentally bilingual community ensuring for the population a choice of Gaelic or English in as many situations as possible. The council regarded bilingual education as the most important element of its policy, and we shall see that the operation of the bilingual education project was the key to establishing a radically different climate for concerns about language, culture and community.

One of the most fundamental parts of the project was a radical pedagogic shift that required an alternative curriculum, different teaching roles, a child centred bilingual approach, and direct exploration of the child's physical environment to enhance verbal expression. The teaching style in the primary classrooms shifted from a hierarchical didactic mode (in keeping with a dependency on another culture and language), to an egalitarian ethic that reflected local cultural preferences. This led to the creation of different classroom materials by teachers and pupils. The pedagogic shift proved to be exhilarating, though sometimes difficult, for children, teachers and the project team (Murray and Morrison 1984). Perhaps herein lies one source of dynamism for the creation of the new emergent climate with regards to bilingualism. The dynamism was tangible in that the quality of work emerging from primary classrooms was astounding (Murray and Morrison 1984:21,36). At the same time language enrichment in both English and Gaelic was occurring at a level not anticipated by the teachers and this was in spite of considerable obstacles due to lack of access to reading and media provisions in Gaelic.

The dearth of adequate reading materials in Gaelic for schoolchildren and the initial steps taken by the project in making up this shortfall, resulted in the establishment of a Gaelic publishing company, *Acair*, in 1977. The bilingual education project was the catalyst for other bodies - *Comhairle nan Eilean*, Highlands and Islands Development Board (hereafter H.I.D.B.) *An Comunn Gaidhealach* - to establish this company. In a similar fashion the project was sufficiently provocative and persuasive to elicit a response from radio and T.V. programmers to broadcast children's programs in Gaelic. Indeed, the project team had considerable input to the *Cuir Car* children's program put out by Grampian T.V. This broadcasting development was particularly important for pre-school children still at home. McKinnon's 1977 study of language retention in Harris demonstrated that one of the population segments least concerned with Gaelic language retention was that of young mothers at home. Gaelic language programs on the radio and T.V. thus provided an essential support mechanism for Gaelic language retention for both mothers and their pre-school children in the home situation.

A dynamic inter-connection of interests was evolving between the bilingual education project and other bodies in community education, publishing, film, the media, drama and on national education committees. This was by merit of overlapping memberships on consultative committees and governing boards. The many hats worn by the same individuals permitted an integrated "climate" to develop which facilitated the initial establishment of bilingualism in the Western Isles. In turn this increased consciousness about language and culture in the *Gaidhealtachd.*

Within the overlapping tendrils of activities, committees and authorities, it is often difficult to discern crucial dimensions in the creation of an effective climate for bilingualism. I tend to think, however, that the establishment of *Acair* was a most critical juncture. This was an implementation with regards to bilingualism that was vital -- a local Gaelic literature production centre and, as such, *Acair* constitutes the hub for the effective continuation and expansion of bilingual/bicultural education in Western Isles communities. This particular point needs some elaboration, and I would like to draw briefly on an evaluation of bilingualism policy in Australia's Northern Territory which has been described as "one of the most exciting events in the modern world" (O'Grady and Hale 1974).

Concerning bilingualism in Australia's Northern Territories, the Watts Committee (1973) stipulated that the major initial need was to create a rich reading environment in the school and furthermore considered that such an environment could be created in the community if materials were available in the following priority:

(1) traditional stories as told by parents to young children;

(2) stories of high interest to young children created by native adults and older school children;

(3) graded reading books for school;

(4) stories and books of high reading interest to various age groups.

Acair and the Bilingual Project team have been effective in the first three of these four domains to date. Since the pilot project, bilingual education was extended in 1982 to all primary schools in the Western Isles. However the education structure was not the sole instrument for the Council's bilingualism policy. A local radio service - *Radio nan Eilean* - was established with Council support, community education projects established since 1978 by the Van Leer Foundation (which worked closely with the education project) use Gaelic as a medium for adult education, and there is a hiring preference for Gaelic speaking field officers appointed to the area by regional bodies such as the H.I.D.B. The Board has also been supportive of Gaelic language and cultural groups. In particular its funding of *Comunn na Gaidhlig* (H.I.D.B. 1984) whose remit is the promotion of Gaelic language, can be seen as part of the changes taking place in established bodies' attitudes towards the language and culture of the Gael.

Since 1975 the Scottish Office has provided funds, personnel and policies that provide a framework for change through regional development agencies and local government authorities. Whether this framework is adequate remains to be seen but the point to emphasize is that the State, at three different levels, has intervened with regards to Gaelic language and cultural issues. It should be noted that this has taken place within the last decade (1980-1990), which indicates that social and structural change does not always have to be a pedestrian process. The onus on effective change in the Western Isles lies pragmatically with the local level of government - *Comhairle nan Eilean.* There are fears that budget cuts and competing priorities for scarce finances may make it impossible to extend bilingual education into the secondary school sector or provide the reading materials in Gaelic that teenagers and young adults would require to remain interested in the language.

The greatest demand on Council finances and manpower lies in the educational field, and if bilingualism can be retained as a priority then mother tongue literacy in schools and adult education can act as a significant revitaliser with regards to community life. This is because a climate is created for distinctive cultural/linguistic events to occur on a voluntary basis. In particular, the institution in 1980 of an annual Barra *Feis* - a cultural festival that functions as a medium for instruction in Gaelic music, dance and drama certainly owes its genesis to the vision of its community leaders (see Appendix B). But the climate created by the Council's bilingualism policy clearly had a considerable influence in facilitating such a cultural event and others like it. In 1979 a *Mod nan Eilean* was held in Stornoway and this has evolved into an annual Stornoway *Feis* which is virtually all Gaelic. It differs in scope from the Barra *Feis* but all these activities are part of a growing awareness of the general public's participative role. Gaelic language and culture are thus being kept to the forefront of public attention so that there is positive feedback in terms of fostering a new consciousness about language and culture.

This could eventually lead to a situation of distinct advantage, since the feedback effect of bilingualism is such that Gaelic usage at the institutional and community level produces a social world of solidarity and self confidence, yet at the same time individual culture bearers have access through English to the metropolitan world. The advantage is that they can keep the alienative aspects of a de-industrializing mass society at arm's length (McKinnon 1983). In questions of cultural style and quality of community life the balance of advantage may have actually passed from the core to the periphery as the implications of effective bilingualism provide the minority culture with the opportunity to have its cake and eat it too!

The Barra *Feis*

Barra is located in the southern end of the island archipelago known as the Western Isles. These closely knit islands stretch 130 miles from Lewis in the north to the uninhabited island of Bernera in the south. The beads of a shattered necklace, they constitute a massive breakwater, shielding the inner islands and coastal Scotland from the immense fury of the North Atlantic, which runs unremittingly from Labrador 2,000 miles away. Barra is considered to be the most beautiful island in the Hebridean chain, a claim that is disputed by the residents of other islands! Its north and west coast has low lying plains of primrose laden machair -- an arable mixture of shell sand and peat humus -- which are fronted by breathtaking silver sand beaches. The southern and eastern coastlines are rocky and indented and shelve into moorland and mountains in the centre. Barra consists of 22,000 acres and its main part is approximately four miles wide by eight miles long. This is connected by an isthmus to the north that links it to the township of Eoligharry. The easternmost beach between these two parts of the island provides a landing strip for light aircraft -- when tides and grazing cattle permit. The population of the island is about 1400 people.

The Barra *Feis* was first held in 1980 and owed its local genesis and inspiration to Father Colin McInnes who was then the parish priest of Northbay. The aim of the *Feis* was to provide a vehicle for Gaelic arts and language to be an everyday part of island life. To this end a two week summer festival was organised, which was accompanied by a year round structure of tuition in the performing Gaelic Arts (see Appendix B). The formal structure of The *Feis* evolved from a small ad hoc group of helpers to a formally constituted Festival Association - *Comann Feis Bharraigh* - which acts as the parent body for a number of local cultural groups under its umbrella. These different groups - dancing, clarsach, heritage, Island Games, etc. - are encouraged to organise their own activities and fund-raising and furthermore conduct their own elections. They are co-ordinated by the Festival Association in terms of general policy and practice. As we will see below this co-ordinating function is essential for the emergence of a distinct *Feis* ideology.

The summer festival is the single biggest promotion undertaken by the Festival Society and is regarded as the bedrock upon which all other activities rest. The structure of the summer *Feis*, which runs for two weeks in early July, is based on four one hourly classes each day, with a compulsory Gaelic language class for all participants. Classes include Gaelic song (traditional and modern), clarsach, chanter, pipes, drums, tin whistle, accordion, guitar, fiddle, Celtic folk and rock, drama and shinty. Gaelic classes for the general public were also held on a daily basis. In addition to the emphasis on tuition, pupils and tutors gave performances throughout the Festival fortnight in community halls, schools and in Ciesmul Castle, so that their cultural involvement and enjoyment could be shared in by the community at large.

The year round *Feis* begins in August when schoolchildren register for one or more of the 10 different classes that are organized on a voluntary basis by parents and local tutors. Each musical instrument or activity e.g. accordion, gaelic song etc. -- has an organizing committee which is responsible for securing local tutors and getting them together with island children to continue the work of the Summer *Feis*. This is a monumental undertaking by the community, as the tutors for the Summer *Feis* were professional performers, musicians, drama and music teachers, whereas the year-round tutors were drawn from the local community. Yet despite the lack of professional background approximately thirty adults from Barra would keep the *Feis* going on a year-round basis, much to the admiration of the professional tutors who arrived each summer to provide further tuition.

There were two main themes underlining both the Summer Festival and the year-round *Feis*. The first was a commitment to Gaelic language, the second was a commitment to a generational transfer of cultural activities. The language issue was at the forefront of all *Feis* activities. Gaelic was its official language, and activities to give greater prominence to the language on a year round basis was the bottom line or validation for all *Feis* activities. In fact the slogan for the 1982-1983 *Comann Feis Bharraigh's* annual report was "Gaelic in our Homes". The Gaelic classes for children and the general public became an integral part of the summer *Feis* catering to both native and non-native speakers. The summer *Feis* tutors were perhaps in the best position to notice any significant changes in their pupils' readiness and ability to communicate in Gaelic. They frequently commented on the slow but steady change in their pupils' attitudes towards Gaelic language use (Comann Feis Bharraigh 1982-1983, 1983-1984).

The generational transfer of cultural activities was a crucial factor in producing community solidarity, and this draws on the work done by the local tutors and organizing committees of the year-round *Feis*. It is true to say that the first public event of the summer *Feis* -- the concert put on by local tutors and children to demonstrate the fruits of their year round collaboration -- is perhaps the most memorable event of each *Feis* fortnight. Here was tangible and irrefutable evidence of the adult generation passing on their skills and knowledge of the Gaelic arts to the island's children and this was publicly acknowledged by the rest of the island population. The context was Gaelic, the location was the community, the result was cultural cohesion and community solidarity. All this in five short years from a situation of gloom and despair about the island's cultural and linguistic heritage. Much of the turnaround is due locally to the informal style of the *Feis* and the enthusiasm of pupils, tutors and the community. However, the reader must be aware that the *Feis* was taking place within a changed institutional climate. I would argue that prior to the ramifications of official bilingualism in the Western Isles, which created a different "climate" about Gaelic language and culture, it is doubtful if the Barra *Feis* could have been so successful.

Institutional support for the *Feis* comes from the H.I.D.B., the Scottish Arts Council and *Comhairle nan Eilean*. This grant support covers approximately 50% of *Feis* expenses, the remainder being raised by the community. The *Feis* has become increasingly expensive to promote (approximately £23,000 per annum) and although the support from the local community and other institutions has been generous, the Festival Society has tried to negotiate financial assistance from grant aiding bodies on a three year basis. This would permit forward planning and ensure a financial commitment to *Feis* objectives.

The greatest expenditure is on accommodation and fees for the summer tutors. About one third of the *Feis* budget is allocated to this expense. But this is money well spent because the tutors are professionals of the highest calibre in their respective fields of music and drama and their commitment to the *Feis* is part of what I referred to earlier as *Feis* ideology. In the early, often chaotic, days of each Summer *Feis* it is the tutors who establish the tone of the Festival fortnight introducing a structure and flexibility to the process of tuition that gives a particularly open character to what would otherwise be little more than a summer school. They donate instruments to the children, help with the organisation and structure of winter tuition, frequently waive their fees and many make visits during the winter months to monitor and encourage activities and performance within their respective domains. I must emphasize that they are not simply paid tutors who turn up every summer for two weeks. They are professionals who allocate their performing time, skills and energies to the *Feis* because of a sense of commitment to its objectives. This ideological component of the tutoring system is most important, as the summer tutors' liaison with the winter committees and local tutors provides an ongoing anticipation of co-operation that is now a renewed part of community dynamics.

The ideological component is also found in the widespread community support and involvement of the Barra population in *Feis* activities. The summer *Feis* has an enrollment of over 200 children, with groups travelling from the neighbouring islands of Uist, Mull and Islay to participate in the Barra festival. The year round *Feis* has an enrollment of approximately 250 local children. Some classes were obviously more successful than others but when one considers that thirty adults were directly involved as tutors and organizers, one begins to realize that there is hardly a household on the island that is not directly involved in the *Feis* on a year round basis.

This direct involvement may be highlighted by a brief allusion to the Barra Games which are held at the midpoint of the summer *Feis*.

The Games were a resurrection of an annual Highland Games that had not been held on Barra for twenty-five years. The Games, like the *Feis*, started on a very modest basis, but have evolved into an event that draws practically the entire island population to the westside Barra machair on Games Sunday. The Games are organized by a separate committee, responsible for fundraising and organization -- and as such resemble in structure and autonomy the other cultural and activity groups that come under the *Feis* umbrella. The Games organising committee secured the support of local businesses to donate handsome trophies and could confidently draw on a wide sector of the community to help organise and run the event. *Feis* dancers and pipers put on exhibitions of their skills and every pupil has the opportunity to perform. It was not just an occasion for accomplished performers. Special events such as Barra-wrestling - with no known connection to any sport other than Japanese Sumo - were anticipated with relish by the crowds. The Games illustrate how the entire community has drawn together. They support it financially, participate and attend. It confirms their solidarity, and mutual support, highlights the *Feis* after its first week and provides an arena for great fun and enjoyment. The community commitment and solidarity that has become so evident since the inception of the *Feis* has had dramatic spinoffs in other areas of island life that I will briefly examine below.

Within the Summer *Feis* itself there has been a discernible evolution from the faithful reproduction of existing Gaelic arts to the production of new compositions in music and drama. This came about partly due to a crossfertilization between classes as different music groups would join together for classes, provide backing for the dancers and drama groups and generally evolve into their own distinctive expressive forms. This cross-transference was encouraged by *Feis* organisers and tutors and was particularly evident in the singing classes. Here the children, particularly the five to eight year olds, avidly explored the lore and background of different songs, placing them in an imaginative metaphysical and paranormal context that frequently amazed their tutors. This creative exploration was in Gaelic. The bottom line once again was language, in that new Gaelic art and expressive forms can emerge only in situations where language use is creative and ongoing. This notion lay behind the one year experiment in Gaelic community drama sponsored by the *Feis* (1983-1984) which provided financial support for a professional Gaelic actor and drama tutor to work in Barra's schools and in the community promoting Gaelic drama. The Scottish Arts Council provided 50% of the budget with the remainder coming from the H.I.D.B., *Comhairle nan Eilean* and the community.

The political dimension to this specific cultural activity and general ideological commitment has been community pressure on the local government to provide music and drama teachers for the island schools on a permanent basis. The interest and enthusiasm generated by *Feis* activities did not have any reflection in school curricula -- simply because teachers in music and drama had not been appointed by the regional council. Political activity by the *Feis* and the community is being directed at the council so that a policy decision can be taken to provide the necessary teachers and resources. This political activity may be seen, ironically enough, as one consequence of the success of the council's bilingualism policy. The climate fostered by the council provided fertile soil for the Barra *Feis* to take root such that further demands are now being made on the council to extend its stated commitment to bilingualism in specific ways. Political activism in general areas concerning Gaelic language and culture has yet to become part of *Comann Feis Bharraigh's* activities. It was mooted in the 1982-1983 Annual Report but was not taken any further. I suspect that the immediate concern of the *Feis* committee is with internal consolidation in terms of island needs. The formation of a Heritage Society in 1984 for adults and children and the institution of a society to promote Hebridean Dancing - a dance form quite different from Highland dancing - are part of this consolidation.

I do anticipate, however, that *Feis Bharraigh* will eventually emerge as a campaigning force for Gaelic issues. It already has done so by its example and activism. It has yet to emerge with clear political statements about broadcasting and media coverage of Gaelic, bilingualism in schools and community, Gaelic play groups etc., but I do anticipate that it will. There are *Feis* connections with the Irish language and educational movement - *Slogadh* - and it is simply a matter of time before the *Feis* ideology that has emerged from community commitment to language and culture will have stated political and economic ramifications.

These ramifications can already be seen indirectly in terms of a renewed solidarity and self reliance in other spheres of island life. For instance; (a) the formation in 1984 of a Barra Water Sports Association which provides lessons in water safety, sailing and kayaking for children, (b) the determined activity of parents and children from 1983 to 1986 to reverse a decision by the Scottish Office and local council not to proceed with the construction of a swimming pool, (c) in 1985 the ambitious plans to extend the activities of the community co-operative and (d) the formation of a Heritage Society in 1984. These activities and others like them are mostly due to a significantly changed attitude within the community towards what it now defines as possible which twenty years earlier would have been largely unthinkable (Prattis 1987). The movement towards self reliance rather than dependency, reflected in the many independent activities taking place since 1980, could not have happened in the 1960's or 1970's (Prattis 1987). In the decades prior to the 1980's there was not the commitment to language, culture or community that could have provided the ideological basis for the cultural, economic and political activity that took place in the 1980's.

The turning point was the 1975 commitment to bilingualism by *Comhairle nan Eilean*. The expression of this commitment through the bilingual education project provided the stage for a voluntary community response that provided the driving force for regenerating the Barra community. What is emerging here is a reversal of the usual equations about community development and economic well being. My emphasis is on culture, language and community dynamics as being prior to economic and political developments. This basically is what *Feis* ideology is all about.

Conclusion

Implicit in the earlier theoretical discussion are concepts of ethnic legitimacy, boundary maintenance, structural and voluntary feedback, variations in the bilingual language situation, a model of dependency, and voluntary responses to institutional changes. The advantages of bilingualism apply at a psychological (Lambert 1977) and social level (Barth 1969). When experience, institutions and activities - in this case in Gaelic - reinforce ideas and categories of difference then cultural identity can be retained and reinforced and operate as a galvanizer for community solidarity. The corollary also holds -- if experience falsifies the categories or demonstrates the lack of relevance of the categories for interaction and day to day life, then cultural identity will not persist (Mitchell 1974).

Given the situation of general dependency described for the Western Isles (Prattis 1977, 1979; Hunter 1977; McKinnon 1983), part of the solution to linguistic and cultural erosion concerns the reduction and elimination of such dependency (Prattis 1980a; Prattis and Chartrand 1990). However, work on the nature of ethnic relations by various scholars (Berreman 1979; Enloe 1973, 1979) indicates that it is a mistake, in the situation we have above, to focus only on class relations of political economy. The grassroots commitment to minority language and culture has not been maintained in spite of wider societal pressures for acculturation, but precisely because of them. This argument applies to the generation which was brought up before the communications revolution. This generation is now slowly disappearing and the present population now faces overwhelming external and media pressures to assimilate to the mass culture. Later generations would, all other things being equal, lose the traditional language and culture (Prattis 1979). But in the Western Isles all other things have not remained equal, as definite attempts have been made to arrest this trend.

The first step in reducing dependency was the 1974-1975 reorganisation of local government in the U.K. The creation of *Comhairle nan Eilean* with a responsibility for the entire Western Isles removed Lewis and Harris from the mainland authority of Ross and Cromarty; while the Uists, Benbecula, Barra and Vatersay were similarly removed from the dictates of mainland Inverness-shire. This re-organisation reduced in one stroke a significant part of mainland hegemony. The second step was the *Comhairle's* declaration that it was officially bilingual and committed to bilingual education. The third step was a variety of community responses to these institutional changes of which the Barra *Feis* is perhaps the most spectacular. The result is that in those areas where bilingualism has been implemented on a systemic basis, the young now have a better knowledge of the minority language than the generation immediately before them, and communities have the opportunity of responding culturally to a changed set of institutional constraints.

The blueprint of minimum conditions for successful bilingualism (Prattis and Chartrand 1985; Appendix A) is designed to secure and pursue these changes. It is not antithetical to the inevitability of social change nor is it concerned with preserving distinctive cultures at all costs. Rather it leads to a constructive, ongoing modification from within minority language communities instead of entrenching conditions of cultural, political and economic dependency. Furthermore, the blueprint implies that given specific preconditions, cultural revival and continuity is not a difficult nor necessarily slow process.

The bilingualism policy of *Comhairle nan Eilean* and the institutional ramifications of the education project succeeded in producing an integrated set of interests that changed the climate of concern with respect to Gaeldom's language and culture. Different levels of the State apparatus were involved (H.I.D.B.; Scottish Office; *Comhairle nan Eilean*) in allocating funds, personnel and policies such that a perceived shift in attitudes was discernible. Critics have argued that the institutional support for Gaelic is inadequate and I agree with them, but this objection obscures the symbolic importance (to the Gael) of different state bodies declaring an active interest, implementing an official bilingualism, and providing tangible measures on the ground in pursuit of their varied declarations.

At once the "stigma" and uncertainty about the value of Gaelic language and culture erodes in the face of official statements to the contrary. The symbolic significance of *Comhairle nan Eilean* declaring itself to be officially bilingual cannot be underestimated, even though the council cannot deliver all of its services in two languages and may not ever be able to do so. The question of delivery of services in two languages is distinct from the changed perceptions of language, culture and self that the Gael received from the symbolic steps taken by the *Comhairle's* commitment to bilingualism for the Western Isles. It was within this set of preconditions that the Barra *Feis* took root, and without them I doubt if it would have become an established part of island life. As it was, given the changed perceptions of community residents on Barra, latent community commitment to the language and culture were mobilised by the *Feis* articulating the two major premises of its activities. First the commitment to language, and secondly the commitment to an intergenerational transfer of cultural material. These twin themes underlie the achievements of the *Feis* and the potential for cultural revival and continuity.

These themes may be most dramatically illustrated by the revival, through the *Feis*, of a particular Gaelic cultural form and its transformation into an organisation that will regulate the activity on a national basis. I am referring to Hebridean Dancing, a distinctive dance form that had died out in the islands. There was only one teacher of this dance form still alive. Farquar McNeil, retired in Southwest Scotland, became a *Feis* tutor in 1982 and revived a dance form that children and tutors responded enthusiastically to, because it was a distinctive form unique to their own Hebridean heritage. Hebridean Dancing assumed a primacy in *Feis* objectives and in 1985 an official dancing board was formed, known as *Bord Daunsa nan Eileanach* with a remit to promote Hebridean dancing locally, nationally and internationally. In other words to make of it an institutionalized form to rival the more well known Highland Dancing. In three short years (1982-1985) a "dead" Gaelic performing art had been revived, transformed and institutionalized on an ongoing basis. This example perhaps best exemplifies the cultural revival and continuity that the Barra *Feis* has brought about. The *Feis* itself has become institutionalized as a major component of everyday life on Barra and has political implications that will stretch way beyond its insular confines.

The intellectual concern about Gaelic language and culture by academics and well-wishers has been reflected for many years in institutions of higher learning in North America and Europe. This is indeed necessary and supportive as a secondary activity but the plaudits must go to those people on the ground, who work diligently to maintain, enrich and entrench Gaelic consciousness. This consciousness is radically different to current rationality, mostly because it is not antagonistic to life on this planet. Those academics that have shared in it and understood its significance have the added responsibility of communicating the results of their privileged experience. This chapter is dedicated to the tutors (local and professional) and children on the Island of Barra for their stewardship and co-creation of the Barra *Feis*, and to the visionaries in different levels of the state apparatus for establishing the institutional framework. They may not realize it, but they have created something very dynamic that may eventually reverse current notions about situations of dependency.

Appendix 1: Blueprint of Minimum Requirements for Effective Bilingualism

1. Official recognition of the minority language;

2. use of the minority language in administrative, bureaucratic and legal structures;

3. agreement and support of the local community for the introduction of bilingual education that is part of a wider community education program;

4. support and financing for minority language medium instruction at all levels in the education system;

5. major centres for teacher training, curriculum design and the production of literature in the minority language;

6. reading schemes, at all levels, in the minority language;

7. teachers fluent in the minority language;

8. support for measures to use the minority language in community education and cultural programs, to increase its social standing;

9. support for minority language in the mass media; radio and television programs for schools, children at home and general broadcasting.

These minimum conditions for effective minority language bilingualism are, I believe, generalizable and will have relevance to situations of multiculturalism on a global basis. The concentration in previous work has been on bilingualism as a systemic issue and not simply a consideration of what medium of instruction is used in schools. This emphasis places bilingual education within an ongoing process of bicultural education involving the entire community rather than schoolchildren only. This is part of an argument that a necessary prerequisite for successful bilingualism is a "climate" of vigorous biculturalism and broad based community education programs.

Appendix 2: Structure of the Barra *Feis*

COMANN FEIS BHARRAIGH - The Barra Arts and Festival Association provides the overall organizational "umbrella" for (a) activities that have their own autonomy - Barra Games, Heritage Society, Hebridean Dancing Society and (b) for activities more closely directed by the *Comann Feis* - clarsach, fiddle, accordion.

SUMMER FEIS - Held first two weeks in July with the Barra Games at the midpoint. Classes from 10 a.m. to 3:45 p.m. with four one hourly periods of instruction plus a compulsory Gaelic class. Concerts, dances, parades, performances every night in community halls, Ciesmul castle, and village square provided by tutors and pupils.

Figure 7.1: Summer *Feis*

Activity	Pupils: 1983	Pupils: 1984	Professional Tutors 1983	Professional Tutors 1984
Piping	7	9	2	2
Chanter	25	24	2	3
Tin Whistle	60	66	1	1
Fiddle	20	27	1	1
Clarsach	20	30	2	3
Accordion	25	27	1	1
Singing	63	67	3	2
Teenage Workshop	44	60	4	3
Folk Groups	-	26	-	1
Drama	79	103	1	2
Dancing - Highland and Hebridean	86	89	4	4
Shinty	24	26	1	1
Gaelic	238	245	6	6
			28	30

YEAR-ROUND FEIS - Organized by a committee and local tutors for the following activities

Figure 7.2: Year Round *Feis*

Activity	Pupils: 1983*	No. of local adults and tutors 1983
Accordion	16	3
Fiddle	8	2
Clarsach	14	3
Song - Traditional and Modern	42	6
Dancing - Highland and Hebridean	107	6
Chanter	18	4
Tin Whistle	28	3
	233	27

* A precise breakdown of figures for 1984/85 is not available. Numbers did increase to 250 registrants (1985).

Acknowledgements

I am grateful to Jean-Philippe Chartrand for a timely critique and review. The *Feis* organisers and participants also receive my thanks, particularly the athletes competing in the veteran's 1/4 mile race of the Barra Games. In two successive years they managed to fall by the wayside or run in the wrong direction permitting the author to obtain his one and only gold medal. An elderly gentleman had the audacity *not* to do this in 1985 so keen was he on the gold medal for himself!

Bibliography

Balkan, L.
1970 Les Effets du Bilinguisme Francais-Anglais sur les Aptitudes Intellectuelles. Bruxells: Aimav

Barth, F
1969 Ethnic Groups and Boundaries. Boston: Little, Brown and Co.

Ben-Zeev, S.
1972 The Influence of Bilingualism on Cognitive Development and Cognitive Strategy. Unpublished doctoral dissertation, University of Chicago

Berreman, G.
1979 Social Inequality: A Cross Cultural Typology. In Prakash, V. (ed.): Caste and Other Inequities. Vatuk: Meerut

Comann Feis Bharraigh
1982-1983 Aithris Bhliadhnail

1983-1984 Aithris Bhliadhnail

Comhairle nan Eilean
1976 The Bilingual Policy, a Consultative Document. Stornoway

Dubé, N.C. and G. Herbert
1975a St. John Valley Bilingual Education Project: Report to U.S. Department of Health and Welfare. Madawaska: Maine

1975b Evaluation of the St. John Valley Education Program, 1970-1975. Madawaska: Maine

Enloe, C.
1973 Ethnic Conflict and Political Development. Boston: Little, Brown and Co.

1979 Multinational Corporations and the Making and Unmaking of Ethnic Groups. In Grant, R. and E.S. Wellhoffer (eds.): Ethnonationalism, Multinational Corporations and the Modern State. Monograph, Science and World Affairs, V.1, 15, 4. Denver: University of Denver

Fennell, D.
1981 Can a Shrinking Linguistic Minority be Saved? Lessons from the Irish Experience. In Haugen, E., J.D. McClure and D.S. Thomson (eds.): Minority Languages Today. Edinburgh: Edinburgh University Press

Gaarder, A.B.
1967 Organization of the Bilingual School. Journal of Social Issues, 23

Hechter, M.
1975 Internal Colonialism: The Celtic Fringe in British National Development, 1536-1966. Los Angeles: University of California Press

Highlands and Islands Development Board
1984 Annual Report

Hunter, J.
1977 The Making of the Crofting Community. Edinburgh: Donald and Sons

Lambert, W.E. and E. Anisfield
1969 Note on the Relationship of Bilingualism and Intelligence. Canadian Journal of Behavioural Science 1:123-128

Lambert, W.E., H. Giles and A. Albert
1974 Language Attitudes in a Rural City in Northern Maine. Montreal: McGill University Mimeo

Lambert, W.E., H. Giles and D. Picard
1975 Language Attitudes in a French American Community. International Journal of the Sociology of Language, 4:127-152

Lambert, W.E.
1977 The Effects of Bilingualism on the Individual: Cognitive and Sociocultural Consequences. In P.A. Hornby (ed.): Bilingualism: Psychological, Social and Educational Consequences. N.Y.: Academic Press

McKinnon, K.
1977 Language, Education and Social Processes in a Gaelic Community. London: Routledge and Kegan Paul

1983 Power at the Periphery: The Language Dimension in the Case of Gaelic Scotland. Paper presented to British Sociological Association. Cardiff, April

Mitchell, G.C.
1974 Conceptions of Ethnicity and Ethnic Behaviour: An Empiricial Exploration. In Cohen, A. (ed.): Urban Ethnicity. London: Tavistock Publications

Murray, J. and C. Morrison
1984 Bilingual Primary Education in the Western Isles, Scotland. Stornoway: Acair

O'Grady, G. and K. Hale
1974 Recommendations Concerning Bilingual Education in the Northern Territory. Darwin: Australian Department of Education

Prattis, J.I.
1977 Economic Structures in the Highlands of Scotland. Glasgow: Fraser of Allander Institute, Strathclyde University

1979 The Survival of Communities. Current Anthropology, V.20, 2:361-375

1980a The Structure of Resource Development in the Canadian North. Carleton University, Department of Sociology and Anthropology Working Paper, 80-6

1980b Ethnic Succession in the Eastern Townships of Quebec. Anthropologica V. XXII, 2:215-234

1981 Industrialization and Minority Language Loyalty. In Haugen, E., J.D. McClure and D.S. Thompson (eds.): Minority Languages Today. Edinburgh: Edinburgh University Press

1987 Organisational Change and Adaptation - Community Cooperatives and Capital Control in the Western Isles of Scotland. American Anthropologist V.89, 3

Prattis, J.I. and J.P. Chartrand

1985 Minority Language Bilingualism: The Case of Inuktitut in the Canadian North. Anthropologica, V.25, 1

1990 The Cultural Division of Labour in the Canadian North. Canadian Review of Sociology and Anthropology, V.27, 1

Reitz, J.G.

1980 The Survival of Ethnic Groups. Toronto: McGraw-Hill Ryerson Ltd.

Scott, S.

1973 The Relation of Divergent Thinking to Bilingualism: Cause or Effect. Unpublished research report, McGill University

Torrance, E.P. and J.C. Gowan
1970 Creative Functioning of Monolingual and Bilingual Children in Singapore. Journal of Educational Psychology, V.61:72-75

U.N.E.S.C.O.
1953 The Use of Vernacular Language. Paris: U.N.E.S.C.O.

Watts, B.H., W.J. McGrath and J.L. Tandy
1973 Bilingual Education in Schools in the Northern Territories. Darwin: Australian Department of Education

Withers, C.W.J.
1985 Culture and Hegemony: The Cultural Status of Scottish Gaelic. Paper presented to Iona Foundation Conference. P.E.I., Canada, July

Chapter 8

Sacred Dance and Cultural Bridges

To the Universe
belongs the dancer.
Whoever does not dance
does not know what happens.

Acts of John 95:16-17

For many years I have been fascinated by cultures that dance their myths. The ritual preparation, the total theatre of the mythic enactment produced a cultural dynamic that seemed to provide a bridge between the history, culture and present day consciousness of the cultures observed, as dance moved from the secular to the sacred domain. What was presented was not performance or entertainment, as we usually think of it, but rather a ritual process deeply rooted in the mythology and traditions of a particular culture whereby some transcendent significance was given to a way of life. It is as though sacred dance traditions take people out of the mundane and awaken them to life and reality in a higher sphere. As Professor Sam Gill points out "There is no message in the dance short of the meaning of life itself" (1979:3).

In recent years I have had a number of opportunities to experience and participate in this phenomenon and thereby gain insight to the coherence produced by sacred dance and provide some validation for the implicit conceptual overviews I had about it. One opportunity was in the personal domain, another in the public domain of collaborating with a modern dance company - The Karen Jamieson Dance Group of Vancouver - which I will refer to later in this essay.

The personal domain occurred in my practice of Tai Chi. I had moved to this martial art form after practicing and teaching judo and jujitsu for some twenty years. It was only very recently that the realization dawned on me that in doing Tai Chi, I was in fact dancing the I Ching, the ancient Chinese system of divination. The I Ching itself was a manifestation of a series of creation myths about the location of the human being in the cosmos. This realization -- which came relatively slowly for someone supposedly well versed in symbols, mythology and ritual -- totally changed both the performance of the Tai Chi form and its effects. In recognizing that Tai Chi was enacting in physical movement a mythology of human location in the cosmos, my preparation and attention to detail altered. Tai Chi was done only after meditation with focused attention on breath control, and this was accompanied by a much greater attention to posture, precision in movement and body-breath co-ordination. The effects on the body were dramatic. I felt the movements deep inside, affecting the cellular level of my body which in turn produced profuse sweating on even the coldest of days and trembling and shaking in the body as energy moved from the cellular level into the physical. All this was activated through a different mental awareness of the symbolic significance of the choreography inherent in the sequences of Tai Chi. So for me, doing Tai Chi had moved from a martial art to an energy dance to a sacred dance. It was not so much that I was performing Tai Chi as moving within its parameters. In other words it was now total theatre in the ritualistic sense (Turner 1974). The form had stayed much the same, however the practice had radically altered because my consciousness had changed about the symbolic imprinting at the cellular level that the symbolic sequence of Tai Chi had activated. This assertion requires some elaboration as to mythology, sacred dance as total theatre, breathwork and symbols in the body.

The approach to mythology that I subscribe to is outlined in Chapter 4 - *"Reflections" as Myth* and will not be repeated here. Suffice it to say that I think of myth as providing the general foundation from which the specific features of sacred dance emerge, providing a symbolic transformation vehicle for both dancer and audience. In other words sacred dance is a mythic enactment. This interweaving is discussed by Anne-Marie Gaston (1982) in her fascinating discussion of classical Indian dance - *Siva in Dance, Myth and Iconography*. She states:

> Dance in traditional Indian culture permeated all facets of life, but its outstanding function was to give symbolic expression to abstract religious ideas (1982:6).

She notes an intriguing connection between the mythology of Siva, the ancient temple sculptures of Siva's postures and the choreography of contemporary Indian classical dance (1982:15). She considers the Nataraja temple at Cidambaram in South India to be the most important sculptural source for the delineation of *karanas* -- the combined movement of hands and feet in classical dance. The temple sculptures at Cidambaram date from the twelfth and thirteenth centuries and document a timeless version of the Siva myths, that has great utility for modern choreographers within the classical Indian dance tradition. Gaston points out that:

> With the recent trend to create new compositions, however, many sculptural poses are being re-introduced into the dance, the choreographers claiming to be discovering and recreating an older more authentic form than has previously been seen (Gaston 1982:15).

Gaston attributes to myths the function of conveying spiritual guidance and arousing a particular spiritual state in individuals (1982:33). The classical dance tradition recognizes two aspects of dance - *natya* and *nrtta* - mime and pure dance (Gaston 1982:14) with an underlying template known as *rasa*. Concerning *rasa* she states:

> Rasa pervades all the classical Indian arts and results from the awakening of latent psychological states (sthayi-bhavas) in the beholder by the use of appropriate formalized imagery... The expression of certain bhavas by a dancer was considered an important way to worship God and was one of the reasons dance became a necessary and integral part of religious worship... the dancer... sang the religious songs, externalizing her feelings with facial expressions and danced using stylized movements. These are only three of the many elements used to evoke an emotional response in the beholder (Gaston 1982:14).

So the dancer steps into the experience of *bhavas* and draws the audience in turn into a different state, described by the term *rasa*. In their close association between iconography, dance in mythology and classical (live) dance form the dancer's knowledge of myths, and symbolic gestures (mudras) introduces a flexibility and spontaneity into the form.

Analogous to the concept of *rasa* is the direct correlation many folk societies make between ritualized dance forms and altered states of consciousness (Price-Williams and Hughes 1994:7-8). Katz (1981, 1982) has documented how the !Kung bushmen of the Kalahari desert in South Africa believe that ritualized dance brings individuals into a direct experience with *n/um*, a special energy that can best be described as Kundalini energy -- which is evoked and activated through specific spiritual practises. The pivotal event of their healing traditions is the all night sacred healing dance. The singers, mostly women, gather round the fire chanting and clapping while the men dance in a highly stylized manner around them. As the dance intensifies a particular kind of energy known as *n/um* is activated in the male dancers who are healers. They move into a state of experience called *!kia* which is recognized as a form of enhanced consciousness, and while in this state they heal everyone at the dance by drawing them into the same energy (Katz 1981:60). Price-Williams and Hughes (1994) posit a general correlation between dance, movement and human consciousness without developing an in depth or systematic argument to enhance their claim. This essay may provide the evidence and argument to support their correlation.

A common element shared by all sacred dance traditions is the attention given to breath control. This has a very ancient tradition and no less an authority than the Buddha addressed the significance of breath in the *Anapanasati sutra* on the Mindfulness of Breathing. He also addressed the postures of the body in the *Satipatthana sutra* on the Foundation of Mindfulness (Hanh 1987:113,123), the significance of which will become evident later in this essay. The Vietnamese Buddhist master, Thich Nhat Hanh, (1987:23) has this to say about breath:

> Our breath is the bridge from our body to our mind, the element which reconciles our body and mind and which makes possible one-ness of body and mind. Breath is aligned to both body and mind and it alone is the tool which can bring them both together, illuminating both and bringing both peace and calm.

The yogic system of breath control, known as *pranayama*, consists of an infinite set of breathing ratios, methods of alternate nostril breathing, explosive breaths and breath retention. This system is consciously used to experience elevated states of spiritual consciousness which are different from everyday waking consciousness. The different techniques of breath control at some point bring to the practitioner's awareness the recognition that the mind and body is moved by the same energy that pervades the planet and the entire universe. Thus the science of breath in the body is regarded as part of the respiration of Cosmic Breath (Iyengar 1966). I point out (Prattis 1996:170) in my discussion of meditation structures how symbols, mantras, sacred posture, dance, mandalas and other forms of focus are used at different levels of meditative entrainment. Furthermore, I identify the key to all this as being the conscious use of breath and symbolic focus. Heinze discusses breath control as a vehicle to move individuals into a state of spiritual awareness they would not otherwise experience (Heinze 1994:10). So, when conscious breathing and the attention to breath control is connected in sacred dance to (1) the repetitive nature of the choreography, (2) the symbols and mudras shaped by the hands and body postures, (3) the chants, mantras and music that accompany sacred dance; then it becomes obvious that in sacred dance we are dealing with a very powerful symbolic complex of transformation.

The significance of sacred dance and total theatre as a symbolic complex is manifestly evident in Balinese culture. Artaud (1958) has commented on how sacred dance in Balinese theatre creates a new language for performers and audience alike. The use of dance, voice and ritual gestures follow precise musical indications (1958:57) and draw specifically on Balinese creation myths. The theatre, in a ritualistic sense, is almost mathematically defined in its precision. This is not entertainment in the usual sense of the word -- it is an educational reminder of where human beings are located in the cosmos and the basic dramas they play out in life. This is necessarily so, given the mythological basis of the entire enactment. Artaud states; "The Balinese productions take shape at the very heart of matter, life, reality. There is in them something of the ceremonial quality of a religious rite... The thoughts it aims at, the spiritual states it seems to create, the mystic solutions it proposes are aroused and attained without delay" (1958:60). He refers to the dancers as "metaphysicians of natural disorder" who in dancing the myths restore us to a greater sense of ourselves.

It should come as no surprise given my previous argument about breath work and spiritual states that the dancers and actors in Balinese theatre are ritually prepared for their mythic enactments with exacting attention paid to training in meditation and breath control. This correlates with implicit ideas I have long entertained about the significance of body posture in the domain of the sacred. My hypothesis is that there are particular body postures that create the shape of a symbol, and when breath is drawn with awareness into this created symbol it "electrifies" the body because it has hit upon a corresponding symbolic structure deep in the unconscious, and this is felt physically due to cellular memory. From this perspective sacred dance is simply an extended choreography of symbols provided by the sequential postures of the body. The symbols so created act as a lens through which breath magnifies the whole effect of the body symbol on the unconscious symbols, thus producing a match between the external form (sacred dance) and the internal form (unconscious symbols). This is why all traditions of sacred dance pay such meticulous attention to body posture and the precision of choreographic sequence, as well as to ritual preparation and breath control. All of this provides an entry point into the biggest mysteries of life. This brings me back to the head note:

To the Universe
belongs the dancer.
Whoever does not dance
does not know what happens

From the gnostic Acts of John, these are the words spoken by Jesus of Nazareth when anticipating arrest in the garden of Gethsemene. He gathered his followers into a circle to dance, while he stood in the centre intoning a mystical chant (Pagels 1979:7), asking his disciples to "Answer Amen to me". Although Pope Leo the Great condemned the Acts of John as heresy in the fifth-century, I agree with Joseph Campbell (1988) that this is one of the most magnificent passages in the entire Christian tradition. Consider this excerpt of Jesus speaking to his disciples:

I am a mirror to you
who know me. Amen
I am a door to you
who knock on me. Amen
I am a way to you
the traveller. Amen
Now if you follow
my dance,
see yourself
in Me who am speaking
and when you have seen what I do,
keep silence about my mysteries...
You who dance, consider
what I do, for yours is
this passion of humanity
which I am to suffer.
For you could no means
have understood what you suffer
unless to you, as the Word
I was sent by the Father...
Now if you follow
What I am you shall see
when you come yourself.

Acts of John 95:25 - 96:40

What is the mystery here? Jesus explains in the Acts of John that everyone who dances this sacred dance is to "see yourself in Me who am speaking" -- in other words acknowledge their own identity with Christ and learn to transcend human suffering (Pagels 1979:9). When the dance ends, Jesus walks out into the garden, to be taken and later crucified. Campbell comments that "when you go to your death that way, as a god, in the knowledge of the myth, you are going to your eternal life" (1988:109). Thus when dance moves from the secular to the sacred domain there is an opportunity for glimpses of eternity to come through the mythic enactment, for revelation to touch one's insights while in the liminal phase of sacred dance. This is so for both the participants in sacred dance and for the audience, as a deep part of the psyche has been touched and stirred in persons through the mythic enactment (Progoff 1970:188). This is what is so different about cultures that dance their myths -- the audience know the myths and are moved right along with the dancers into the mysteries of human consciousness.

This brings me finally to my collaboration with the Karen Jamieson Dance Group. I shared with Karen Jamieson a common interest in mythology. She had described to me a particular dance her company performed and the strange effects on the dancers afterwards -- members of the company felt nausea, illness and were generally out of sorts. The dance was "Rainforest", one of her company's classics, and the basis of the choreography was Karen Jamieson's interest in myths, masks and posture from North West Coast Indian culture. The choreography featured postures and expressions drawn, in particular, from transformation masks which were used in North West Coast traditions to initiate dancers into other states of consciousness. This information acted as a catalyst for the implicit ideas I had about body symbol, posture and the unconscious and how they all interconnected in sacred dance. It became clear to me that the company were straying into the area of sacred dance, posture and expression but without the appropriate training in the ritualistic sense. In emulating the expression and postures inherent in transformation masks the dancers were forming shapes with their bodies that corresponded to symbolic structures embedded in the unconscious and in the body. Thus a release was experienced that did not have breath control or meditation as a necessary safety valve. This then became my work with the company -- to impart to them very simple techniques of meditation and breath control so that the symbolic correspondence between choreographic sequence and internal symbols enabled the dancers to perform with a different awareness of what they were creating.

It of course developed into much more than that. The dance company was composed of superb young athletes and artists, trained in a variety of dance forms with a sensitivity to movement and energy that was startling. After we had all progressed in the area of symbolic correspondence I asked the company to dance their meditative experiences. The result was instant choreography in the moment that was astonishing in its fluidity, power, grace and effect on the observer (see Progoff 1970). It was not directed or ordered, yet a perfect synchronicity between dancers resulted. They had the dance skills and sensitivity to collectively sense what everyone else was creating. It was simply awesome! To give an example: one meditation involved a visualization about being under the sea (the unconscious realm) swimming and playing with dolphins. At one point in the directed meditation I asked the company to visualize a baby dolphin swimming towards them and tapping them gently in the middle of the chest (the heart centre or chakra). To simulate this part of the visualization I asked the dancers to tap their chest with their hands at the time of impact of the dolphin beak on their heart centre. The meditation then continued for a further fifteen minutes of silence.

Afterwards I asked the four women dancers to stand back to back facing the four cardinal directions (North, South, West, East) and to move and synchronize themselves as a single heart beat of a dolphin. The four men stood some ten feet distant, facing away from the central circle of women dancers. The men were to start dancing the moment they felt the women at the centre synchronize their movements as one heart beat. The women started to move, individually restrained by the grip they had on one another's hands until with an almost audible click their movements were in total harmony and synchronicity. At that precise moment all four male dancers on the outer circle, who had their eyes closed, began to dance in accordance with the harmony created by the women at the centre. This wonderful, instant choreography continued for approximately twenty minutes and we were all stunned at what had been created.

This particular experience was later incorporated into a site specific work the company created for the National Art Gallery in Ottawa. This piece was called "Passage" and it was loosely based on Joseph Campbell's "The Hero's Journey". So the company were dancing the structure of myth, creating a choreography from inner experience. They were also using meditation and breath control to remain centred during the experience of symbolic correspondence between choreography and internal structures in the unconscious and the body. In the creation of "Passage" the company had taken a step away from the secular into the sacred domain of choreographic expression.

The next step for the company was a collaboration with the Gitksan First Nation of British Columbia, in the dancing of a Gitksan creation myth. It is mythology that provides the underlying core of the company's transition from "Rainforest" to the present day. "Rainforest" drew on modern dance and fused it with the masks and myths of traditional North West Coast cultures. "Passage" was a choreographic creation that portrayed the structure of the Hero's mythology. In collaboration with Gitksan artists, hereditary chiefs and historians a further mythological step was taken to create *Gawa Gyani*. In this collaboration the full impact of a sacred dance tradition was felt. For the first time First Nations dancers were involved and they and their Gitksan advisors were properly trained in breath control and Gitksan sacred dance traditions, and this was taught to the Karen Jamieson Dance Group.

Gawa Gyani is a title in the Gitksan house of *Go'onu* and the term may be understood as a principle of mediation whereby groups in conflict are brought to a resolution of difference. The performance revolves around the story of *Sc'a waa*, a Gitksan creation myth which tells of the unity between heaven and earth in the creation of the original Gitksan people. A Gitksan hereditary chief - Alice Jeffrey - taught the dance to the company and another hereditary chief Kenneth Harris narrated the myth while the performance unfolded. So, for the dance company there was a collective interaction with First Nations dancers, with a Gitksan sacred dance tradition and the enactment of a Gitksan creation myth. The interaction was based on mutual respect. This was demonstrated very clearly in a simple circle ceremony held after each presentation of *Gawa Gyani*, whereby an eagle feather was passed round inviting anyone - native and non-native - to speak as a prelude to a common expression of thanksgiving. The presence of Chief Kenneth Harris as narrator of the myth, in Gitksan and English was essential as his family - the *Gisghaast* clan - owned the dance and had to be present to ensure integrity of performance. His narration was crucial as the tone of vocal expression and facial structure are key elements in the Gitksan tradition of relating myth. Needless to say, the performance was electric. Michael Scott's review captured something of what was created:

> In a sense it is dance, since much of it is imparted through movement; but it is also a communal story-telling, laced with the memories of the people who collected and organized it; it is a storehouse of myth, from the images that flicker in individual dreams to the epic poetry that reflects entire cultures; it is theatre, quickened with singing, chanting and spoken text, it is a gazeteer that leads us back and forth between native culture and the noisy and paradoxical communities that have come afterward; it is a musical document of surprising resonance (Scott 1991).

That's as close as a dance critic in our culture can get to saying -- This is sacred dance!

The final problem, however, is how does one study this phenomena as an anthropologist; to do justice to its full compass and avoid the pitfalls of cultural appropriation and academic projection. Let me recall some of the major points. The phenomenon I have briefly presented is the joint collaboration between the Karen Jamieson Dance Group of Vancouver and the Gitksan *Gisghaast* clan in the creation of *Gawa Gyani* - a dance drama that is rooted in a sacred Gitksan creation myth. When this kind of phenomena is introduced into mainstream popular culture, difficulties arise in documenting it as an ethnographic event, as the ethnographer must be able to participate in diverse symbolic worlds and comprehend them while at the same time respecting the narratives and point of view of the different cultural participants. This is the major issue of postmodern anthropology. The joint creation of *Gawa Gyani* is based on a Gitksan principle of mediation whereby groups in conflict come together in a neutral space to formulate an appropriate resolution. The Gitksan decided to share their tradition with the wider public as they felt that the discord of Meech Lake and later constitutional debates in Canada could benefit from a symbolic mediation process that they knew had traditionally worked for them.

The scope of the ethnographic enterprise here is to document the genesis, performance and evolution of *Gawa Gyani* from its first to its last performance and examine effects on audiences, performers and cultures involved. My prior work with the dance group and with the Gitksan (in terms of land claims) permits me to step into their symbolic worlds with appropriate respect. Yet I can only provide a limited perspective that is bound by my own conceptual overviews and assessment of critical patterns of symbolic behaviour and their correspondence with other levels -- behavioural and physiological. I cannot speak on behalf of either the dance company or the *Gisghaast* clan of the Gitksan. Thus the most crucial part of the research design is to invite them to speak for themselves. The ideal research would produce a text or film - "Sacred Dance and Cultural Bridges" - that would include narratives and perspectives from the Gitksan hereditary chiefs, from the dance company, and from me, within an overall compass provided by the navigational skills we are all able to provide. This is not a piece of research I can simply go in and do, irrespective of the voices of the different cultural participants, for their voices and the expressive mode they choose is the most important ethnographic data to elicit. So the unfolding of this piece of research depends less on my particular interests in the domain of sacred dance; it depends more on whether the participants in the creation of the dance drama choose to have it represented at all. And at the moment they do not, and this must be respected. In postmodern anthropology this respect for the other is an important blueprint for contemporary fieldworkers to digest, as it may well lead to research not being done at all.

There is also a particular time perspective involved in this study. The first performance of *Gawa Gyani* was in June 1991 and the final collaborative act was presented in March 1993. The Karen Jamieson Company have since moved on to an artistic expression that is very similar to the Balinese theatre discussed earlier in this essay. That, however, is another story. The creation and evolution of *Gawa Gyani* as a mythic enactment presented a dance drama that stirred deep levels of the psyche -- of participants and audiences alike. To research and document this collaborative dance drama calls for a research perspective somewhat different from that usually pursued by anthropologists -- it is to ensure that the voice of the "other" speaks for itself so that we may be more fully informed of the creative process at hand; also, to accept the situations when that voice chooses to remain silent.

In this essay sacred dance is analyzed as mythic enactment, a process that produces a cycle of meaning between symbolic form (choreography) and symbolic structures contained in the human unconscious and body. I argue that mythology provides the blueprint for the ritual performance of sacred dance to root itself in individual consciousness, as it prepares the ground for symbolic sequences to penetrate unconscious memory and take human awareness to new dimensions of insight and understanding. I also make a direct correlation between the precision of movement and sound in sacred dance and altered states of consciousness. Classical dance traditions in other societies are examined to portray the attention paid to ritual preparation, breath control, meditation and trance experience. I see the sequence of postures in a sacred dance choreography as a succession of symbols formed by the body through which breath is drawn to take the dancer into an altered state. Breath control, the precision and repetitiveness of dance steps, the symbols shaped by the body, and the chants and music that accompany sacred dance are the "drivers" that take audience and dancer alike into an experience of shared archetypal memory. My own phenomenology and physiological responses from performing Tai Chi as sacred dance was one data source. Other data sources were drawn from shamanic and classical Hindu cultures to develop a model that guided my collaboration with a modern dance group, as it moved from the secular to the sacred domain of expression. Finally, I raise problems of research methodology in terms of the postmodern concern with respecting the voice of the "other".

Bibliography

Artaud, A.
1958 The Theatre and Its Double. N.Y.: Grove Press

Campbell, J.
1988 The Power of Myth. N.Y.: Doubleday

Gaston, A-M.
1982 Siva in Dance, Myth and Iconography. Oxford: Oxford University Press

Gill, S.
1979 Focus. Parabola V. vi, 2:May 1979

Hanh, Thich Nhat
1993 The Blooming of a Lotus. Boston: Beacon Press

Heinze, R-I.
1994 Applications of Altered States of Consciousness in Daily Life. Anthropology of Consciousness V.5, 3:8-12

Hennecke-Schneemelcher
1964 New Testament Apocrypha. Philadelphia

Iyengar, B.K.S.
1966 Light on Yoga. N.Y.: Schocken Books

Katz, R.
1981 Education as Transformation: Becoming a Healer among the !Kung and the Fijians. Harvard Educational Review 51, 1:57-78

1982 Boiling Energy: Community Healing among the Kalahari !Kung. Cambridge: Harvard University Press

Pagels, E.
1979 To the Universe Belongs the Dancer. Parabola V. vi, 2:May 1979

Prattis, J.I.
1996 Living Breath. (Forthcoming)

Price-Williams, D. and
D.J. Hughes
1994 Shamanism and Altered States of Consciousness. Anthropology of Consciousness, V.5, 2:1-15

Progoff, I.
1970 Waking Dream and Living Myth. In J. Campbell (ed.): Myths, Dreams and Religion:176-195. Dallas: Spring Publications

Scott, M.
1991 Vancouver Sun, June 10, 1991

Turner, V.
1974 Dramas, Fields and Metaphors. Ithica: Cornell University Press

Chapter 9

Death Breaths and Drivers: The Phenomenology of Shamanic Experiences

Introduction

In 1991 Stanley Krippner of the Saybrook Institute in San Francisco reviewed various research strategies in the study of shamanism (Krippner 1991). Drawing on an extensive literature of reported shamanic events lead him to concede the anomalous nature of this phenomenon due to the lack of consensus amongst scientists about the validity of the data. The data for the most part was derived from interviews and second hand reports. To tidy up the methodology, Krippner proposed two lines of investigation; 1) informal first hand observations and 2) controlled observations and experiments. In his timely methodological rebuke to anthropologists and psychologists studying shamanism there are two important factors which are missing. First of all he overlooks the phenomenological capacity of the observer to experience the events associated with shamanism and this, to my mind, produces a disjunction in communication and coding irrespective of whatever line of investigation is favoured. Secondly, the phenomena are not anomalous, it is the conceptual vocabulary and terminology of the observer that is insufficient. Shamanic experiences are quite natural, only our culture has become so removed from them that even our scientific observers do not possess the appropriate concepts to understand them.

Many of the events associated with shamanism that are labelled as anomalous have to do with the shaman's ability to move into and through a series of related altered states of consciousness (A.S.C.). Without a corresponding ability to enter into an A.S.C., it becomes exceedingly difficult for the observer to understand or code what may be communicated to him or to her. A shaman may communicate to the observer about experience and events several times removed from the reality in which the observer is located. Thus the shaman communicates S and the observer codes and understands it as O, thereby misrepresenting the features, structure and process of whatever the shaman participates in and communicates about. To reduce this disjunction in communication and the associated distortion in coding of information requires of the observer the willingness and ability to suspend disbelief, and travel through the shamanic experience (or something similar) in order to code information from a different level of personal phenomenology.

This is what this work is about. The experiences described are my own. For the past decade I have conducted intensive experiential research with a number of shamans in North America - in Arizona, British Columbia and Ontario. One shaman is a female Ojibway medicine woman, another is a male Algonquin shaman and the final teacher is a medicine man with the Apache in the American Southwest, all of whom prefer that their identity remain confidential.[1] The work with these shamans was a highly privileged encounter as I was taught a great deal that was not made available to other aspiring pupils. My education in this area was consistent with my participation in the healing and meditative arts over the past twenty years. There is a more general model of healing that underlies my understanding of shamanic experience and I intend to make this explicit so that my conclusions may be anticipated. Thus my understanding and experience of shamanic practice will be part of a general model of healing that is applicable to non-shamanic contexts. Before I get to the phenomenology of Death Breaths, which is the title of this essay, I would like to put the building blocks in place. I will proceed to outline an alternative model of healing, then highlight the therapeutic role of an A.S.C. and show why I place such an emphasis on breath control, particularly in the context of near death experiences (N.D.E.). This is before I come on to the phenomenon of Death Breaths and the shamanic journey. Finally, I will derive a model from all this in the form of a healing ceremony. This progression is summarized in Figure 9.1.

Figure 9.1: "DEATH BREATHS AND DRIVERS"

1. MODEL OF HEALING
2. ALTERED STATE OF CONSCIOUSNESS
3. BREATH CONTROL
4. NEAR DEATH EXPERIENCE
5. DEATH BREATHS AND THE SHAMANIC JOURNEY
6. HEALING CEREMONY

Model of Healing

In keeping with many indigenous cosmologies and eastern philosophies, I assume a mind/body/soul unity as the potential state of being fully human. The impediments to experiencing this state are a series of internal blockages and disjunctions that draw their origin from social and cultural conditioning, genetic heritage and karma (Prattis 1996). This combination of factors creates disjunctions in the body and mind and prevents the mind/body/soul unity from taking shape. From the perspective I prefer, the disjunctions are regarded as the underlying cause of physical and psychological illness. When the disjunctions become too great, connection to the soul is lost and intervention is necessary to restore connection and balance and therefore health. Given this perspective, what is required in the healing process is attention to, and dialogue with, the disjunction, so that which blocks inner unity from taking shape is identified, understood, transformed and then transcended. This process is at the core of most healing and meditative systems, and the remedies involve a process of surfacing and clearing (Prattis 1996). This has been clearly identified in the Buddhist system of thought. The fears and anxieties that lie deep in our unconscious are known as *anusaya* -- latent tendencies (Hahn 1993:68). Thich Nhat Hahn, the Vietnamese Buddhist master, has remarked that

> Because we are not able to resolve the anusaya, we repress them, and they grow stagnant and cause sickness whose symptoms can be recognized in everything we do (Hahn 1993:69).

He goes on to say that

> Buddha taught that rather than repressing our fears and anxieties, we should invite them into consciousness, recognize them, welcome them ... quite naturally they will lose some of their energy. When once again they return to our subconscious, they will be that much weaker ... they will continue to grow weaker (1993:69).

This overview of dialogue and interaction with the inner disjunctions and latent tendencies will be incorporated in the model of healing that I will later derive. The basic idea is that when we dialogue with painful material that has been repressed, we reduce the potency of that material. In other words we rob it of the energy that can render us dysfunctional -- physically and mentally -- which is basically what illness is all about. Thus my understanding of the healing process is in energy terms. Let me elaborate on this. The traumas from our upbringing, in our genetic memories and from karma lodge themselves as energy in our bodies and minds, and create an internal formation described as *samyojana* in Sanskrit (Hahn 1993:77). Thich Nhat Hahn describes them as *fetters* or *knots* of suffering deep in our unconscious. Afflictive emotions such as fear, anger, insecurity, sadness, jealousy and attachment keep the knots of suffering in place, and this produces the disjunctions in mind/body/soul unity that cause illness. The knots of suffering "are forged by confusion and lack of understanding, by our misperceptions regarding our selves and our reality" (Hahn 1993:77). Thus it is obvious that perception and cognition have to change and the Buddhist methodology for this is mindfulness -- self-awareness and seeing reality (both internal and external) clearly. Mindfulness is often incorrectly interpreted as an intellectualist remedy and this interpretation overlooks the storage of trauma as energy in the body. It is absolutely necessary to bring more than just the mind to bear on the deeply hidden distress, violence, anger, fear and control that lie within. These energies have to be transformed or sublimated, not just intellectually, but by being discharged physically from the body in an atmosphere that is both safe and sacred, and preferably in a state of altered consciousness. The reasons for these preconditions will become apparent as this essay proceeds.

By and large, in the Western allopathic system of mainstream psychotherapy, it is the mind that is addressed -- neither sacredness nor safety for the body and soul are considered. Thus major components of the healing equation are ignored due to differing perspectives about energy, trauma, and how the mind integrates with the body and soul. While there are increasing numbers of medical practitioners in our society who may be open to the ideas expressed here, mainstream medical practice remains firmly opposed (Winkelman 1992). The model of healing I intend to develop is one that is designed to surface and clear the energies of trauma from the body/mind so that body, mind and soul can be integrated at a different level. The strategic arena for this to take place is that of an A.S.C. but I will develop these ideas later in this work.

The importance of surfacing and clearing, both physically and mentally, is so one can be free of the knots of suffering and experience a deeper level of personal integration. However, the emotion and pain of old wounds and deep hurts must first of all be identified, surfaced and then released. We all have scars and emotional wounds deep within us from upbringing, genetic heritage and karma, and this is repressed in the unconscious as the scars and wounds are too painful for our awareness to deal with. So when an event is presented to us that touches these old scars, that event acts as a trigger and starts to accumulate power and it is this power that generates and fuels those knots of suffering and latent tendencies associated with repressed painful memories. This force increases and comes charging up from the unconscious, so that by the time it gets to conscious awareness it has the power of a runaway express train -- nothing is going to stop it. And so it charges out of us. We react, go out of control, say, do and think things we often regret, for this runaway express train is necessarily directed outwards and projected onto others. This projection process continues until, as Coward points out (1990), an individual achieves sufficient self-awareness to turn her critical energies inward. As Coward puts it,

> This represents the overcoming of the Freudian defence mechanism of projection by which we seek to deal with our own weakness by projecting them on to another and then ruthlessly criticizing the other (Coward 1990:62).

I think about anger and fear as convulsive, reactive emotions triggered by the repression of deep hurts and wounded feelings into the unconscious. One must, as Jung points out, make the unconscious conscious by becoming aware of what lies underneath anger, fear and other forms of distress. Thus one must identify the deeper hurts, feel them, understand them and then release them. The process of identifying, feeling, understanding and releasing requires an acute candour and honesty with oneself. The part played by conscious awareness and mindfulness in this process is of paramount importance because once one acknowledges and experiences the hidden emotional wounds then they can be surfaced and released from one's body and mind. When that is done, anger, fear and their derivatives -- violence and control -- have less raw material of hurtful emotion to latch on to. The energy of trauma gets weaker and the knots of suffering unravel. The roots of trauma can persist only in ignorance and with the assistance of afflictive emotions. Once they are brought to awareness and due attention is directed to the afflictive emotion they then wither away and become inoperative. Denial of the deep emotional wounds, however, is highly dangerous as denial provides the opportunity for anger and fear to strike from within in the form of out of control reaction.

So if one finds that one is angry or fearful, the first step is to identify the deeper emotional pain and distress that anger or fear is reacting to. The pain of abandonment and of feeling unloved are common emotional wounds that we all experience in some dimension of our lives, yet we cover them up with angry and fearful reactions. To go beyond the anger and fear one must first of all surface the emotional distress then clear it from the body and mind. This means giving up on the denial of feelings and having the courage to recognize the presence of emotional wounds within one. This is not easy to do as there is a tendency to bury our wounded feelings under a mask, and so we hide from the blackness that lies underneath our public face. Yet the deeper the blackness is buried the more likely it will manifest itself in chronic illness or explode into compulsive acts of self-destruction and violence. Thus it is imperative that we become consciously aware of all that constitutes the hidden blackness and this often requires the support and guidance of a good therapist, shaman or spiritual teacher. The recognition of that which is repressed as being part of ourselves is the first and most crucial step in surfacing and clearing. It is a step in learning to be what we are without pretence or artifice and requires that we dig out all the hidden compulsions and repressions by becoming aware of them. It is a most crucial understanding to clearly see ourselves and our internal patterns and to be mindful of them. The most effective arena for this process of surfacing and clearing to take place is that particular A.S.C. associated with meditative and shamanic practices.

Figure 9.2: MODEL OF HEALING

ASSUMPTIONS:

1. MIND : BODY : SOUL UNITY
2. BLOCKAGES FROM CONDITIONING, GENETICS AND KARMA CAUSE PHYSICAL AND MENTAL ILLNESS
3. *ANUSAYA* : LATENT TENDENCIES
} ENERGY IN THE BODY
SAMYOJANA : KNOTS OF SUFFERING
4. SURFACING AND CLEARING
5. A.S.C. AS ARENA FOR HEALING

Altered State of Consciousness (A.S.C.)

The classic description of an A.S.C. in modern literature was provided by Ludwig in 1966, in which he identified a number of characteristic factors. These include: alterations in thinking, disturbed time sense, loss of control, change in emotional expression, body image change, perceptual distractions, change in meaning, sense of the ineffable, feelings of rejuvenation and hypersuggestibility (Ludwig 1963:13-17; Price-Williams and Hughes 1994:2). Charles Tart gives a more encompassing definition of an A.S.C. as a state in which the individual:

> ...clearly feels a qualitative shift in his patterns of mental functioning, that is, she feels not just a quantitative shift (more or less alert, more or less visual imagery, sharper or duller, etc.) but also that some quality or qualities of his mental processes are different. Mental functions operate that do not operate at all ordinarily, perceptual qualities appear that have no normal counterparts, and so forth (1969:2).

These definitions indicate that we are clearly dealing with a dramatic cognitive and perceptual shift of which the individual is fully aware. Furthermore, Bourguignon (1973) and others maintain that the capacity to experience an A.S.C. is part of the psychobiological heritage of our species. In other words, it is a universal feature or process innate to *homo sapiens* that is expressed in culturally variable ways. There is a major implication here. Mainstream medical science refuses to recognize that this is so (Winkelman 1992:121,123), which raises some very interesting questions about the western allopathic medical system and its assumptions about healing, particularly as scholars such as Weil (1972) and Siegel (1989) claim from their research that there is a species-wide innate drive to experience A.S.C. (Price-Williams and Hughes 1996:2). One implication may be that mainstream western medical science is flying in the face of what we are biologically programmed to experience.

Eliade's ground breaking work on shamanism (1964) referred to A.S.C. as archaic techniques of ecstasy. Scholars from Peters and Price-Williams (1980) to Winkelman (1992), Harner (1990) and Wolf (1993) have all identified the A.S.C. as the most important element of the shaman's healing repertoire. One of Wolf's hypotheses

(1993:287) is that shamans perceive reality in a state of altered consciousness which they do in fact control. Peters and Price-Williams (1980:398-399) refer to the ability of the shaman to induce and exit from an A.S.C. at will. While in an A.S.C. the shaman sees self and clients in a mythic light -- a different and broader conception of reality -- and it is in this context that healing takes place. The aspect of control, however, is that the shaman also remains in the ordinary reality of waking consciousness so that an effective process of monitoring is also at work while the shamanic journey - for shaman and clients - takes place. Grof has referred to this as "dual consciousness" (Grof 1993). The imagery of the shamanic journey has similar psychotherapeutic effects as Jung's notion of "active imagination" (1960) and other similar techniques (Singer 1974), in that the imagery creates a situation whereby a dialogue is initiated by the client with archetypal material from his or her own unconscious.

The visual imagery experienced by the shaman and invoked for the client is usually interpreted by many Western observers (including myself) as metaphorical of internal symbolic processes. My view of the internal dialogue with different figures that appear in the shamanic journey is that this is a communication with archetypal material that facilitates individuation. The shaman, on the other hand, tends to see them as objective events (Peters and Price-Williams 1980:405), not unlike the methodology proposed by Jung for active imagination (1960:185). It should be remembered that Jung frequently referred to the collective unconscious as the "objective" psyche. In other words, the appropriate attitude towards the inner images, events and dialogues is to treat them as von Franz (1976) argues "as-if-they-were-real" (Peters and Price-Williams 1980:406). The shamanic journey is about mediating between different levels of consciousness and integrating them. Winkelman points out that in an A.S.C. the brain/mind interface is also affected:

> permitting conscious (mental) control and regulation of what are typically unconscious organic bodily processes. A.S.C. involve conscious -- unconscious integration through activation of unconscious material which permits abreaction and the resolution of conflicts. Traditional healing practices suggest that recovering and giving expression to repressed aspects of the self and conflicts is achieved through ritual A.S.C. activities (Winkelman 1992:188).

So how does one get into or induce an A.S.C.? There are a diverse set of procedures used by shamans to induce an A.S.C. These can be referred to as drivers and range from rhythmic drumming and the use of sound in chants, sacred songs, and percussion instruments (Olsen 1975), the repetitive motor activity of dancing (see Chapter 8 this volume); the use of symbolic imagery (Noll 1985); fasting, meditation (Gellhorn and Kiely 1972), physical austerities and sensory deprivation (Mandell 1980) to the use of hallucinogens and other psychoactive drugs (Siegel 1989). Drivers are used in combinations and the intent is to alter the relationship between the conscious and the unconscious parts of the human mind (Winkelman 1992:119). Winkelman claims that cross-cultural research on the psychophysiological effects of the various drivers supports the contention that a common set of psychophysiological changes in brain functioning occur (Winkelman 1992:95). In other words, each driver reinforces the effect of other drivers and they all zero in on that part of the brain which pushes the mind into an experience of an A.S.C.

Figure 9.3: ALTERED STATE OF CONSCIOUSNESS (A.S.C.)

1. QUALITATIVE AND QUANTITATIVE SHIFT IN MENTAL PROCESSES
2. PART OF OUR PSYCHOBIOLOGICAL HERITAGE
3. DIALOGUE WITH ARCHETYPAL MATERIAL IN THE SHAMANIC JOURNEY
4. "DRIVERS" INTO AN A.S.C. : SOUND, DANCE, SYMBOLIC IMAGERY, MEDITATION, DRUGS

Breath Control

The driver I wish to address in this work is that of breath, in particular that of Death Breaths as this is the most significant phenomenon I experienced in my research with shamans. As the derived model will demonstrate, it is used in conjunction with other drivers -- meditation, drumming, music, chants, symbolic imagery --

but my experience shows that it is a primary vehicle for inducing an A.S.C. This contention is supported by the perspective taken by Stanislav Grof (1988, 1993) on the significance of breathwork. His earlier work on A.S.C. relied on the use of drugs - in particular LSD - to induce a different state of consciousness. He later discovered that intensive breathwork was just as significant, but was safer in terms of no side effects and maintenance of a sense of control over the process. He then developed a healing system he called Holotropic Breathwork, an unstructured, free flowing process of breathing that stimulates the spontaneous physical release of pent up traumas and emotions (Grof 1993).

The Buddha addressed the significance of breath in the *Anapanasati sutra* on the Mindfulness of Breathing whereby he precisely described sixteen different methods of using one's breath to achieve mindfulness. The yogic traditions considered breath to be the great connector between body, mind and soul and the ultimate force of redirection and transformation. Thich Nhat Hahn talks about breath as the bridge that connects life to consciousness. It "unites your body to your thoughts. Whenever your mind becomes scattered, use your breath as the means to take hold of your mind again" (1987:15). In a later book he says "to practice conscious breathing is to open the door to enter the domain of concentration and insight" (1993:6).

This factor of concentration and insight has been perfected in the yogic traditions through a system of breath control known as *pranayama*, which is designed to connect the meditator experientially with Cosmic Breath -- which eastern cosmology regards as the prime mover of the Universe. In meditation, one's body is regarded as the Universe and its vital energy - *prana* - is brought to one's experience and awareness through *pranayama*. This is Conscious Breathing in practice, a revitalizing and purifying force that is consciously used for spiritual growth and evolution. Particular patterns of nostril breathing, of breathing through a constricted throat, following appropriate patterns of Inbreath : Holding Fullness : Outbreath : Holding Emptiness -- activate the entire respiratory system and induce a state of calm in the body and mind thus enabling one to enter more deeply into meditation. In the yogic traditions, mastery of the science of breath is the process that enables one to still the mind and turn inward. Without such mastery one is subject to the bondage of the mind's attachments and projections. The human mind is only one portion of the equation that unites cosmic intelligence, human consciousness and the universe's potential. In yogic traditions, the integration of the mind with the soul through breath permits one to seize the arrow that allows human spiritual evolution to take place. The arrow is the mind/soul integration and meditation is the powerful bow that drives the arrow outside of time and space. It works as a "driver" to propel individuals from an everyday state of consciousness into a different state of spiritual awareness (Heinze 1994:10). I now want to examine the relationship between breath control, A.S.C. and near death experiences, but first let me turn to a recent publication.

Figure 9.4: BREATH CONTROL

1. GROF AND THE BUDDHA'S *ANAPANASATI SUTRA*

2. EVERYDAY LIFE ↓ → BREATH CONTROL → DIFFERENT CONSCIOUSNESS ↑

BREATH CONTROL ↑ YOGIC PRANAYAMA SYSTEM ↑ BREATH AS "DRIVER" INTO AN A.S.C.

Near Death Experience (N.D.E.)

In December 1994 Newberg and d'Aquili published a very interesting article on "*The Near Death Experience as Archetype: A Model for "Prepared" Neurocognitive Processes.*" They drew on Jung's archetypal hypotheses and argued that the neural activation of certain archetypes may be involved in the N.D.E. (1994:2). They note that the issue of the neuropsychological mechanisms underlying archetypal activation is a contentious one (1994:7) which gives me some room to speculate. The authors state that most N.D. experiencers report that they feel their cognitive functions are very clear and sharp (Moody 1975; Ring 1980), that they possess a hyperalertness:

> in which they have heightened visual and auditory sensation in addition to mental clarity. Time and space, however, are not perceived in the normal way. There seems to be a slowing or absence of time, and space is usually perceived as being either infinite or non-existent (1994:2).

This correlates with the previously discussed properties of an A.S.C. and also with the qualities associated with mystical visions in different meditation traditions. Ring has discussed the close relationship between mystical experience and the N.D.E. as representing an awakening to a higher spiritual reality (Ring 1984; Newberg and d'Aquili 1994:4). From the reports of N.D. experiencers it is clear that a major cognitive and perceptual shift takes place during the N.D.E. and afterwards. Newberg and d'Aquili point out that the experiencers report:

> not only a persistent sense of the ultimate reality of the N.D.E. even after they return to this world, but they experience a transformed life in this world as a direct result of experiencing that reality in terms of decreased materialism, increased altruism, greater care for others and a lack of fear of death (1994:12).

Here they draw on the extensive research of Kubler-Ross (1969), Ring (1980), Noyes (1980) and Bauer (1985).

The N.D.E. is triggered by two circumstances: firstly, the actual and imminent prospect of physiological death, and secondly the *perception* of being in a life threatening situation. This distinction is important in terms of how the authors correlate it with different archetypes and how I then use the notion of perception, archetype and death breaths. But that is jumping ahead a little; let us stay with Newberg and d'Aquili. The authors assert that N.D.E.s activate both the archetype of Dissolution and the archetype of Transcendent Integration. Dissolution refers to the kind of hell states reported in *The Tibetan Book of the Dead* (Freemantle and Trungpa 1987) as the Chonyid state of grisly dismemberment, torture and other imagery of that nature. This visual imagery is a symbolic representation of both the physical body's disintegration and the final deterioration of the sense systems, and has to do with an individual's personal physiological death. Transcendent Integration is the archetype of transformation -- of ego and self into a universal structure of integration and wholeness.

This experience is actively cultivated by most meditation traditions and it is obvious there are certain shared characteristics between meditative experiences and N.D.E. in that they both cause major cognitive shifts into a similar kind of A.S.C.

The authors point out that while the first archetype has a physiological basis, the second one is *perceptual*, and can be triggered without any immediate physiological distress. The authors point to the numerous documented N.D.E.s where there was only a conscious perception about almost certain death without real physical danger. It is the perceptual pole of the N.D.E. that I will now be focusing on. I will be arguing that the *perception* of imminent death provokes an enormous release of material stored in the collective unconscious. It could be argued that our main focus in ordinary waking consciousness is on survival of the body and a vast amount of our energy and attention is directed to body survival. My contention is that the N.D.E. moves the focus of energy away from the body's survival, and redirects it to the collective unconscious, a realm of consciousness that very little attention is paid to in the ordinary waking state. This, in fact, is what Death Breaths do!

Figure 9.5: NEAR DEATH EXPERIENCE (N.D.E.)
NEWBERG AND D'AQUILI (1994)

1. NEURAL ACTIVATION OF ARCHETYPES

2. TRIGGERS INTO A N.D.E:

(a) PHYSIOLOGICAL DEATH IMMINENT	(b) "PERCEPTION" OF LIFE THREATENING SITUATION
↓	↓
ARCHETYPE OF DISSOLUTION	ARCHETYPE OF TRANSCENDANT INTEGRATION

"DEATH BREATHS"

1. CONVINCE MIND THIS IS THE LAST BREATH, ENERGY SHIFTS FROM BODY SURVIVAL TO A.S.C.

2. DRAMATIC PHYSIOLOGICAL AND COGNITIVE EFFECTS

Death Breaths and the Shamanic Journey

The first act of a new born baby is that of inhalation. The last act of a person who is dying is that of exhalation. The focus of death breaths as a process is on extending the component of exhalation in order that the mind becomes convinced that this is the last breath to be experienced. This also creates a different internal "space", and it is at this juncture that energy shifts away from body survival as the mind's primary focus and is diverted to the realm of the collective unconscious. This brings about dramatic somatic and cognitive effects. Death breaths are part of a cycle of breathing that I was taught by my shaman teachers. Also, in the yogic traditions, this form of breathing is termed "*Asparsa* Yoga" and is known colloquially as "dead man's yoga" for reasons that will become very apparent. The breathing cycle begins with deep breathing -- Inbreath : Holding Fullness : Outbreath : Holding Emptiness. There is a slow count for the Holding Fullness and Holding Emptiness portions of the deep breathing. This is the same basic pattern that is used in yogic breathing. The count increases until the individual holds the fullness and the emptiness for slow counts of twelve. This build up can take approximately twenty to thirty minutes. It is then followed by several minutes of short explosive breaths -- similar to the *kapalabhati* breaths of the yogic *pranayama* system, after which the death breaths begin. These are long inbreaths and retention of breath for a slow count of twelve, followed by the outbreath and holding the emptiness for a slow count of thirty. This continues to expand so that one builds up to holding the emptiness of breath, after the exhalation, for as long as is possible. What does this do? Obviously there are variations depending on an individual's preparation, openness and willingness to enter an A.S.C.

My experience of this cycle -- cognitively and physiologically -- did vary in the many shamanic journeys I have undertaken[2], but there were common patterns of experience. First of all, the deep breathing took me into a state of mental calm. Secondly the short explosive breaths produced a sort of portal or gate that I could feel myself going through. I also felt light headed and dizzy. The death breaths, however, really did the trick. On the inbreath and retention I would feel stable, on a particular plateau of experience. On the outbreath and holding emptiness for as long as I could, my limbs and body would shake and tremble. There would also be periods of profuse sweating and extreme cold particularly in my hands and feet. Then on the last gasp of holding emptiness I would take an inbreath. The trembling and shaking would stop, and while holding the fullness of inbreath for a count of twelve I would experience a deep clarity. Cognitively, I felt hyperalert and hyperlucid. The next outbreath and the holding of emptiness for as long as I could would again produce trembling and shaking throughout the body, extreme sensations of heat and cold but from a different level of experience. Once more on the last gasp of holding emptiness after the outbreath, the inbreath produced a feeling of cognitive calm but at a different level. In doing the death breaths over a period of time I felt as though I was taking a series of steps to different plateaus of cognition. In the process, however, I always felt a sense of control, totally cognisant of what was taking place at different levels of awareness; "dual consciousness" once more (Grof 1993). The other drivers I would experience with my shaman teachers during the breathing cycle were music of a repetitive, rhythmic nature, drumming, rattles, and nature-based music that incorporated the sound of animal calls.

Each cycle of deep breathing, explosive breaths and death breaths would have a period of respite -- of normal breathing for several minutes -- then the entire breathing cycle would be repeated and I would experience similar cognitive and physiological shifts, once more climbing further stairs of cognition. I was quite aware of being in an A.S.C. yet simultaneously aware of myself in conscious waking reality. What was happening with the death breaths was that a different "space" was being created as my mind was being convinced that this was the last breath my body would experience. In actual fact it was not, but the trick is to move the mind into the *perception* that this is so, in order that the energy devoted to the survival of the body can be switched into triggering connection to archetypal material that can then be experienced and dialogued with. Then one is considered to be ready for the shamanic journey. This can be guided or non-guided. The former involves the symbolic imagery of a guided meditation while you are in an A.S.C. and provides a loose structure so the individual can dialogue with archetypal material about his unique personal scars, traumas and also about her creative potential. The dialogue experienced in the journey can continue afterwards through journalling, communicating the experience and exchanging views with the shaman facilitator. At the end of the shamanic journey there is a return and you come back to where you are sitting or lying down. I will provide an example of this process but first of all I want to refer to some personal experiences.

Over a period of five months in the spring and summer of 1994 I experienced very intensive shamanic journeys that I had prepared for through fasting, meditation and sexual abstinence. The cycles of death breaths were over an hour each time. On five separate journeys I met in turn, and dialogued with, the ancient shaman from the South, the ancient shaman from the East, the ancient shaman from the North, the ancient shaman from the West and the ancient shaman of the Centre. I knew this was an experience and dialogue with five facets of the same archetypal material from the collective unconscious. At the same time it is important to note that in the experience of each of these journeys I was always met, and then lead to the ancient shaman, by a female figure. In previous work on the Parsifal myth (1991, Chapter 2, this volume) I had stated very clearly that primary access to the collective unconscious for males in our civilization was through the female archetype -- the anima. The existential significance of this assertion was right before me in the experience of being met by a female figure in each of these five specific shamanic journeys. Yet I did not make this very obvious connection until much later, when I reviewed my field notes more than a year after these particular journeys took place. It was with an almost visible shock that I noticed I had missed something so significant and so obvious. There it was -- the anima staring me in the face from my field logs from March through to July of 1994. There were other fascinating consequences that I was also not immediately aware of.

At my home in the middle of Gatineau Park in Quebec, I had a small circle of large stones in my front yard with a beautiful fern growing at the centre. I had an overwhelming compulsion that summer to build a medicine wheel with this circle of stones as the centrepiece. I had been taught by an Apache shaman from Arizona the appropriate state and procedure of respect necessary to construct a medicine wheel. So I enlisted the assistance of two friends who shared my respect and we carried out the appropriate ritual, reverence and construction. As we proceeded on a very hot and humid summer's day, a silence settled on all three of us in a very tangible way. Something was happening inside and around us while we were creating this architecture of incredible grace, power and beauty. I had collected the stones for the medicine wheel from my garden and the surrounding forest. They were some of the most ancient rocks on the planet -- the hard granite of the Canadian Shield and they were part of the very ground where the medicine wheel was being built. After wheeling in fresh earth from the rest of my garden to fill in the four quadrants of the medicine wheel, we contemplated what had been created. I realized with a start that it was completely related to my shamanic journeys over the previous two months. The cardinal points of the wheel are the four directions, North, South, West, East, all leading from an outer circle to an inner circle at the centre. So what had taken place was a symbolic recreation of my archetypal experience of the five ancient shamans. The medicine wheel was a symbolic map of my internal dialogue. It just took me a while to realize that I was re-inventing the wheel for myself from my own experience. This led to the insight that medicine wheels, mandalas, sweat lodges etc., are symbolic formations of the collective unconscious that take an individual from her present existential location into a dialogue with an archetypal map that is common to all human beings. Although this may be well travelled ground it was important to verify the insight from my personal experience.

This brings me finally to the derivation of a model or ceremony of healing that draws in part from my experiences with shamanism. Here I combine my expertise and training in the healing and meditative arts over the past twenty years with more recent research on shamanism over the past decade.

Healing Ceremony

Figure 9.6: HEALING CEREMONY

SEQUENCE		DRIVERS
1. BREATH FOCUS		1. MUSIC : SOUND
2. EXTERNAL SYMBOL OF PURIFICATION	↔	(a) SACRED FLUTE
3. INTERNAL SYMBOL OF PURIFICATION	↔	(b) ETERNAL OM, GREGORIAN CHANT
4. BREATHING CYCLE (4 times) - DEEP BREATHS - EXPLOSIVE BREATHS - DEATH BREATHS - PAUSE	↔	(c) TONAL (d) CHARIOTS OF FIRE (e) DRUMMING (f) MANTRA
5. JOURNEY		2. SYMBOLIC IMAGERY
	↔	(g) NATURE BASED MUSIC
6. MEDITATION ON LIGHT		

The healing ceremony is based on the principles of safety, sacredness and responsibility, and draws in particular on two traditions -- shamanism and yogic meditation practices -- and my experience of both. The traditions are not as far apart as one may suspect, as Eliade (1958), Mironov and Shirokogoroff (1924) point to a continuity between pre-Vedic shamanism, Vedic practices and later yoga. Furthermore, shamanic practices used in the Tibetan Bon religion were incorporated into Tibetan Buddhist practices over 1300 years ago, indicating a cross fertilization between the two traditions. This is endorsed in a recent publication by Geoffrey Samuel (1996). His fascinating book, *Civilized Shamans: Buddhism in Tibetan Societies*, examines both the monastic and the shamanic traditions in Tibetan Buddhism. He shows how the need for shamanic services by the majority of the population dovetails very neatly with the journey to enlightenment pursued by a minority of the people -- the lamas, monks and yogis. The shamanic use of altered states for healing and divinatory purposes were incorporated into tantric Buddhism, and Samuel illustrates how the lamas in Tibetan Buddhism have subtly reconciled shamanic and monastic traditions in their teachings and scholarship.

The ceremony begins with a stated verbal emphasis and focus on the attention to breath, so that everybody's awareness becomes attached to inbreath and to outbreath. The circle motif is maintained and emphasized during the opening symbol of external purification. Individuals gather in a circle, and burning sage is passed from person to person in a clockwise direction; one person holds the sage while the next one in the circle takes the smoke with their hands over their heads and bodies. This manner of conducting the "smudging" is intended to reduce perceptions of hierarchy. During this opening process -- the external symbol of purification - a musical driver is in operation. Sacred Native American flute music is played quietly as people gather for the ceremony, form a circle and participate in the opening purification. It is emphasized that persons are responsible for themselves, that they validate their experiences from their own internal recognitions and that this can be discussed and verified at the end of the ceremony through guidance from the ceremony's shaman facilitator. Once again this caveat removes dependency on any hierarchy and reveals the influence of Krishnamurti on my thinking (Krishnamurti 1984) about the absolute necessity of knowing for oneself the significance of one's experiences, rather than relying on what someone states should be experienced. Unless it is one's own experience there is no real self-knowledge.

The next step is a symbol of internal purification; a simple Buddhist heart centre meditation. During this meditation the sound driver changes from the opening sacred flute music to religious chants. The sound of the eternal Om being chanted or Gregorian chants facilitate the deepening of the internal symbol of purification -- the Buddhist heart centre meditation. This meditation is straightforward. As you fill your lungs on the inbreath, visualize white light coming in to the middle of your chest -- your heart centre. You can visualize this as light floating gently down to the area behind the sternum, or as a funnel of light coming directly into your chest from the Universe. Whatever works. If you do not visualize easily, then *think* the light coming into your heart centre. Feel this white light as a gentle glow and take it through the heart centre, inside the chest and throat, up to your crown. All this is on the inbreath. At the end of the inbreath, at the top of the crown, hold the breath for a moment and place a thought into the procedure. The thought is "Send this light to every cell in my body". Then on the outbreath imagine the white light moving from your crown, filling your entire body right down to the toes. Complete the breathing cycle by grounding the energy through your feet into the floor. Do this quite a few times until you feel something different in your body, a different sensation or a greater feeling of relaxation.

Then add a wonderful meditation that Thich Nhat Hanh describes in his book, *The Blooming of a Lotus* (1993:15). Accompanying the inbreath and outbreath say mentally within:

1. Breathing in, I calm my body.	Calm
Breathing out, I smile.	Smile

After a while proceed to:

2. Breathing in, I dwell in the present moment	Present Moment
Breathing out, I know it is a wonderful moment	Wonderful Moment

Do this for a while then abandon the words and remain within the silence and energy of the meditation for approximately twenty-minutes. If thoughts distract you from the process, as they surely will, simply come back to the focus and direction of breath, light and word in the meditation, and register with the information the body provides as feedback. This meditation is a centering vehicle; it grounds the person in her body and is an important step in ensuring safety for the participant.

The next stage introduces two drivers used in combination. The first breathing cycle of -- deep breaths / explosive breaths / death breaths / pause -- begins, and is accompanied by a different sound to that of the chants used in the prior meditation. Particular qualities of tone, rhythm and repetition correlate very closely with the experience of altered states (Olsen 1975) and changes in tone and rhythm intensify the driving effect of music, particularly during the breathing cycle. As Winkelman has pointed out (1992:95) the various combinations of drivers in sequence are designed to induce the experience of an A.S.C. The initial breathing cycle of -- deep breaths / explosive breaths / death breaths / pause -- is to the accompaniment of a tonal musical driver; for example, New Age synthesizer music that is repetitive, relaxing and harmonic. After the first breathing cycle is finished, everybody relaxes their breathing during the pause and prepares for the second breathing cycle. This cycle is accompanied by music that has a more insistent, repetitive, driving beat along the lines of the electronic synthesizer music from, for instance, *Chariots of Fire*. Once the second cycle of -- deep breathing / explosive breaths / death breaths / pause -- is complete, the third cycle begins but the sound driver changes to a ten minute period of drumming. Once this is complete the fourth, and final breathing cycle is entered and the sound driver moves into the repetitive sound of the Gayatri mantra. This is the most powerful mantra of purification and transformation known to the yogic traditions and I would like to elaborate a little on the effects of the Gayatri mantra, as sound, on human consciousness as this discussion will demonstrate the incremental steps taken into an A.S.C. during each stage of the healing ceremony.

The Gayatri mantra comes from the Vedas - the ancient religious tradition of India. The successive sounds of the Sanskrit syllables and words are designed to move the individual into different states of spiritual consciousness (Saraydarian 1989), first of all by calming the mind and body, then through activating the energy centres of the body which brings about a deeper connection with internal essence. It is an invocation for enlightenment that can have the effect of drawing other individuals into the same state. The repetition of the Gayatri mantra creates a unique vibration that integrates a person's mental awareness with deeper levels of the unified energy system that is believed to be at the core of being. Progressively, the mantra takes the individual into the experience of stages of expansion of consciousness, thus propelling the invoker into different cognitive/perceptual states. The tonal design of the sounds produces purification and integration so that the individual at the physical, emotional and mental level becomes more open and receptive to inner guidance. From this foundation other levels of enlightenment and openness are believed to ensue.

Figure 9.7: THE GAYATRI MANTRA

OM	*OM*
BHUR BHUVA SVAH	*ALL ON EARTH, MID-WORLD AND HEAVEN*
TAT SAVITUR VARENYAM	*MEDITATE UPON THE LIGHT ADORABLE*
BHARGO DEVASYA DHIMAHI	*OF THE DIVINE SUN OF LIFE*
DHIYO YONAH PRACHODAYAT	*TO ENLIGHTEN OUR SOULS*

The Gayatri mantra has been described as the most universal, non-personal invocation of integration and transformation which anybody can use irrespective of culture, language or religion (Bharati 1995). Although it is drawn from the Vedic traditions of India, in this healing ceremony the cultural associations drop away as being irrelevant. Recall the arguments made earlier about drivers and altered states (Winkelman 1992), the N.D.E., perceptual states and archetypal stimulation (Newberg and d'Aquili 1994). As drivers and breath cycles combine to take an individual into an A.S.C. and prepare them for a dialogue with archetypal material, the culturally specific significance attached to any form of driver is stripped away because they are zeroing in on *species* specific material, viz. archetypes; rather than on the *culturally* specific material unique to the particular form of the driver.

The four breathing cycles are associated with four distinct sound drivers. Once the fourth breathing cycle is complete, normal breathing ensues and the sound of the Gayatri mantra continues, allowing the sound and experience of the mantra to penetrate more deeply into the mind and body. The individual by now should be in an altered state, extremely relaxed, and it is at this point that the shamanic journey begins, introducing extended symbolic imagery and a different sound driver. The journey proceeds to the accompaniment of nature-based music that incorporates animal and bird calls and other sounds drawn from the world of nature. This is played softly. I use Dan Gibson's "Algonquin Suite" as an appropriate tonal musical driver for the journey. There are many variations to a shamanic journey -- into the past, into the future, under the sea, into the earth, beyond time and space, and they can be guided or non-guided. I will document only one form of guided symbolic imagery, and ask the reader to suspend disbelief sufficiently to accompany me on this journey.

Journey:

See yourself walking through a beautiful meadow, full of flowers. You hear the sounds of insects humming and birds singing. The sun feels warm on your face and a slight breeze ruffles your hair. As you walk, look up into an endlessly clear blue sky and for a moment allow yourself to merge with it, and enter such clarity. (Pause) Then notice a small shape hovering in the sky that gets bigger as it comes closer to you, and see a golden eagle slowly circling above you. He is your guardian and will watch over you and keep you safe on your journey. As you walk, the meadow slowly gives way to a stream, that runs over hills and rocks before eddying into deep, still pools. Follow the bank of the river in the direction of the sun. There is a path to walk along. Notice the mallard ducks at the water's edge, with their ducklings, and a kingfisher sitting patiently on a branch overhanging a deep, still pool. The sun filters through the trees at the stream's edge and the light dances on the rocks and water like a crystal cloak that shimmers and moves with every swirl of the water. Walking round a bend you see that the stream empties into a clear lake fringed with forests, reflecting snow capped mountains in its still surface. Find a spot by the side of the lake, sit down and enjoy the intimacy of nature that is around you. At the end of the lake you see a cow moose with her calf at the water's edge. In the distance you hear wolves calling to one another, then you notice two rabbits beside a shrub close by. A doe and two fawns walk slowly and tentatively from the forest into the sunlight. Skylarks hover motionless in the sky, then descend to earth with their lilting song. Your eyes are drawn to a stately grey heron standing motionless in the reeds at the lake's edge. These creatures and more are there to remind you of your connection to the world of nature. Take a moment to be with the grass, the trees, animals, birds, insects, and bring to this place your favourite animals. (Pause)

Then ask one of the creatures to accompany you on your journey and wait to see which one comes forward. It does not matter if none come forward, the golden eagle still circles overhead as your guardian.

Then after sitting by the lake's edge for a while, stand up and slowly walk into the water. It is icy cold, fed by glaciers from the snow capped mountains. But it is a cold that is easily bearable because it purifies, stripping you of your anxieties, stress and worries. Slowly walk into the water up to your hips, your chest and then submerge yourself in the icy cold embrace of purification. Underwater you can breathe and move around with ease. Notice the rays of sunlight coming into the water, fish swimming swiftly past and see the rocks and submerged tree trunks on the lake floor. As you move around and adjust to the water you see a cave at the bottom of the lake and you swim strongly and powerfully to it and enter the cave. There is light at the end of a long underwater passage and you swim through and emerge out of the water into a cavern covered in crystals. The sound from the crystals shimmers through your body. At the edge of the cavern is a waterfall. Stand underneath it and feel the water washing over and right through your body. Feel the energy of the waterfall taking away any anxiety, tension and distress you may feel inside. (Pause)

Then leave the cavern and follow a trail that takes you through a pine forest. Beautiful tall pines are on either side of you, stretching up into the sky. Take a moment and see the entire sky endlessly clear and enter such clarity. (Pause) Then see how the forest opens up into a large clearing with a big flat rock in the centre. There is a fire prepared for you by the rock. As you warm your hands by the fire and feel its warmth on your face, you feel a presence next to you. Turning around you see a beautiful old woman with clear brown eyes that look right into you. She smiles in welcome and you feel she knows all about you and embraces you in a simple, heartfelt love. She is a very powerful healer and a wise shaman and is there on your journey to serve you. (Pause) Standing next to her is a handsome old man, with weatherbeaten features and a gentle smile that lights you up. From his eyes you feel an overwhelming compassion and understanding. He is a very powerful healer and a wise shaman and is there on your journey to serve you. (Pause) Standing between the old man and old woman is a young woman who sparkles. She is fresh, vibrant and beautiful and she is aglow with life's vitality. She also greets you with a smile and a love and understanding that you know is unconditional. She is a very powerful healer and a wise shaman and is there on your journey to serve you. (Pause)

Know that these three shamans come from the deepest part of yourself and they represent your own powers of creativity and self healing. The three shamans approach you and invite you to speak to them. Choose whoever you wish to communicate with and talk to them about whatever distresses you; the anxieties of the day, the stresses at work and at home, then if you wish, go deeper into your distress. Talk to them about growing up, the neglect and abuse you may have experienced, the isolation, separation and lack of understanding you encountered as a young person, adolescent and adult. Talk about the damage caused to you and the damage you may have caused others. Talk about the hatreds, angers and insensitivities you experience and perpetuate. You can say anything to these three shamans. They understand and love you and are there to heal you. Talk about whatever you feel free to communicate and feel the distress and trauma leaving your body. And when you run out of things to say, just be with that loving and supportive presence. (Pause)

Then ask each one of them if they would transfer their power of creativity, understanding and healing to you. And of course they agree. Look into the eyes of each one of them in turn and feel the transfer of their healing power with a jolt or energy circulation within your body. Thank them for this gift, then ask if you could speak to someone from the other side. Someone who has passed on that you did not have the opportunity to say what you wanted to say, or hear what you would have liked to have heard. Wait and see if anyone comes and do not be disappointed if nothing happens. It is not the time (Pause)

Take your leave of the shamans, thank them for their support, love and power of healing. Turning round you see a beautiful child surrounded with a golden aura. This golden child is you -- without trauma, hurts or damage -- and the child comes directly to you and takes your hand and leads you to a cliff edge where the beautiful golden eagle is waiting for you. He has been there as a guardian throughout your journey and is now ready to take you home. Ask your golden child if he or she wants to come with you, then climb onto the back of the eagle and feel him take off from the ledge and soar high on the updrafts. Below you, see the mountains, lakes and forests of your journey. Smoke curls lazily skyward from the fire by the rock and as you fly with the eagle feel how beautiful this earth is. Then when you feel ready to do so, part company from the eagle and fly on your own. With your arms spread wide as wings, catch the air currents and soar, then swoop low over the streams and mountains and enjoy the strength of flying on your own. (Pause) Then after awhile slowly fly back to the edge of the lake where you were sitting. Once again notice the animals, birds and insects and see how happy they are to see you again. Sit there for a time. (Pause) Now see yourself sitting or lying down in the healing circle. Form a circle of brilliant white light around where you are sitting or lying down, then step through the light and slowly return to your body. Breathe deeply on the inbreath and deeply on the outbreath. As you breathe in, say quietly to yourself "I am home". As you breathe out, say quietly to yourself "I have arrived". Continue to do this breathing exercise for at least five minutes or until you feel "arrived" in your body.

After the safe return a final meditation with light is conducted. Once more in a circle a tray of lighted candles is passed round in a clockwise direction and each person acknowledges the light in the other from the light that is in them. The entire healing ceremony has been about surfacing and clearing fetters, knots and blockages -- in other words, energy "sinks". The internal dialogue with the shamans at the rock is a dialogue with the powerful archetypal material of creative self healing, and throughout the breathing cycles and journey other material will surface and it is essential to be aware and dialogue with all of it -- so that the energy of trauma is steadily diminished. If trauma and distress come to the surface and are left there on their own, it is dangerous and destructive both for individuals and for the others they inevitably project onto. It is absolutely necessary to bring to the surface the awareness of mindfulness and the power of self healing to accompany the trauma, so that an individual can begin to see deeply, clearly and take the steps to release the energy of trauma. The final meditation with light acknowledges that there is more to consciousness than trauma, suffering, blockages and energy "sinks". There are seeds of happiness, joy and grace that acknowledge the inherent Divinity within everyone. The acknowledgements in the final meditation water these seeds and create a critical and crucial finale to the healing ceremony.

Conclusion

The healing ceremony draws together and synthesizes my theoretical discussion with personal experiences in meditative and shamanic practices. The ceremony is based on a model of healing which assumes that disjunctions and blockages in the mind/body/soul system are caused by traumas from conditioning, genetic heritage and karma, and these traumas lodge themselves as energy "sinks" in the body and mind. The removal of such blockages, therefore, must also be in energy terms in order that a higher level of integration can take place. In the process of surfacing and clearing the distress caused by energy "sinks", it is essential that any distress brought to the surface of awareness be accompanied by mindfulness and the power of creative self-healing. This ensures that distress is surrounded by energy processes that facilitate transformation and at the same time reduce the potency of the energy "sink". The focus on meditation and initial breathwork secures the individual within the safety of his or her own body, quietens the mind and provides a foundation for the knots and fetters of suffering and distress to surface, both during the breathing cycles and the journey. The surfacing can be somatic, mental and emotional, particularly during the dialogue with the three shamans at the rock --- who represent the archetypal symbolism of the power of creative self-healing.

One significance of the dialogue process is that each individual chooses which level of distress to communicate about. They are not pushed to deal with more than their organism can cope with -- the consideration of safety once more. The ceremony clearly emphasizes the therapeutic role of an A.S.C. The death breaths focus on the extension of exhalation so that "space" is created within the individual for distress to more readily surface. The A.S.C., and the use of breathwork as a driver to enter this state, magnifies the effects of both the dialogue with archetypal material and the "space" created for distress to surface. Indeed, the intent and focus of the entire ceremony is to heighten the significance of the dialogue by creating a different "space" to facilitate healing and integration. Furthermore, I would argue that healing and integration are complementary facets of the same archetypal material. The release of the energy causing distress is in response to the imagery of the journey and the psychophysiological triggers induced by the breathwork. The particular type of breathwork used in the healing ceremony directs attention and energy to the archetype of Transcendent Integration and *not* to other archetypes.

The theoretical discussion of A.S.C., N.D.E., models of healing, breathwork and my personal experience of the same are the two essential components of this work and reflect how I think about doing science. Theoretically, one of course needs a set of conceptual reference points to construct models of understanding. The insights and knowledge from personal experience, however, provide the driving force to construct a level of meaning that would otherwise be impossible to achieve.

Notes

1. My understanding of the experience of each shamanic journey was communicated to my shaman teachers and confirmed by them as accurate in terms of their view of the teachings they imparted, and the experiences they initiated.

2. Over a period of five years (1990-1995) I undertook over 200 shamanic journeys.

Acknowledgements

Many audiences and scholars have heard presentations of different aspects of this work. In particular I thank Ruth-Inge Heinze for critical feedback on the issue of shamanic experience as anomaly, Dr. Sean Kelly directed me to rethink Stanislav Grof's work, Radhika Sekar double checked my use of Sanskrit terminology and meanings, and Derek Blair provided an excellent critical response to my talk about "Tribal Epistemologies and Death Breaths" at the 1996 American Philosophical Association meetings in Seattle. Previously I received a great deal of encouragement from members of the Society for the Anthropology of Consciousness at their 1995 meeting in San Francisco. They sent me back to the drawing board to resculpt how I may better communicate my thoughts and experiences.

Bibliography

Bauer, M.
1985 Near-Death Experience and Attitude Changes. Anabiosis, V.5:39-47

Bharati, Swami Raju
1995 Personal Communication

Bourguignon, E.
1973 Religion, Altered States of Consciousness and Social Change. Columbus: Ohio State University Press

Coward, H.G.
1990 Joseph Campbell and Eastern Religions: The Influence of India. In D.C. Noel (ed.): Paths to the Power of Myth:47-67. N.Y.: Crossroad

Eliade, M.
1958 Yoga: Immortality and Freedom. Princeton: Bollingen Foundation

1964 Shamanism: Archaic Techniques of Ecstasy. Princeton: Princeton University Press

Freemantle, F. and
C. Trungpa
1987 The Tibetan Book of the Dead. Boston: Shambhala

Gellhorn, E. and W. F. Kiely
1972 Mystical States of Consciousness: Neurophysiological and Clinical Aspects. Journal of Nervous and Mental Disease 154:399-405

Grof, S.
1988 The Adventure of Self Discovery. Albany: S.U.N.Y. Press

1993 The Holotropic Mind: The Three Levels of Human Consciousness and How they Shape our Lives. San Francisco: Harper San Francisco

Hahn, Thich Nhat
1987 The Miracle of Mindfulness. Boston: Beacon Press

1993 The Blooming of a Lotus. Boston: Beacon Press

Harner, M.
1990 The Way of the Shaman: A Guide to Power and Healing (3rd Edition). San Francisco: Harper and Row

Heinze, Ruth-Inge
1994 Applications of Altered States of Consciousness in Daily Life. Anthropology of Consciousness V.5, 3:8-12

Jung, C.G.
1960 [1916] The Transcendant Function. In the Collected Works of C. G. Jung, V.8. Princeton: Princeton University Press

Krippner, S.
1991 Research Strategies in the Study of Shamanism and Anomalous Experience. The Anthropology of Consciousness, V.2, 1-2:13-19

Krishnamurti, J.
1984 Krishnamurti's Notebook. San Francisco: Harper and Row

Kubler-Ross, E.
1989 On Death and Dying. N.Y.: MacMillan

Ludwig, A.M.
1966 Altered States of Consciousness. Archives of General Psychiatry 15:225-234

1969 Altered States of Consciousness. In C. Tart (ed.): Altered States of Consciousness. N.Y.: John Wiley & Sons

Mandell, A.
1980 Toward a Psychobiology of Transcendence: God in the Brain. In D. & R. Davidson (eds.): The Psychobiology of Consciousness. N.Y.: Plenum

Mironov, N.D. and
S. K. Shirokogoroff
1924 Sramana-Shaman: Etymology of the word Shaman. Journal of the Royal Asiatic Society, North China Branch 55:105-130

Moody, R.A.
1975 Life After Life. Atlanta: Mockingbird Books

Newberg, A.B. and
E. G. d'Aquili
1994 The Near Death Experience as Archetype: A Model for "Prepared" Neurocognitive Processes. Anthropology of Consciousness, V.5, 4:1-15

Noll, R.
1995 Mental Imagery Cultivation as a Cultural Phenomenon: The Role of Visions in Shamanism. Current Anthropology 26:443-461

Noyes, R.
1980 Attitude Change following Near-Death Experiences. Psychology 43:234-242

Olsen, D.A.
1975 Music-Induced Altered States of Consciousness among Waro Shamans. Journal of Latin American Lore 1, 1:19-33

Peters, L.G. and
D. Price-Williams
1980 Towards an Experiential Analysis of Shamanism. American Ethnologist 7:397-417

Prattis, J. I.
1991 Parsifal and Semiotic Structuralism. In I. Brady (ed.): Anthropological Poetics:111-131. Savage, Maryland: Rowman and Littlefield

1996 Living Breath. Forthcoming

Price-Williams, D. and
D.J. Hughes
1994 Shamanism and Altered States of Consciousness. Anthropology of Consciousness V.5, 2:1-15

Ring, K.
1980 Life at Death. A Scientific Investigation of the Near-Death Experience. N.Y.: Quill Publishers

1984 Heading Toward Omega: In Search of the Meaning of the Near Death Experience. N.Y.: William Morrow

Samuel, G.
1996 Civilized Shamans: Buddhism in Tibetan Societies. Washington, D.C.: Smithsonian Institution

Saraydarian, T.
1989 Five Great Mantrams of the New Age. Sedona, Az.: Aquarian Educational Group

Siegel, R.K.
1989 Intoxification: Life in Pursuit of Artificial Paradise, N.Y.: Dutton

Singer, J.L.
1974 Imagery and Daydream Methods in Psychotherapy and Behaviour Modification. N.Y.: Academic Press

Tart, C.
1969 Altered States of Consciousness. N.Y.: John Wiley & Sons

von Franz, M.L.
1976 Confrontation with the Collective Unconscious. Los Angeles: C. G. Jung Cassette Library

Weil, A.
1972 The Natural Mind: A New Way of Looking at Drugs and the Higher Consciousness. Boston: Houghton Mifflin

Winkelman, M.J.
1992 Shamans, Priests and Witches. A Cross-Cultural study of Magico-Religious Practitioners. Arizona State University Anthropological Research Papers No. 44

Wolf, F. A.
1993 The Eagle's Quest. N.Y.: Touchstone Books

Chapter 10

Metaphor, Vibration and Form

"I'm picking up good vibrations ..."

- The Beach Boys -

Introduction

The exploration of the rich diversity of symbols in different cultures and their enactment in ritual contexts presents a staggering array of phenomena. It seems an overwhelming task to catalogue, classify and understand their systemic meanings. Initially one can embark on a descriptive journey, touching base for instance with the fire dance performed by elderly peasant women in the mountain villages of northern Bulgaria, then with the masking traditions of Northwest Coast societies such as the Salish and Tlingit, the rites of passage into secret societies of the Mende in West Africa, and the rituals of role reversal in Swaziland. Descriptions can continue with Blackfoot naming rituals, mourning rituals in the New Guinea Highlands, first menstruation ceremonies for young women of the Apache nation, initiations into manhood among the Kota of the Congo, right up to the formal rituals surrounding high school proms in North America.

On their own these descriptions have exotic value only, that is until attempts are made at some form of classification. Anthropologists have been keen to classify symbolic and ritual life into some kind of total schemata, and most have been easy targets for Sir Edmund Leach's charges of "butterfly collecting" (Leach 1961). But nevertheless the classifications of symbolic phenomena into categories of similarity and difference was a necessary first step in understanding the regularities and common processes underlying the enormous diversity and richness of human symbolic activity. In past studies, many classifications were concerned with aspects of control and order, with how symbols and rituals were used to coerce and constrain behaviour. While symbolic activity does have factors of control as a political correlate, that is not the emphasis of this essay. I intend to argue that the more significant, and frequently neglected, aspect of symbolic systems is not simply that of producing order, but that of bringing about transformation and change. In other words, I see symbolic systems as inclusive systems of transformation and order, rather than exclusive systems of coercion and control. By this I mean that the transformative aspect of a symbolic system creates order at different levels and the latter cannot be understood without the former. In other words, order and transformation are to be seen as dialectical components of an ongoing symbolic process.

My perspective on symbolic process is tutored by Jung, Turner, Campbell and Lévi-Strauss, and involves considerations of context, structure, process and phenomenological experience. I think of symbols as multi-levelled and polyvalent. They connect to other symbols and complexes in ways that are often unrecognized. I believe that it takes human experience, and understanding of symbol, to open doorways to yet deeper understandings of that same symbol. Thus a symbol -- the Cross or the Om mantra -- can have meaning at different levels for different people, but can also change meanings as individuals engage more deeply with that symbol in an ongoing phenomenological relationship. Furthermore, symbols that are loaded with archetypal meanings have a similar impact on different people. Symbols are thus not merely abstract, intellectual constructs -- they have to be experienced and engaged with in an almost visceral manner for their meanings to surface. In this sense the symbolic process is a continual feedback system in which the symbol has to be integrated with "real" experience if a deeper understanding of it is to be the end result.

What I add to current conceptions about symbols is that they are communication vehicles that operate as pointers to the unknown, and as mediators between different levels of consciousness and reality. Symbols begin deep in the human mind and are then projected into mythology which provides the basis for symbols to be enacted in ritual contexts as well as in everyday life. (The term "ritual" is used in the liturgical sense, in that it denotes religious connotations, as distinct from the everyday sense where it does not.) The mythological process is to my mind a vital organizing template for symbolic life cross-culturally. I have argued elsewhere that these sacred narratives draw on archetypal imagery from the human unconscious, and furthermore that the symbolic sequences of mythology activate deep unconscious structures (Prattis et alia 1995:46). The world's mythologies are complex protohistories of religion that are coded and multi-levelled, providing a guidance system for the integration of awareness with the unconscious. Ritual provides an effective arena for the operation of this system, which works with precision. The ritual enactment of mythology in ceremony, festivals, sacred dance, shamanism, rites of passage, etc., provides individuals with a phenomenological encounter in which they engage with universal structures contained in the unconscious by bringing them to the level of personal experience.

There is a cycle of understanding here which proceeds from symbols in the human unconscious to mythology then to ritual enactment. The next part of the cycle goes from ritual enactment back to human awareness. The argument is that the deep mind in the unconscious projects symbols into mythology which then become the basis of liturgical reinforcement. The liturgical acting out of the myths thus enables the devotee to experience the power of the symbols being liturgically enacted. This cycle can be tracked as follows: deep mind > symbol, myth > liturgy > reconnection with deep mind.[1] So if we can begin to understand and decode mythology we will have a grasp on one part of the cycle of understanding which then takes us to the deep workings of the human mind. This was, in different ways, the preoccupation of both Joseph Campbell (1949, 1960, 1974) and Claude Lévi-Strauss (1972, 1973, 1978). Furthermore, it caught the attention of Carl Jung (1959), Victor Turner (1969), Mircea Eliade (1964), Charles Laughlin's biogenetic structuralist group (1990, 1995) and many others, in particular Paul Ricoeur (1969) and Roy Wagner (1986). This same preoccupation surfaces in the teachings and writings of seers, saints and shamans from time immemorial. There is a very rich legacy to draw upon, and not just from twentieth-century scholars, which converges on questions about the symbolic basis of our humanity.

Process

Scholars throughout this century have searched for pattern and process in the symbolic diversity presented by the world's cultures. Joseph Campbell underscored the astonishing similarities in the world's mythologies with his analysis of the Hero's Journey (1949), the stages of which take adventurers on a search for Truth through successive experiences of personal liberation. In terms of process his ideas were closely allied to Jung's (1959) concept of individuation, Eliade's quest for archetypes in the history of religions (1969) and the classical Hindu concepts of the stages of spiritual life. Jung, Campbell, Eliade and Eastern religions shared a common theme about consciousness transformation and how mythic enactment in ritual facilitates this (Underwood 1990:16). Campbell, Eliade and Jung, the mythological troika of this century (Doniger 1990:182), were drawn to a study of Eastern religions, particularly Hinduism and Buddhism, because these belief systems allowed

> ... for a direct identification of the individual searcher with the divine consciousness. The gods of the various religions are understood to be simply masks by which universal consciousness manifests itself in different times and places (Coward 1990:56).

According to Campbell myth provides a metaphor, in these terms, for an internal spiritual journey. By referring us to a transcendent, non-dualistic reality that exists in radical contradiction with the dualities and separations we create everyday in life, Campbell argues that myth guides us through the crises of our existence (Campbell 1986).

Victor Turner's ground-breaking work on rites of passage (1969, 1992) focused on the liminal phase as the crucible of change and transformation. He identified liminality as the locale of rich ritual dramas, provided concepts to describe it (communitas, gnosis and anti-structure), implied a necessary synchronicity between symbol, experience and structure, and showed how dominant symbols can unify the normative and emotional poles of meaning (Bynum 1984). In addition he demonstrated the multivocal nature of symbols by identifying three levels of meaning: exegetic, operational, positional; and permanently changed how anthropologists think about symbols. Grimes has pointed out that "Before Turner ritual was static, structural, conservative. After Turner it is imagined as flowing, processual, subversive" (Grimes 1993:6). No longer could symbols be regarded in the strictly functional sense of order and social solidarity, as Turner very skilfully and dramatically exposed order as the subversive target of liminal processes. His ideas on the dialectical tension between structure and anti-structure (1969) provided specific insights into the nature of ritual, which were about change, transformation and redefinition. As Laughlin and McManus have remarked,

> ... Turner taught that certain types of ritual produce states of consciousness that effectively unstructure the "natural attitude" of participants and then restructure a new attitude, one that is considered more appropriate, functional, adaptive or mature by the society. The classic case of such a ritual is a rite of passage which transforms an initiate to a more mature level of social status. The key to the operation of any such ritual is the involvement of *embodied* consciousness in activities that produce transformations of consciousness (literally, the reorganization of the structures mediating consciousness). These activities destabilize the habitual patterns of neurobiological processing, and guide the growth of new patterns (Laughlin & McManus 1995:38).

Laughlin's biogenetic structuralist group developed a model of the Cycle of Meaning (adapted from Ricoeur's hermeneutic circle), to describe the process of symbolic penetration into unconscious realms, and the tutoring of that experience through shamanic intervention in order to construct new cognitive and perceptual realities (Laughlin, McManus and d'Aquili 1990; Laughlin 1995). They were interested in levels of belief, understanding and realization in the interaction between religious worldview, brain cognition, neural structures and direct experience, whereby the mythic enactment and interpretation of the worldview was mediated through ritual processes and rewired into the brain.

Claude Lévi-Strauss (1972) chose a semiotic, linguistic approach to plot the archaeology of the structuring process from which he thought all symbolic systems were derived. This entailed the eventual relegation of cultural categories to the cutting-room floor, as Lévi-Strauss felt that an understanding of the deep, hidden mental processes required an identification of the relations between categories first of all, then an investigation of the structure of relations between relations. Cultural categories were merely a starting point in his exploration of the innate structuring capacity of the human mind. He argued that this capacity was expressed in culturally discrete ways yet the structure driving the symbolic constructions was beyond cultural constraints and configurations. Hence his famous comment about mythology, where he claims not to be interested so much in the myths themselves but rather with how myths think themselves out in the minds of men, without men knowing (Lévi-Strauss 1972). While I do not think the workings of the deep mind can be fully encompassed semiotically and do agree with Turner's exposé of the limitations of semiotic structuralism (Turner 1992), I have extrapolated on Lévi-Strauss' contentions by arguing that mythology and other systems of symbolic action are an implicit acting out of humankind's deep mentality (Prattis 1973). The obverse also holds true -- that *not* to act out the symbolism, to be without mythic enactments and the physical experience of embodied consciousness, has dire consequences for civilization. I will return to this theme in my conclusion.

Perhaps the most sophisticated model of culture, symbol and transformation lies in the science of Kundalini Yoga as represented variously in Buddhism and Hinduism. The chakras, arranged in ascending order from the sacrum to the crown, provide a lexicon of the stages of transformation of an individual's consciousness. The chakras are thought of as an ultimately connected energy system that can be integrated through the vehicle of conscious breath, meditation, and ritual focus. Each centre corresponds to a particular level of psychological awareness and spiritual growth and is associated with specific mantras, symbols, colours, and meditative practices. The aim of this transformation system is to advance through ritual practice and mental entrainment from the first chakra at the base of the spine (*Muladhara*) to the seventh chakra located at the top of the crown (*Sahasrara*), which represents the fully opened thousand-petalled lotus of awakening, beyond all duality. The kundalini energy in this system passes through each chakra, activating and integrating it with other chakras, creating a centred consciousness which evolves to a transcendant state that is beyond the level of body, mind, and experience dualities.

I do not intend to review every tradition of thought which has endeavoured to identify the underlying patterns of symbolic process, although I should point out Geertz' important critique on the transformative use of symbols in his book on the Balinese Theatre (1980). Furthermore, Clifford and Marcus (1986) have led the postmodernist charge into re-evaluating how we understand texts and narratives about symbols in the first place. There are, however, many other significant scholars not duly mentioned. I must confess that I have explicated those scholars that provide the most plausible foundation for my own discussion of the symbolic process of behaviour transformation. Thus I selected the transformational grammar of semiotic structuralism, the cyclic processes of the Hero's Journey and the Cycle of Meaning, the dialectics between ideology and structure in rites of passage and the enduring progression of change inherent in individuation and Kundalini Yoga.

Metaphor, Vibration and Form

I now intend to identify a particular process. The movement is from metaphor to vibration and finally to form. I will discuss the properties of each component of this process, and draw on my personal experience of meditative and shamanic practice as data, before providing two examples of the processual movement from metaphor to vibration then to form -- one of which "works", the other of which does not. The examples are necessary to fully amplify the conceptual distinctions I employ to describe and understand transformation through phenomenological engagement with symbols.

The term metaphor, in this essay, is used to describe the qualities, meanings and properties assigned to symbols. The importance of metaphor and the process of analogy is that it enables a symbolic concept to register with the mind and senses. As metaphorical meaning is imparted to symbol by our minds in the first place, there is then an engagement of the mind's products with the mind's sensibilities. As I intend to demonstrate, when this engagement occurs within well defined and orchestrated ritual sequences, an inordinate impetus for behavioural transformation is engineered. Vibration is nothing other than the physical experience of the metaphysical and "numinous" meanings attached to symbols. Rites of passage, cycles of meaning, meditative practices and ceremonial dramas provide the context or arena for the symbolic metaphor to be experienced in ever deepening ways, as energy circulations and vibrations that are felt physically in the body.

The progression from metaphor in the mind to vibration in the body is essential because without it the individual is left with mental constructs and intellectual curiosity, but no physical experience. Without such experience it is impossible to take the next step into the ineffable (Jacobi 1967:54-59), which by definition cannot be adequately described. It does, however, have connotations with the idea of the "numinous" -- a spiritual connection with both other human beings and the metaphorical manifestation of divine presence, the *unio mystico* of Christianity and the experience of the union of opposites *conjunctio oppositorum* (d'Aquili 1983:263). The midpoint of the progression from metaphor to vibration then to form usually involves entry into an altered state of consciousness (A.S.C.) so that the individual experiences an oceanic sense of interconnectedness, harmony and integration with the universe. Without the experience of this state, I would argue that behavioural restructuring and personal transformation is highly unlikely. This is what form refers to; the cognitive/perceptual changes in the individual that are reflected behaviourally. When the physical experience in the body deepens and is interpreted and understood through continued ritual focus, the initiate becomes aware of differences in attitudes and behaviours, as the "numinous" qualities associated with the symbolic metaphor are eventually expressed behaviourally in terms of new and different modes of acting. The new behaviour forms are supported socially and through repeated ritual enactments that entrench the qualities of the symbolic metaphor in the mind, behaviours, and attitudes of the initiate. It is at this instance that one can say the metaphor has come into form, through a model of behaviour transformation based on symbolic focus, "numinous" experience and mental entrainment. This is what rites of passage, the hero's journey, cycles of meaning and so on accomplish.

Much of the consolidation of the movement from metaphor through vibration to form takes place in what has been referred to as the void (Muktananda 1974; Mookerjee 1982; Wilbur 1980). This corresponds, in part, to previous discussions of A.S.C. which I see as the pivotal point of liminal experience (see Chapter 9 on Shamanism). The void is a liminal, transcendant state beyond time and space constraints. It does in fact precede metaphor as it lies beyond all imagery, yet it also contains imagery and metaphor as latency. This latency, however, makes it possible for metaphor to provide a means of accessing the void. The two examples that I discuss later in this essay may make this concept clearer. Being in void energy allows the initiate to experience a heightened awareness of the stimulus provided by symbol. The void also occupies the midpoint in the process of movement from metaphor to vibration and finally to form. It is an experience outside of time and space, where there is nothing in terms of preconceptions or prior experience to hold on to. In this liminal state there is in actual fact a great deal taking place, mostly to do with consolidating within the body the "numinous" qualities of the metaphor focused upon. Metaphor is thus a means for human awareness to connect to symbol, so that the spiritual guidance inherent in all that symbolizes the transcendental, for instance, can initially be grasped. The metaphor -- be it a concept of the Almighty or a symbol for Truth or Eternity -- is an external mental form which corresponds to a latent internal symbolic structure that is not yet known through personal experience.

It is being in energy, through a ritual focus that engenders an A.S.C., which in turn translates the "numinous" qualities of metaphor into personal experience, that the initiate then integrates with physically. So knowledge does not remain a mere intellectual artifice or a series of mental sets; knowledge becomes deeply embedded in the body as physical experience. In meditation and other rituals of transformation the focus on a particular symbolic metaphor brings to the surface specific qualities that are then felt as a physical circulation throughout the body. Ideally the initiate must be in this energy experience in a detached manner so that the qualities of the metaphor become physically encompassed as experience without any accompanying projections, hence the supreme importance of an A.S.C. and the suspension of time and space. In this process the qualities inherent in particular metaphors can eventually be given form. These changes create shifts in cognitive/perceptual mind states and permit the initiate to see a larger picture of interconnectedness that was formerly not possible.

As a result of my immersion in meditative techniques I tend to think of symbols in a musical sense, as tones. I have found that continued meditative focus on symbol produces a particular kind of alignment whereby the symbolic focus strikes a tonal chord with like structures in my unconscious and my cells. At these points of synchronicity, much of what is undiscovered (unconscious structures, cellular memory) is then made available to my conscious awareness. My exposure to meditation and transformation rituals has been through the medium of Buddhist Mahayana practice, Siddhi Samadhi Yoga, and the pranayama practices of Raja Yoga, in addition to shamanic experience over the past decade. I will briefly allude to the understandings I have derived from my personal experience with these traditions.

I have found metaphor and analogy to be very important aspects of meditation as they enable a symbolic concept to register with one's mind and senses. For instance, the qualities associated with the Star of David, the Cross, or the Om mantra take shape in the structure of symbol and sequence of visualization and experience. In meditation these qualities are transformed by being traced out in white light, (as symbol), and experienced in the body, (as vibration). This aspect of physical experience is very important and explains why so much attention was given by my teachers to personal registration with bodily sensations and the discernment of their significance. They signify a connection, through conscious breath, between one's mental awareness and corresponding symbolic complexes structured at the cellular and archetypal level. The point of meditation is to bring all these levels into synchronistic harmony with the highest plane of consciousness that is achievable at the time.

From this perspective, the discipline of meditation can be thought of as the focus through breath, whereby the frequencies of metaphor and symbol are experienced as energy vibrations and circulations in the body in ever-deepening ways. This is the step from metaphor and symbol as mental constructs to vibration -- the physical experience in the body of the tonal frequencies associated with the "numinous" qualities of the metaphor. As this deepens through continual meditation, one suddenly becomes aware of differences in attitude and behaviours. New qualities are expressed from within. The qualities of the symbolic metaphor are thus surfaced, pulled up from the unconscious and activated by a symbolic mental construction that is felt in the body. Without the physical feedback from the body one remains with mental constructs only -- the books and reports of experiences told by others. One does not own the experience of meditation for oneself. The physical aspect of meditation -- the experience of vibration, circulations in the body, energy pulses -- enables one to own the experience of meditation for oneself. If this is not the case, then one is a talking head, full of theological niceties, and other people's jargon. One is not informed by the significance of *one's own internal experience*, which, as anthropologists are beginning to learn, is always one basic referent for ethnographic accounts (Jackson 1989).

In all meditation traditions it is constantly emphasized that the vehicle for transformation is oneself. It may come as a shock to realize that one has all that one needs within oneself, within one's body. This is a metonymic process in which the microcosm (body) contains all the information about the macrocosm (cosmos) (Laughlin et alia 1990). Fully knowing the body means knowing the wonders of the universe. Guidance from teachers and symbolic signposts are essential, hence the necessity for cosmology, ritual and some form of shamanic or spiritual intervention, yet the realization that one is ultimately responsible and alone in one's spiritual evolution, fosters a climate where one embraces such aloneness and moves on with trust in one's own bodily Truth. The Gnostics clearly understood this, but paid the price of expulsion from orthodox Christianity once spirituality had become a matter of relating to a God beyond oneself, mediated through the institution of the church and its appointed officials.

To recap the major points made about meditation: the most important focus is the conscious use of breath and the realization that one breathes with one's entire body. The mind focuses on how breath is brought into the body both with respect to location (energy centre) and to metaphorical construction (symbol and visualization). In this way mental constructs for direction and amplification of the energy associated with symbolic metaphor enter the body with breath during meditation and are felt as bodily sensations. These vibrational frequencies, or tones, represent particular metaphorical qualities that are held mentally and once experienced physically, translate into form in terms of changes in how we think, speak and act. Continued focus on meditations, visualizations and ritual that characterize the properties of a given symbolic complex cause changes throughout one's being -- from the cellular level to the expressive level. What one discovers is that one speaks, thinks and interacts with a new appreciation for the qualities inherent in the symbolic complex focused on. Furthermore, the changed manner of expression draws forth corresponding qualities from those interacted with. It is at this instance that one can say the metaphor has come into form at another level, the metaphysical into the physical - although the process is unending as that which seeks to become physical (viz. the metaphysical) is rarely exhaustively appropriated by the individual. I have written about this at length in a forthcoming manuscript (Prattis 1996) and go on to discuss the dissolution of symbols and structure into emptiness, which I will allude to in my conclusion. The point of this diversion is to root my analytical preferences in personal experience. Now to the examples.

Eagle Dance

The Sky Woman or Winona Myth of the Ojibway and Iroquois Nations is about the first spirit being and ancestor of the human race, Winona, who descended to the Earth from a hole in the sky and landed upon a great turtle, whose back formed the dry Earth. She is supported and nourished by the animal kingdom, attacked by evil spirits from the underworld, guided by spirit guardians sent by the Creator, and after the Creator's intervention she in turn becomes a guiding light particularly for male spirit quests. The most spectacular transformation that Winona guides humans through is the Eagle Dance, a sacred ritual enactment grounded in this creation myth. In the present era this sacred dance is taught to males who seek to transcend the historic and present tribulations and dispossessions that beset aboriginal society, and thereby provide an example of courage and strength for others (White Eagle Woman 1990). Before this sacred dance is enacted the initiate is prepared for the movement into a different state of mind and of being -- through ritual fasting, sweats, sexual abstinence, observation of food taboos, isolation and solitude. During this time frame, which can take up to eighteen months, the steps to the dance are learned, but beyond this, the qualities that are associated with Eagle are taught. The initiates learn the mythologies and rituals that feature Eagle, and draw on the experience of other initiates who have gone through the ritual preparation for this dance. So the initiate gets a feeling for the majesty, power, and grace of Eagle and a sense of the great dignity and wisdom that underlies the power of all that symbolizes the Eagle. The all-seeing eye of Eagle provides an unflinching vision of truth and clarity. This vigilant scrutiny is both of energy brought towards the initiate, and of all that arises internally, and is designed to enable the initiate to take steps towards ultimately seeing every reality clearly, just as it is. Also taught is the sense of how solitary Eagle is in his majesty and knowledge, without reaction or judgment.[2]

With all of these qualities of the Eagle in mind, the point of meditative and ritual focus for the initiate is to enable him to experience these same qualities arising from inside himself. So after a protracted preparation period, when the initiate dances the Eagle dance for the first time, his altered state of consciousness enables him to soar with the energy and spirit of Eagle and he feels he *is* Eagle. This is felt physically, mentally, emotionally and spiritually, all at the same time, and the initiate is taken past internal mental blockages that would formerly prevent the experience and ultimately the expression of the "numinous" qualities that symbolize the Eagle. What begins in the mind as symbolic and metaphorical imagery about the qualities of Eagle is taken physically into the body through careful ritual preparation in order that the energy of the Eagle symbol can be experienced as vibration in both the preparation and the dance. The final step is that after the ritual performance, the initiate incorporates aspects of the metaphorical qualities of Eagle that he has experienced into his daily living. And indeed this is expected of him -- to display some, if not all, of the metaphorical qualities associated with the symbolic meaning of Eagle. This is supported through social expectation and repeated ritual enactments.

The Eucharist

Now let me move to an example that rarely works. This is the mass or celebration of the eucharist in Holy Communion. The bread and wine are symbolic of the body and the blood of Jesus of Nazareth. This symbolic complex originated at the last supper when Christ broke bread for his disciples and bade them eat, that in this way they could partake of his essence (his body). The same directive applied to the wine that was passed around his disciples -- drink and partake of his essence (his blood). In this instant Jesus created a mythic enactment and a means through which this sacrament could be re-experienced in the ceremony of bread and wine that Christians celebrate as Holy Communion. This mythic enactment is a powerful metaphor for all the qualities embodied and symbolized in the being of Jesus Christ. Bynum (1984) describes the eucharist as the central symbol in a processual ritual drama that moves from the last supper to the crucifixion and resurrection. The eucharist symbolizes this entire process in an astonishingly simple and powerful ceremony that nowadays escapes our attention, simply because we remain solely with the intellectual, metaphorical component of what I consider to be the supreme mythic enactment of the entire Christian religion.

For the vast majority of Christians in contemporary society, partaking in Holy Communion is a process of ingesting a wafer and some grape juice in a solemn ceremony usually held on a Sunday. It is rarely more than a surface performance that has become stuck at the metaphorical level. It has intellectual appeal at best, at worst it is a dutiful performance for most participants. Yet look at what has been lost given the perspective I have offered about metaphor, vibration and form. The purpose of the eucharist, a mythic enactment about Christlike qualities, is absolutely immense. This purpose is to feel physically that the bread and the wine *is* the body and blood of Christ; and that the energy of Christ the saviour is at work inside because it is felt physically, and "owned" by the body as experience. It no longer remains a mental or metaphorical concept in the intellect. When people feel the elements of the eucharist inside themselves, as the body and blood of Jesus, then the "numinous" Christlike qualities that are associated with the symbolism of the eucharist (which are also at the same time latent inside the individual) are brought to the surface of experience and then become enacted in daily living. The goal of the eucharist is to be Christ, just as the goal of the previous liturgy is to be Eagle.

This line of reasoning is beyond the experiential reach of most Christian theologians; and they do not have to encounter too many instances of it because participants in the eucharist rarely move beyond the metaphor. This produces a deep sense of loss in the symbolic sense, not just for Christianity, but by the wider culture itself. This loss is often contributed to by the theologians themselves who have never had the experience of what it is they seek to describe. Those who *do* experience the metaphor as the actual physical experience of Christ essence live their lives as exemplary enactments of all that Jesus stood for, or at least endeavour to do so. In the modern context, my educated guess is that such individuals are a very small minority and are totally isolated from the wider civilization of which they are a part. For the rest of us who participate in the celebration of Holy Communion, we rarely get past the metaphor; and the sequence of metaphor to vibration and finally to form does not operate to alter how we as individuals may then perceive and participate in life.

Conclusion

There are a number of loose threads left hanging in the present essay that I would like to return to before I draw it to a close. These threads of argument have to do with symbolic appropriation, levels of reality and the outrageous idea of going beyond symbols.

Recall Lévi-Strauss' views concerning myths thinking themselves out in the minds of men without man's knowledge (Lévi-Strauss 1972). In the early 1970s when I first pondered the implications of this facet of Lévi-Strauss' thought I was led to consider what would happen to a culture, like our own, that becomes demythologized. Opposed to Lévi-Strauss's disembodied view of myth and with a different perspective on process, I wondered (1) if there were deep structures in our minds and bodies; and (2) they were predisposed to be activated in a life of progressive symbolic encounters, (3) that are no longer orchestrated in society; (4) then what might be the consequences? Lévi-Strauss in the last paragraph of *L'Homme Nu* provides one answer to this with an ambiguous word play on the paradoxes of our culture. He arrives at a particular metaphor for our humanity that I have referred to as a rebuke to our lack of consciousness (Prattis 1984:202). He concludes with the words "C'est a dire rien". I explored his conclusion by examining the possibilities of chaos, breakdown and entropy at the individual, societal and global levels (Prattis 1973, 1984), but refused to allow Lévi-Strauss' logic to have the last word. Instead, I maintained that symbolic categories do have transformative potential in their own right and are not to be banished to the cutting room floor as experientially irrelevant, once relations between categories have been established.

A more encouraging yet problematic consequence is the deep hunger for ritual in our contemporary society -- a civilization that has apparently lost touch with the unconscious, the symbolic significance of myth and with how ritual enactments lead to personal transformation. This hunger has lead to a large-scale and indiscriminate borrowing and appropriation of other cultures' symbols, and to the prolific creation of syncretic ritual -- all driven by a deep sadness about the modern world's disconnection from a deeper sense of humanity. Barbara Myerhoff (1984), Ronald Grimes (1990, 1993) and others (Myerhoff and Moore 1977; Driver 1991) have cogently argued a case for new rituals in a society that has become increasingly fragmented and which also lacks the mechanisms to handle the crises and transitions of daily life. New Age movements and prophets of various hues and integrities have appropriated the rituals of other cultures, taken them apart and quite consciously proceeded to create new rituals of their own. Guided more by the spirit of Emerson, the grand do-it-yourselfer, than by an understanding of process, preparation and underlying mythology, men and women are creating goddess circles, wild man retreats, ritual therapy groups and are appropriating, in particular, the sacred ceremonies of Native Americans. This takes me into the delicate area of symbolic appropriation.

It is true to say that cultures have always borrowed symbolic complexes and incorporated ceremonial practices since time immemorial. At the archetypal level of understanding this borrowing is to be expected and perhaps openly permitted -- all other things being equal. But all other things are not equal. Factors such as conquest, dependency, exploitation and colonialism provide a volatile political context as the arena within which symbols are borrowed, reconstructed and used. Consistent with this argument is the notion that humans share common symbolic complexes, located deep in the unconscious, that are expressed in discrete and different regional and cultural manifestations. While recognizing that this is so, it would be naive and irresponsible to ignore the volatile political context within which symbolic appropriation takes place.

Having said this, it is also important to introduce a note of candour into the discussion of symbolic appropriation and syncretic ritual. The communities and populations studied by anthropologists have been subject to varying degrees of capitalist penetration and are part of the global commodification of products, values and symbols. They also participate in the current explosive information era with the combined result that their post-colonial world is largely one of fragmentation, dependency and conflict, involving the breakdown of traditional symbolic systems that once provided meaning and the construction of coherence. Their traditional ceremonies and symbolic maps of coherence are frequently forgotten or have value only to certain elderly segments of aboriginal society. Nonetheless there is in process a worldwide phenomena of populations creatively re-inventing themselves through remembered and borrowed ritual as one means of defining identities for political, moral and symbolic reasons. Thus the issues of syncretic ritual and symbolic appropriation are not unique to western culture, and never have been. There is a growing pan-cultural phenomena of reviving and re-inventing symbolic systems appropriate for the present era of fragmentation and uncertainty on the one hand, and global commodification on the other. The problems and issues of syncretic ritual are generalizable to a much wider context than western civilization. Furthermore, as our civilization has gone further in the demythologizing process than most other cultures, then our attempts at re-inventing identity through ritual practices -- borrowed, remembered, synthesized -- provides a critical empirical arena for research on symbolic process. This directs the observer's focus to examine both the lack of attention to due process and to the overall context that drives the hunger for ritual in our society.

These considerations take us back to Emerson. The effort to build a better mouse trap assumes that short cuts will be taken in order to produce a more efficient and readily available end product. The heirs to Emerson (viz.-us!) have travelled from the richness of mythic narrative to the terse paucity of seven-second-sound-bytes. When this latter logic and communication preference is transferred to ritual activities, the potential for highly dangerous consequences is created. In non-industrial societies the underlying mythology, ritual preparation and attention to due process enables initiates to engage safely with archetypal material. This occurs under the guidance of shamans or medicine people who have the requisite knowledge of entire cycles of meaning and of the symbolic transformations involved. Without this kind of knowledge, preparation and guidance, modern day wild man retreats, healing circles, or masking workshops, for instance, may well do more harm than good in terms of releasing unconscious material in circumstances where nobody has the requisite knowledge or procedures to facilitate archetypal integration. Given the shortcuts, lack of attention to preparation and due process in symbolic appropriation, is it then possible in the modern world to create meaningful symbolic systems that serve the interests of transformation and societal change? Or are we left with a form of mindless psychobabble that characterizes many New Age endeavours? I think the answer is a little bit of both!

When one engages with archetypes, rituals and mythology, one enters an exceedingly powerful set of symbolic complexes. I think there is a supreme responsibility on anthropologists to clearly understand the consequences and processes of this combination and to communicate to, and educate, a wider public audience about the awesome power of rituals that activate archetypal material. By and large I would argue that our society is stricken with a chronic, but not yet terminal, case of symbolic illiteracy. When this spiritual barrenness is allied with a hunger for meaningful ritual, it is inevitable that individuals and groups will indiscriminately tinker with ritual, other people's and remnants of their own -- we are after all the heirs of Emerson and the consumers of seven- second-sound-bytes. Yet anthropologists know enough about ritual to advise against tinkering without knowledge, understanding and respect, and as responsible professionals we can counter the gross misunderstandings about ritual, symbols and archetypes. Rituals that are borrowed and vaguely remembered can be recreated in a manner that is authentic, once one understands the importance of respect, preparation and due process.

My experience and exposure to symbolic complexes from other cultures - shamanic and meditative - is that they do strike a personal chord within me. Twenty years of experience and respect for symbolic complexes has been for me a necessary prerequisite before it was possible to reconstruct meaningful symbolic sequences that were valuable for healing and transformative practices in my own society. As a mediator between symbolic systems my underlying concern, for instance, with deriving a healing ceremony based on shamanic and meditative experience rested on considerations of safety, responsibility and sacredness and were a result of my observations of symbolic reconstructions that did not have these considerations (see Chapter 9 on Death Breaths and Drivers). From the preceding remarks it is obvious that I do not have a solution to the issue of symbolic appropriation and perhaps there is no need for one. However, I do feel it is necessary to map the context, history and further use of another culture's symbols to understand the contingent factors in this sensitive area of symbolic appropriation. I offer only those guidelines I am drawn to through my own experience of the symbolic complexes of other cultures. These are understanding, experience and respect; attention to the principles of safety, responsibility and sacredness; and knowledge and experience of due process.

In this regard we can learn a great deal from Buddhist distinctions between historical and ultimate reality that are directly applicable to our understandings about creating significant ritual processes for our times. Thich Nhat Hanh uses the analogy of how waves and water are connected to understand how different dimensions of reality are interwoven (1992:11-128), and why we must learn to touch both. Waves rise, fall and die when they wash up on a shore -- this is the analogy for the historical dimension. The ultimate dimension is the water that remains constant no matter what happens to the waves. Hanh points out that we generally only touch the wave, rarely do we discover how to touch the water. He goes on to say,

> ... the world of waves is characterized by birth and death, ups and downs, being and non-being. A wave has a beginning and an end but we cannot ascribe these characteristics to water. In the world of water, there is no birth or death, no being or non-being, no beginning or end. When we touch the water we touch reality in this ultimate dimension and are liberated from all of these concepts (Hanh 1992:117).

Ultimate reality thus refers to a transcendant reality, a dimension outside of time and space. Historical reality, on the other hand, is the existential dimension of our day to day existence. The two realities are brought together or at least overlap, through mythology, ritual enactment and meditative practice. I have referred to myths as sacred narratives beyond time and space and to rituals as mythic enactments that bring the mythic dimension into existential reality with unique symbolic performances that are discrete to particular cultures, religions and times. So that which lies outside of time and space is brought *into* the dimension of time and space through mythic enactments. I would argue further that transformation is not possible without this particular interconnection of dimensions. For if we try to symbolically transform time and space elements (existential reality), by applying other time/space elements then very little will take place beyond surface posturing. "A" cannot change or transform "A". But if the symbolic basis of transformation draws on no time/no space elements and applies them to temporal/spatial phenomena then movement towards the transcendant is possible. Here we have "B" working on "A" and transformation is now a possibility. Thus we can begin to appreciate, from another level, the supreme importance of mythology.

I believe that archetypes operate in the same manner as mythology in that they too are symbolic complexes beyond time and space. Jung (1953) implied and Laughlin (in press) insists that archetypes are neural structures of cognition that developed during the evolution of our species. For our present existential reality the archetypes can be considered as symbolic complexes structured in our collective unconscious, the experience of which lies beyond time and space. Laughlin (in press) maintains that the archetypes are the direct window into what he calls the "non-local totality of the Quantum Sea" (Personal Communication 1996). An important part of the human spiritual journey is to recognize and actualize the archetype of Divine Consciousness, often referred to as the God Archetype (Coward 1990; Zimmer 1969). It manifests itself in different religious connotations of the transcendant in different populations, religions and time/space frames. For instance, concepts of God, the Creator, Yahweh, Allah, Bodhisattvas, etc. draw on a similar archetype - that of Divine Consciousness - which lies outside of time and space and manifests in the temporal/spatial dimension as specific, culture bound religious preferences. There is not a time or space boundary on archetypes, thus they are a facet of ultimate reality. Their projection through myths, dreams and enactment in the symbolic sequences of ritual and ceremony brings them into historical, existential reality so that time/space referents are symbolically connected to no time/no space referents. We can then touch both the wave and the water.

Without this kind of equation I do not think ritual can work in a transformative manner. This assertion provides a caveat to assess the quality of emergent ritualizing in our society (Grimes 1993:10); because a secular mentality, applying itself to ritual processes, rarely recognizes the significance of the no time/no space dimension which in turn provides the foundation and symbolic energy for transformation. Yet this is what contemporary ritualizing is so desperately trying to touch. Indeed we are driven to it, for in our collective unconscious lies a no time/no space "programming" in that ultimate reality (the water) lies unrecognized within our minds as archetypes. This is why there is a psychobiological drive, innate to our species, to experience altered states and mythic consciousness (see Chapter 9).

James Joyce once remarked that our existential reality with its trials, tribulations, triumphs and sorrows is an opera, only it hurts! To endure the opera and to transform our beings requires a glimpse or experience of a reality not bound by historical, existential constraints of time and space. Hence the value of Buddhist and other cultural conceptions about ultimate reality. For when the timeless, the spaceless enters the historical reality of daily existential activities, it provides a conduit or path for our consciousness and lives to transform. We yearn for these glimpses, fleeting experiences, and the lack of them drives the hunger in our civilization for meaningful symbol systems. However, in the cobbling together of ritual from different sources, the syncretic end result often ignores or only pays lip service to the no time/no space dimension of ultimate reality that actually spurs our transformation. In other words, drastic or marked changes in consciousness are not attained. This is despite the fact that our myths are good -- for instance the Parsifal myth (Chapter 2), the emerging Gaia myth (Chapters 12 and 13) and the mythology behind the enactment of the Eucharist (Bynum 1984) -- all contain the components of ultimate reality. We can also take the time and discipline to learn, understand and appreciate the myths of other cultures -- otherwise their rituals once borrowed do not make sense, and more importantly they do not carry the energy of transformation as they are taken out of the context of no time/no space.

Symbolic transformation begins in the dimension of ultimate reality beyond time and space that many cultures clearly recognize and articulate in their myths and dreams. The myths of the world, as Jung has pointed out, carry the imprints of archetypal material. Therefore the dimension of ultimate reality is clearly inherent in human beings, in the archetypal level of the collective unconscious. So when we make myths and create rituals we bring into existential reality the deep knowledge of ultimate reality that lies undiscovered within us. In this cycle we take steps to return to what we hold deep in our minds and create a fuller, more integrated expression of ourselves. These recognitions provide important caveats and guidelines in our rush to tinker with ritual. It requires that we become aware of different dimensions of ourselves and realize that a meaningful symbol system is one that brings the historical and ultimate dimensions together in the interests of integration and transformation. The obverse is that if our ritualizing processes are not mythologically and archetypally based then they are a surface practice, a superficial acting out of the deeper connections that are available. With these caveats in mind, our headlong rush into symbolic appropriation *can* be tempered with knowledge about process, connections and dimensions. There is a clear logic to it all, yet it is a logic that requires of us that we first of all experience it.

A final thought is about going beyond symbol. In meditation and ritual dramas a great deal of attention is devoted to the constant surfacing and releasing of patterns that obstruct vision and clarity. Indeed, the different techniques of meditation can be viewed as mechanisms of symbolic entrainment designed to deal with such obstructions. The symbolic forms in meditation are frequently set within mandalic formations (circles) into which the separation and obstructions dissolve. It is no accident that this framework also operates as a physical stage or theatre for Native American rituals -- medicine wheels, sweat lodges and healing ceremonies. By relying on a symbolic focus for "assistance" up the ladder of consciousness, one must be aware that such focus in and of itself incorporates notions of separation. The symbol forms a boundary or veil, and often times a crutch to enable one to journey further along the continuum of consciousness. Yet the focus on symbols, the importance of mythology, and the attention to due process is so that all of these components can ultimately be abandoned. I am asserting that in ritual life the progressive exposure to symbolic encounters ultimately leads one to a recognition of the inherent redundancy of symbol. It too is an obstruction, and focus upon symbol, myth and structure has to dissolve into emptiness and silence. The symbol itself is drawn from historical reality yet its *referent* is that of ultimate reality! Symbols thus bridge the realities kept separate in our minds and experience. When the symbol becomes redundant then the boundaries of separation between ultimate and historical reality become meaningless. For example, the Tai Chi symbol of Yin and Yang energies maps complementary gender and energy polarities framed within a circular mandalic form. The real significance of this symbol becomes apparent when it dissolves into emptiness at the centre of the mandala. This is the point of symbolic exposure and maturity: to dissolve polarities, to release obstructions until the final obstruction is also released -- the symbol itself.

All of this, of course, is very difficult to contemplate and even more difficult to experience. So we rely on progressive symbolic encounters as navigational guides both through the crises of life and for movement along the continuum of consciousness. The Upanisads of India, a most wonderful mythology of consciousness, address these concerns directly. The Vedic notion of the four stages of life (*asrama)* describes how as students and householders, individuals are mostly influenced by biological drives and a host of external worldly identifications (Coward 1990:55). Myth, symbol and ritual are the vehicles that take attention away from the *egosphere* of the first two stages of life (student and householder), and refocus an individual's attention to the internal *ecosphere* of the final two stages. In other words, these vehicles set us up for the transformations in consciousness anticipated for the final two stages of life, which are referred to as the forest and wandering holy beggar stages (Zimmer 1969:155-158). Jung would no doubt describe this as the final steps in the individuation of a person, the insistence by the God archetype that it be recognized and actualized. The forest stage involves the throwing away of external identifications and worldly concerns before discovering the essence of self underneath the masks and identities gathered throughout life. The mythology and symbols that guide an individual to this stage are themselves masks and they too must be abandoned. This is what I mean by going beyond symbol. The Vedas then support a very profound cycle of meaning as the Rishis and Yogis, having gone beyond mythology and symbol, return to society with their experience and wisdom and teach others the necessary symbolic steps to arrive at the state of "no symbol", an awesome yet comprehensible journey of the Hero in both classical and modern life. Now that the threads of symbolic appropriation, levels of reality, and going beyond symbol are loosely tied I can return to summarize the body of this essay.

My text has demonstrated that an understanding of symbolic events cross culturally requires an appreciation for the significance of the interplay between context, structure, process and phenomenological experience; furthermore, with how they connect to different dimensions of reality. This cycle of understanding leads to an emphasis on symbolic systems as models of behaviour transformation, and research may usefully be applied in identifying the limits of process by examining instances in which this process runs its full course, and in which it does not. The two examples -- the Eucharist and Eagle dance -- amplified my model of process. The movement from metaphor to vibration then to form also augments an understanding of the processual analyses of Campbell, Turner, Jung and Laughlin, while at the same time providing a critique of the transformational grammar of Lévi-Strauss. Finally, the model enables one to understand the lack of transformation and change in some symbolic systems, by identifying the component of process where societal attention becomes fixated -- mostly at the metaphorical, intellectual level. The two examples provide graphic illustrations of this. The afterthoughts on symbolic appropriation and the ultimate redundancy of symbol instigates a debate about the professional responsibility of anthropologists concerning the symbolic processes and emergent ritualizing of our times. This raises questions of what and how we communicate, who we communicate it to, and more precisely why we must serve a public much wider than that served in strict academic discourse. I leave the last words of this essay with Thich Nhat Hahn. In discussing the activities of Bodhisattvas he brings the two dimensions of reality together and illuminates the Vedic cycle I discuss in the previous paragraph. He states (Hahn 1992:128):

> Having touched the ultimate dimension, these bodhisattvas return to the historical dimension to help, however they can, to transform the suffering and offer relief. They live the life of a wave, but they also live the life of water, and in doing so, they offer us non-fear.

Dedication

For White Eagle Woman, who taught me so much, and continues to do so.

Notes

1. John Dourley, Professor of Religion at Carleton University suggested this tracking sequence in his very helpful critique of an earlier draft of this essay.

2. My own field experience of these teachings was through the wisdom of White Eagle Woman (1990-1995) and a medicine woman of the Shuswap nation who prefers not to be identified (1988-1990). I present a distillation of their guidance, which has been dutifully checked with them in an ongoing consultation for accuracy in representing their knowledge and teachings.

Acknowledgement

John Dourley and Derek Blair provided very thoughtful critiques of an earlier draft of this essay. Tim Olaveson directed my attention to grammatical mistakes and to my neglect of the concept of the "numinous". Charles Laughlin provided a timely and well received critique. My debt of gratitude is to them all.

Bibliography

d'Aquili, E.G.
1983 The Myth-Ritual Complex: A Biogenetic Structural Analysis. Zygon, V.18, 3:247-269

Bynum, C.W.
1984 Women's Stories, Women's Symbols: A Critique of Victor Turner's Theory of Liminality. In R.L. Moore and F. Reynolds (eds.): Anthropology and the Study of Religion. Chicago: Center for the Scientific Study of Religion

Campbell, J.
1949 The Hero with a Thousand Faces. Princeton: Princeton University Press

1960 The Masks of God I: Primitive Mythology. London: Secker and Warburg

1974 The Mythic Image. Princeton: Princeton University Press

1986 The Inner Reaches of Outer Space. N.Y.: Harper and Row

Clifford, J. and G. Marcus
1986 (eds.): Writing Culture: The Poetics and Politics of Ethnography. Berkeley: University of California Press

Coward, H.G.
1990 Joseph Campbell and Eastern Religions: The Influence of India. In D.C. Noel (ed.): Paths to the Power of Myth:47-67. N.Y.: Crossroad

Doniger, W.
1990 Origins of Myth-Making Man. In D.C. Noel (ed.): Paths to the Power of Myth:181-186. N.Y.: Crossroad

Driver, T.F.
1991 The Magic of Ritual: Our Need for Liberating Rites that Transform our Lives and our Communities. San Francisco: Harper San Francisco

Eliade, M.
1964 Shamanism: Archaic Techniques of Ecstasy. Princeton: Princeton University Press

1969 Yoga: Immortality and Freedom, (2nd edition). Princeton: Princeton University Press

Geertz, C.
1980 Negara: The Theatre State in Nineteenth Century Bali. Princeton: Princeton University Press

Grimes, R.
1990 Ritual Criticism: Case Studies in its Practise, Essays on its Theory. Columbia: University of South Carolina Press

1993 Reading, Writing and Ritualizing: Ritual in Fictive, Liturgical and Public Places. Washington, D.C.: The Pastoral Press

Hanh, Thich Nhat
1992 Touching Peace: Practicing the Art of Mindful Living. Berkeley: Parallax Press

Jackson, M.
1989 Paths Toward a Clearing: Radical Empiricism and Ethnographic Enquiry. Bloomington: Indianna University Press

Jacobi, J.
1967 The Way of Individuation. N.Y.: New American Library

Jung, C.G.
1953 Two Essays in Analytical Psychology. The Collected Works of C.G. Jung, V.7. London: Routledge and Kegan Paul

1959 The Archetypes and the Collective Unconscious. The Collected Works of C.G. Jung, V.9. Princeton: Princeton University Press

Laughlin, C.D.
1995 The Cycle of Meaning: Some Methodological Implications of Biogenetic Structural Theory. In S. Glazier (ed.): Anthropology of Religion: Handbook of Theory and Method. Peterborough: Greenwood Press

In Press Archetypes, Neurognosis and the Quantum Sea. Journal of Scientific Exploration

Laughlin, C.D., and J. McManus
1995 The Relevance of the Radical Empiricism of William James. Anthropology of Consciousness V.6, 3:34-46

Laughlin, C.D., J. McManus and E.G. d'Aquili
1990 Brain, Symbol and Experience: Toward a Neurophenomenology of Human Consciousness. N.Y.: Columbia University Press

Leach, E.R.
1961 Rethinking Anthropology. London School of Economics Mononographs on Social Anthropology, No. 22. London: Athlone Press

Lévi-Strauss, C.
1972 Mythologiques IV. L'Homme Nu. Paris: Plon

1973 From Honey to Ashes (trans. John and Doreen Weightman) N.Y.: Harper and Row

1978 The Origin of Table Manners (trans. John and Doreen Weightman) London: Jonathan Cape Ltd.

Mookerjee, A.
1982 Kundalini: The Arousal of the Inner Energy. N.Y.: Destiny Books

Muktananda, Swami
1974 Play of Consciousness. South Fallsburg, N.Y.: SYDA Foundation

Myerhoff, B.
1984 A Death in Due Time: Construction of Self and Culture in Ritual Drama. In J. MacAloon (ed.): Rite, Drama, Festival, Spectacles: Rehearsals Toward a Theory of Cultural Performance. Philadelphia: Institute for the Study of Human Issues

Myerhoff, B. and S.F. Moore
1977 (eds.): Secular Ritual: Symbol and Politics in Communal Ideology. Amsterdam: Van Gorcum

Prattis, J.I.
1973 Metaphor and Entropy. Mediations, V.1, 1:35-42

1984 Man and Metaphor: An Exploration in Entropy and Coherence. Communication and Cognition, V.17, 2/3:187-204

1996 Living Breath. Forthcoming

Prattis, J.I., D. Blair,
L. Grigas and O. Krassnitsky
1995 "Reflections" as Myth. Dialectical Anthropology, V.20, 1:45-69

Ricoeur, P.
1969 Le Conflet des Intepretations: Essais d'Hermeneutique. Paris: Éditions du Seuil

Turner, V.
1969 The Ritual Process: Structure and Anti-Structure. Ithica: Cornell University Press

1992 Blazing the Trail: Way Marks in the Exploration of Symbols. Tuscon, Az.: University of Arizona Press

Underwood, R.A.
1990 Living by Myth: Joseph Campbell, C.G. Jung and the Religious Life-Journey. In D.C. Noel (ed.): Paths to the Power of Myth:13-28. N.Y.: Crossroad

Wagner, R.
1986 Symbols that Stand for Themselves. Chicago: University of Chicago Press

White Eagle Woman
1990 Personal Communications 1990-1995

Wilbur, K.
1980 The Atman Project: A Transpersonal View of Human Development. Wheaton, Ill: Theosophical Publishing House

Zimmer, H.
1969 Philosophies of India. J. Campbell (ed.). Princeton: Princeton University Press

Chapter 11

Science and Sages: A Small Matter of Paradigms

Introduction: Paradigms, Distortion and Awareness

Since Thomas Kuhn's groundbreaking work on scientific revolutions and paradigms (1970), scholars have been preoccupied with the question of bias and distortion in discourse (Clifford and Marcus 1986; Rappaport 1994). This questioning has provided much of the impetus for the healthy chaos of postmodernism which asks of perpetrators of discourse "What really do you know and do you really know what you are doing?" (Rosenau 1992; Tyler 1987).

Paradigms are very slippery concepts because at one and the same time they provide a blueprint for knowledge yet limit our perceptions of anything that may fall outside of that blueprint. In examining a considered reality any scholar, as observer, deletes from or adds to that reality depending on bias produced by their particular socio-cultural conditioning and education. What is added to the perceptual field of the reality examined are different levels of distortion, making it necessary for methodology to provide controls and checks. Yet much of the methodology employed in science is a collectively agreed upon set of biases that are considered acceptable to the academic community. Thus scientific investigation proceeds on the basis of agreements about what science is to do, who it is to serve and what is to be done with the results. There are vested interests that seek to define scientific endeavour in a particular mould that has very little to do with a search for truth, or an examination of reality as it is. Part of the scientific community then proceeds on the basis of agreements that stem from the control evoked by powerful vested interests. These agreements provide obstacles to knowing reality as it is, yet sooner or later these shibboleths disintegrate because science as constituted cannot explain the increasing number of events that are conveniently labelled as anomalous (Young and Goulet 1994). This, as Kuhn points out (1970), sets the stage for a scientific revolution that will be severely resisted by the "established" yet unsatisfactory code of knowledge presently in place. The business of paradigm shift is thus a messy process and I intend to stir these waters by putting scientific and contemplative traditions together, in order to arrive at a more conceptually accurate level of explanation.

Joel Barker (1985), following in Kuhn's footsteps, made a film on the business of paradigms and elucidates some interesting points. He reiterates that new ideas involve change and create uncertainty and disruption. It comes as no surprise that they are usually considered as dangerous and are therefore strenuously resisted. In the Middle Ages church and state were so antagonized by Galileo's ideas that he was threatened with torture and imprisonment and forced to publicly retract his views, based on meticulous observations, that it was the sun, not the earth, that was the centre of planetary movements. Church and state authorities at that time held to a different paradigm about the earth's primacy and were powerful enough to force Galileo to recant. They operated with a particular set of rules and regulations about acceptable knowledge and Galileo's views lay beyond their conceptual and empirical boundaries. Thus Galileo had to be suppressed, otherwise church and state authority would be undermined and rendered vacuous.

Paradigms influence how we see and understand the world because they act as filters screening the data that comes into our minds. New paradigms are fiercely resisted in order that pre-existing power structures can be maintained. This is as much the case with modern science as it was for the medieval church and state. In science, data that agrees with the scientist's paradigm is easily accepted, but data that does not fit the expectations of the dominant paradigm is often overlooked or rejected. Fig. 1 simplifies these considerations and prompts an alternative to resistance and perceptual blindness to that which lies outside of our conceptual boundaries. We must be prepared to continually re-examine and expand conceptual boundaries. This entails breaking down the perceptual screens that conditioning, education and training have put in place, as the major way to overcome distortion is to expand awareness.

Figure 11.1: Distortion and Awareness

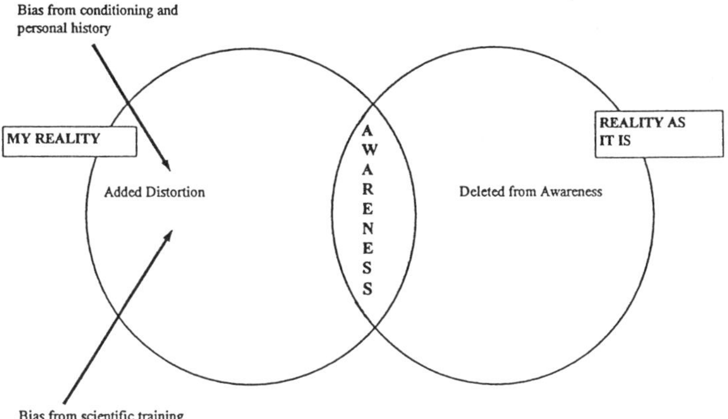

In this vein Barker (1985) provides some interesting observations about the global watchmaking industry. He makes the point that when a paradigm shifts, past success guarantees nothing and everything goes back to zero. For example, in 1968 Swiss watchmakers controlled 65% of the world market, garnering 80% of the profits. By 1978 they had less than 10% of the world market and had laid off 50,000 of their 65,000 workers. By contrast, in 1967 Japan had no real participation in the world market for watches but by 1980 had become the dominant exporting nation. What happened?

It was the invention of the quartz electronic watch, 1000 times more accurate than the mechanized watch with its gears, springs and bearings. The quartz watch was invented by a Swiss researcher in 1967 who worked for the Swiss watchmaking industry. His invention was rejected by the manufacturers as they thought it could not possibly be the future of watches. This invention was displayed at an international watch conference, and so little was it thought of by the Swiss manufacturers that it was not protected by patent. Texas Instruments and Seiko of Japan saw it, snapped it up and took over the global market. The Swiss watchmaking industry went back to zero; they were blinded by the success of the old paradigm and by their level of investment in it. They could not see the data that did not fit their paradigm of watchmaking which involved springs, gears and bearings. The Japanese on the other hand have never been reticent about encountering new phenomena, rapidly adapting it to their own uses, and in effect switching paradigms.

So we see that paradigms dramatically and powerfully affect our judgments, because they not only influence but also distort our perceptions; we see best what we are supposed to see. Paradigms are common facts of life in science and religion -- indeed in life in general -- and they are a useful focus for attention, but when alternatives are rejected out of hand, and a paradigm becomes THE PARADIGM, we enter the terminal disease of certainty -- a form of paradigm paralysis that supports the emergence of the Hitlers of this world with variations of the paradigm of Aryan superiority. Heisenberg warned against this in the 1920's with his "principle of uncertainty".

Joel Barker and Thomas Kuhn both note that the people who create new paradigms are outsiders, not part of the paradigm community, therefore they have nothing to lose -- new rules are almost always written at the edge. When paradigm paralysis becomes terminal, that is a sign that one can choose to change the rules and regulations and see the world anew; in other words break down the perceptual screens by expanding awareness. Once this happens, and a paradigm shifts, different questions are asked and different solutions to problems are created. This is what is happening in a dramatic way in quantum physics, where the current research on subatomic particles is promoting a worldview that is closely related to the views of mystics of all ages and traditions (Capra 1979:1983). This has become known as the new physics.

> The fact that all particles can be transformed into other particles shows us very vividly that the constituents of matter do not exist as isolated entities but as integral parts of an inseparable network of interactions. The whole universe is thus engaged in endless motion and activity -- in a rhythmic dance of creation and destruction .....
>
> The eastern mystics have a dynamic view of the universe similar to that of modern physics, and consequently it is not surprising that they, too, have used the image of the dance to convey their intuition of nature. The metaphor of the cosmic dance has found, perhaps, its most beautiful expression in Hinduism in the image of the Dancing God Shiva. According to Hindu belief all life is part of a great rhythmic process of creation and destruction, of death and rebirth, and Shiva's dance symbolizes this eternal life-death rhythm which goes on in endless cycles.
>
> For the modern physicist, the dance of Shiva is the dance of subatomic matter. As in Hindu mythology, it is a continual dance of creation and destruction involving the whole cosmos; the basis of all existence and of all natural phenomena (Capra 1979:65).

However, despite what is going on in the new physics the overarching conception of science does not recognize that our perceptions and cognitions are intricately intertwined with a consciousness that includes ourselves, the planet and the universe. The perspective I take favours a rethinking about the nature of these multiple realities and I regard human consciousness as the connecting link between levels of correspondence that are presently kept separate in our minds and conceptions. Science is actually a beautiful creative choreography if we can only begin to understand and appreciate it from a different vantage point.

New and Old Science

I intend to discuss science from the perspective of paradigm shift, of expanding awareness to the extent that bias and distortion can be radically reduced. This involves a transgression across established boundaries, but I do this in order to emphasize the importance of a metaphysical component in general and to focus on meditation practices in particular. First of all I will talk about science from this perspective then give two examples to support my contentions.

I see science as the engagement of a conceptual dance, whereby that which the observer perceives continually evolves and is sculpted as the observer's level of awareness begins to expand. As the subject-observer recognizes the importance of self-awareness in the journey toward scientific and conceptual discovery, the groundwork is laid for a quantum leap into a new foundation from which science and civilization may then progress. The present scientific paradigm inherited from Descartes, refined through Newton and implemented through the Vienna school of positivism often abandons the relevance of the interactive nature within the subject-object relationship (Prattis 1996a, Chapter 5 this volume). This has led many scientists and philosophers to question the status of knowledge in science because descriptions of atoms, nature and social behaviour have become connected only to the properties of the observer through the measuring instruments used (Bohr 1938). The properties of that which is observed have become obscured. The epistemological issues raised by this neglect include the implications for clarity and truth within perceptual accuracy, particularly when one considers the level of self-awareness of the observer in the scientific process of investigation.

Observation is an interactive engagement that influences the feedback loop between subject and object, self and other. The interactional relationship created links the observer to the observed and co-determines the "reality" that emerges from their engagement. So one requires clarity about what constitutes Truth in perception. Lack of clarity produces constraints on perception which are then compounded when projected out and placed upon the object of study. Scientists, therefore, must be clear in recognizing the influence of their own culture, ideology and discipline before too much can be said of that which is observed, as the scientist's personal level of self-awareness, personal history and conditioning underlie the foundation for how science is conducted (Prattis 1996).

It is apparent to me that the epistemological separation between subject and object is nothing other than an extension and projection of the separation that exists within the self. Such separation is in fact encouraged by the Cartesian paradigm that separates the body, mind and spirit, while emphasizing and defining mechanistic priorities of investigation for all levels of natural phenomena. The paradigm of separation places limitations on scientific investigation and could be enhanced by the conceptual re-integration of body, mind and spirit through an emphasis on the reflective self-awareness of the subject as a starting point in scientific enquiry. It thus becomes necessary for scientists to recognize and resolve personal internal patterns of separation so that science in general may take a quantum leap into a more conceptually accurate foundation of enquiry.

Separation between the scientific and reflective mystical domains is relatively new in the history of humankind. Several thousand years ago it was assumed that the physical and metaphysical interpenetrated at many different levels and it was impossible to understand one without the other (Campbell 1986). The positivist revolution in rationality vigorously separated these domains of comprehension, producing an incomplete understanding of science on the one hand and a total denigration of all that a contemplative tradition had to offer on the other. This was illusory, for the domains of science and contemplation are complementary, particularly as the latter induces detachment from observation in order that reflexivity enters enquiry as self-awareness.

This is the major shortcoming of science at present, as the perceptual mind state of the observer in science is a random variable in the conduct of enquiry. Many scientists do not realize that the subject-object disjunction that underlies their methods of enquiry precisely describes the state of awareness of the scientific observer. Thus the instrument of observing, mapping and reporting is highly random in an enterprise that prides itself on rigor. The rigor of the contemplative tradition assumes that through the discipline of meditation the perceptual-cognitive apparatus of the observer evolves to an awareness of multiple dimensions of reality, and that phenomena and events exist as connected levels of correspondence. As the individual evolves through different levels of awareness; then pattern, order and connection change, simply because the apparatus doing the perceiving, the human mind, has also changed in moving to a higher level of consciousness (Iyengar 1966; Barysenko 1994). Modern science is by and large on the bottom rung of this ladder of reflective self-awareness, whereas individuals who are disciplined in a contemplative tradition are sitting on the top of the ladder with a clear view of all the preceding rungs and steps, awaiting the appearance of the next ladder at which time one's present awareness will constitute the bottom most rung.

In the contemplative traditions this is what meditational techniques are designed to do in a rigorous and progressive manner. The particular steps, techniques and sequences of meditation provide one's awareness with a boost up the ladder of perceptual accuracy so that current levels of conscious awareness are transcended and one comes closer to perceiving reality as it ultimately is. The major stumbling blocks to this progression are the biases, distortions and perceptual barriers to our understanding the multidimensional nature of self and of reality. The task in overcoming this obstacle becomes one of recognizing the internal barriers to one's own perceptual clarity, so that one may more readily see things as they are. Here an analogy with superconductors in physics may be useful: when there is no resistance in the conduction of information or energy, a quantum leap in the quality and quantity of what is being communicated takes place. This analogy implies that the next step in human and scientific evolution requires the removal of internal resistances so that higher levels of conscious awareness and perceptual clarity may be achieved, both within oneself and science. Thus, as one experiences and integrates higher levels of conscious awareness, radically different kinds of perceptions and understandings are possible. This proposed direction for the nature of research has the potential to move one's reflexive self-awareness through to a resistance-free communication system with others, all within the domain of a higher order of knowledge. However, one must be aware of first steps. So, how does one remove those illusive internal barriers?

The Importance of Breath, Focus and Meditation

I would argue that the first step is through breath, with focus, in meditation. Meditation is often described as the space between thoughts, yet there is much more to it than that. Associated with meditation is a focus on form, colour, sound, movement or symbol that precisely keys in to an individual's level of awareness. In this way the tools associated with meditation can be applied to taking the next step up the ladder of consciousness (Prattis 1996b). The form of meditation varies according to particular personality preferences, cultural prescriptions and individual levels of awareness, yet the process of movement from one level of awareness to a yet higher level is universal. The propelling vehicle for movement is meditation in its many forms. For through this diversity a unitary process emerges, a common human experience of stillness.

Throughout one's journey to stillness there is an important constant of focus. It is the *conscious* focus through breath to integrate mind, body and soul. At different stages the focus is on particular meditation sequences, at yet other stages it may well be upon symbols, chants, mantra, mandalas or sacred dance. The symbolic forms and sequences are designed to cut through one's mental clutter and bodily agitation in order that the meditative focus penetrates to deeper and more integrative levels of consciousness. As thought, phenomena and other distractions arise in meditation one simply returns to the symbolic focus of the meditation, to once more cut through one's mental clutter and bodily agitation. The experience of nothingness is the ideal state in meditation, yet it takes considerable self-awareness to experience this state. Without a conscious focus through breath there is a fragmentation of experience. So one emerges through form and structure in meditation - variously expressed in different traditions - to a conscious focus, through breath, which becomes the constant in everything one does.

Science and Synchronicity

In the scientist's struggle to understand general laws and principles it is often paradoxical to find that the bigger picture, once it is revealed, turns out to be a simple and straightforward equation. The bigger picture includes everything -- the Universe, the earth, humankind, animals, plants and the cell -- and connects each of these elements into one interrelated system. The procedure to study the interconnectedness of each component is not by starting with the object of study, but by starting with the subject doing the studying. As scientific method moves to include the scientist's self-awareness as an integral part of enquiry, the implications for an exponential leap in discovery are elicited and revealed, together with a higher understanding of both subject and object. Thus the exponential rate of discovery is balanced out as the object of study, and the subject doing the study, move toward a different order of enquiry into both subject and object. It is those scientists who are involved in the practice of internal discovery who will extend the foundations of scientific enquiry beyond present parameters. Indeed the procedure to study the interconnectedness of all phenomena starts with individual responsibility for self-awareness and continues with what that awareness leads to. The enormous exponential power of this consideration has wider implications. It is that individuals in their own right can make a difference to science, civilization, the planet and human evolution by simply taking responsibility for their own internal journey.

The implications of science as synchronicity are perhaps a trifle astonishing. First, there is a fundamental axiom about the necessary conjointness of the metaphysical with the physical. Secondly, this conjointness is expressed holographically on multiple levels that are interconnected. "Holographic" refers to the communication of a total energy event, whereby each part of the event is encoded with the structure of the whole (Grof 1993; Wilbur 1985). An identical structure is found on corresponding levels -- the Universe, the planet, the human brain, body, cell and subatomic particles. The task for science is the exploration of the intricate systems of connection that enfold these multiple levels of correspondence into one comprehensible system. This is why science must study the largest possible set of correspondences rather than reduce the material of study to the smallest set of elements (Bohm 1980).

This approach may enable the human brain, which currently operates in fragmentation and within the limits of specialization, to be entrained to function as a whole holographic energy event, placing all levels of phenomena within one synchronistic system (Wilbur 1985). Thus the physical and metaphysical may be seen as mirrors for one another, in that they have identical structures with different manifestations. The holographic paradigm required for one to entertain this perspective does not have correlates within standard notions of time and space. Thus mythology is invited onto the centre stage of enquiry as it is not restricted to time and space constraints (Campbell 1968; Noel 1990). The microcosm-macrocosm series of linkages from cell to body, body to planet, planet to cosmos is programmed into countless mythologies that liken the Universe to a living body that is fashioned from cellular structure. As an industrialized civilization imbued with science, we are now only dimly aware of this documentation encoding synchronicity with mythology. The current scientific worldview is unrelated to any sense of mythology -- personal or collective. It is based on the conditioned brain reproducing specialization and separation. The essence of being human calls for something different, so that science does not lose sight of the quest for the structure of the harmony enfolding multiple levels of correspondence (Bohm 1980).

This is what science as synchronicity is all about. The creative spiral of the intuitive leap and disciplined research procedure brings unity into practices that currently remain separate -- the mystical and the scientific. They are in fact complementary, for they investigate the same material -- the fundamental properties of matter. The connecting intricacies between levels of correspondence may be unravelled in the stillness experienced in meditation. This discipline is inescapable and is part of an unfolding implicate order that could lead the sage and the scientist to similar conclusions (Weber 1985).

The basic structure of matter unfolds through the connections instituted by conscious breath. The investigation of meditation is into the deepening relationship between one's awareness and one's inner consciousness, and connecting this to the bigger Universal picture. This is the fundamental relationship of matter and as this understanding changes and evolves then so does one's understanding of, for example, cellular material and interplanetary structure. The deepening knowledge of how energy works with breath in meditation and how it connects to cellular information, reveals the template of the fundamental relationships of matter that are replicated in multiple dimensions. The primary investigation is an internal one and the premise of investigation is very simple -- physical and metaphysical, internal and external are mirrors for one another.

Interpenetrance of Physical and Metaphysical: Two Examples

I would like to give two examples to support the views I have expressed. First of all attention is paid to the OM mantra, then I will discuss the cell from both a metaphysical and physical perspective.

In the yogic traditions of meditation, mantras are Sanskrit words of power considered to be essential for the internal journey of self-knowledge. The resonance of the sound of the mantra operates as a total energy system that first of all engages with and calms the clutter of the mind so that stillness can be experienced. I think of each syllable in a mantra as a set of tonal frequencies that resonate with cellular templates and activate energy centres in the body, connecting and unifying them into a single integrated system (Prattis 1996b; Saraydarian 1990).

The variation in pitch, tone and resonance adjusts the effect of the mantra's set of frequencies to the energy centre's capacity to receive activation. The repetition of mantra is to take one deeper into the resonance of syllables (external form) with activated energy centre or chakra (inner essence). The energy encased in the vibrational structure of mantra works on multidimensional levels within the cell and being. Furthermore, the combinations of different syllables in mantra have different effects when one moves from the external form to the inner experience. The external form is when one chants the mantra out loud. The next step is to form the sound of the mantra without chanting it. This is a prelude to the penultimate step of thinking the mantra quietly within. The final step is not to think at all, nor is it to shape the sound of the mantra. One allows it to arise spontaneously from deep within one's being. The same mantra thus has four levels of experience that moves one progressively from external form to transcendental experience, from the periphery of one's true expression to the essence of it. The different mantras, and the levels within each mantra operate on different wavelengths, i.e. with discrete resonances. Thus each mantra affects specific parts of one's cells, body, mind and being, producing connection and transformation.

One of the most widely known forms of mantra is the omniscient sacred syllable OM. It is a primordial sound, inherent in the Universe, and the Vedas teach that when one goes deep into one's own being that is the sound that is heard, spontaneously arising. After it is chanted out loud on the out-breath there is a pause and a long silence and its internal sound in one's mind can extend over several breaths. The sound of OM allows the statement of where an individual is and their potential for oneness to be put out into the Universe. The Universe is already one and whole and responds to the resonance of OM's sound in the following silence. This secures a foundation for the next issuing forth of OM, which deepens the experience through repetition. One can then move to other levels of this mantra, until one allows it to spontaneously arise from within.

OM as mantra has four phases. In Sanskrit there are three letters A, U, M and a following silence that constitutes OM, Divinity without limitations. As it is practiced in meditation A, U, M denotes at one level the impure state of the meditator and at the same time OM is the pure Universal state of consciousness. It is the necessary silence between the ending and the new beginning of each OM that enables one to abandon self-consciousness and personal afflictions and allow the exalted nature of Universal mind, speech and body to become part of one's transformation (Prattis 1996b).

It is common knowledge in physics that the energies of the Universe can be categorized as the forces of creation, maintenance and destruction (Capra 1983). In Hindu cosmology these energies are represented by the deities of Brahma, Vishnu and Siva. The sound of the mantra OM (A-U-M), takes this connection a step further. The Sanskrit symbols for A, U, M correspond at one level to the deities of Brahma, Vishnu and Siva respectively, and therefore to the categories of Universal energy identified in physics. When the OM mantra is chanted these cosmological metaphors of Universal energies enter the body directly, because different parts of the breathing system are affected through its vibration. The A syllable which begins at the back of the mouth is felt in the abdominal area of the breathing system, the U syllable in the middle of the mouth impacts the chest area and the final M syllable chanted through closed lips activates the respiratory system in the throat and head. Each sound activates specific energy flows from the cellular level to the respiratory level and the combination of A-U-M activates and enlivens one's entire breathing system. In this example one begins at the level of science and the cosmological representations of the forces and functions recognized by physics -- creation, maintenance and destruction. This connection is taken from the mind into the body and cells through the vibrations of the OM mantra. Thus one begins with the Universe and proceeds through mental concepts, symbolic metaphor and vibration to encompass physics, cosmology, mind, body and cell. All of this rests on a simple axiom -- internal and external, physical and metaphysical are not different, rather they are synchronistic levels of correspondence of the same underlying reality, and the connection between all of them is human awareness (Prattis 1996b). Figure 2 illustrates these connections.

Figure 11.2: Om Mantra

O M (A - U - M)

PHYSICS	HINDU MYTHOLOGY	O M	BODY
CREATION	BRAHMA	A	ABDOMEN
MAINTENANCE	VISHNU	U	CHEST
DESTRUCTION	SIVA	M	THROAT

The Cellular Dance

My second example is one that involves a metaphysical and physical perspective on the cell. I think of cellular activity as a dance, with a master choreographer at the centre -- the cellular nucleus -- which orchestrates how all the parts contribute to the whole. The purpose of this dance is to provide the body with a continual source of energy for cell regeneration and reproduction, so that the body remains healthy and vital. In the process of the cellular dance genetic information is released and new cellular form takes shape. I think that the dimensions of this cellular form are best understood as having both physical and metaphysical properties.

"The mind in the cell" and "the soul in the cell". These phrases appear in much contemporary literature on religious philosophy (Chopra 1991; Dossey 1992). What do they mean? A metaphysical explanation views the cell as having more than just physical properties. Intrinsic within each of us lies the capacity and potential to draw from inner consciousness an innate wisdom and knowledge that may guide us throughout life. From this perspective the cell may be seen as the holder of the knowledge and wisdom, deep within one's being, that serves one's mind -- i.e. cellular memory. Furthermore, it is the source through which the soul may guide one toward fulfilling our own unique potential as one learns to "listen" to what one's body is saying through the cell - body - mind communication system.

It is also necessary to consider the physical properties of the cell to see how the metaphysical and physical aspects work together as one integrative system. So we need to understand how energy moves proteins, enzymes and molecules from one part of the cell to another. This is an essential component in comprehending the working of the bigger integrative system -- physical and metaphysical. So, to fully appreciate the cellular dance of evolution our perspective on the cell must change so that different answers can emerge to questions about cellular activity, questions like "How does the mind influence the body's cellular activity?" "How is cellular activity either mobilized or exhausted?" "What triggers protein activity to move information bearing molecules from one part of the cell to another?" and "What activates the genetic information that puts enzymes to work repairing cellular damage?"

A first step toward answering these questions is to consider the cell's activity from a different perspective -- that of the molecular level. Instead of seeing the cell as a minute part of the physical organism, the molecular view may be seen as a vast array of different cross cutting transport systems that operate independently of one another. The cell would appear to be like a modern city with bus, railway, rapid transit and underground systems. Taxis, trucks, skytrains, helicopters, escalators, hovercrafts, boats and even hot air balloons complete the analogy. All of these transport systems, and more, are there to move energy around this vast city, from one part of the cell to another. However, in the cellular city things are highly discrete. Not all of the transport systems are available to take all molecules and enzymes from one part of the cell to another. Different systems of connection come into operation only when particular proteins are ignited to provide both the vehicle and the discrete commuter pathway for particular information bearing molecular passengers to get on board. In other words, particular types of transport system are only appropriate for particular types of molecules. There is a series of transport systems in the cellular city that lie dormant. This implies that there are many molecules that are not transported from one part of the cell to other parts. Thus specific areas of the cell are underused and information is not moved to where it may otherwise activate cellular templates. A.T.P. (adenosine triphosphate) is the super unleaded gas of the cell, and it too must be activated and burned off to provide the high grade fuel to set hundreds of different transport systems into motion.

The transport analogy goes only so far in helping to map the nature of cellular activity. This initial understanding is helpful, however, as a stepping stone to seeing the cell as a multidimensional series of layers of transport systems, activated by proteins and enzymes so that information is moved from one part of the cell to another. Everything is connected to a central nucleus. The cellular nucleus co-ordinates and directs the cellular dance within the body. It has the job of organizing genetic information so that proper reproduction takes place. It organizes a highly complex internal energy system and also responds to externally introduced energy. However, this central conductor does not always have a full orchestra to play with, as particular transport systems and connections are not wired in to commands that permit the cell to operate at its maximum potential. It is as though half the violin section is missing and the trombones do not come in on time.

So there are great puzzles to unravel about the remarkable activity that takes place within the cell. This is particularly apparent in the way the cellular nucleus organizes repair work to damaged D.N.A. (Fiess 1989). (D.N.A. - deoxyribonucleic acid is the molecular basis of heredity and evolution. At cell division the double helix of D.N.A. opens up with half of the helix going to each new cell, so that the stored genetic information is transmitted to the next generation). Environmental hazards such as ultraviolet light and radiation damage D.N.A. Yet at the same time a response is triggered from the cellular nucleus to repair the damage in complex and highly efficient ways (Fiess 1989). Certain enzymes become activated and remove damaged sections of D.N.A. for repair, while other enzymes knit the D.N.A. structure back together. So, there are genes that regulate the repair functions of D.N.A. and the genetic repair instructions are activated by environmental damage. Unrepaired damage to D.N.A. interferes with the proper reproduction and release of genetic information and results in malfunctioning and mutant cells that are the instigators of disease. But in some individuals the cellular nucleus is unable to activate the repair enzymes, and mutant information is passed on to the next cell generation. This leads to a number of questions. "How is it that cellular repair is activated in some individuals and not others?" "Why are there latent, inactive parts of the cell?" "Can enzymes that repair D.N.A. damage be activated through externally introduced energy?"

The answer to these questions, and questions like them cannot be fully addressed from the physical level of biology alone, so a metaphysical level must be entertained. The dimension that I think is most pertinent is the conscious use of breath and symbolic focus in meditation. One effect of conscious breathing with focus is to accelerate the natural functions of the cell and boost the movement of molecules aboard proteins -- this enhances what already takes place at the cellular level (Prattis 1996b). The multidimensional levels involved place the cellular nucleus at the core of this synchronistic connection. Synchronicity implies that the structure of the Universe is replicated in many domains -- on the planet, in the body, in mythology as it emerges as stories from our unconscious and finally as a structure imprinted at the cellular level. The question then arises as to how one may access these different information systems connected in multiple layers around the cellular nucleus. Herein enters the passage of mind, i.e. human awareness. Balanced synchronicity between levels occurs when the soul in the cell, the entire Universal structure encased at the cellular level, meets one's mind -- viz. we become aware of all the connections, and this is facilitated through the experience of stillness in meditation. The mind in the cell and the soul in the cell is a meeting place that each one of us is uniquely ordained to enjoy, yet there is so much blocking this appointment that the meeting frequently becomes permanently postponed.

The integration with one's soul in the cell takes one to deeper levels of awareness of cellular knowledge, for herein dwells the inner consciousness I have referred to. This boundless reality of being is, however, cluttered with debris from genetic heritage, conditioning and karma. These dimensions are real, they have vibrational frequencies of energy that structure molecular strands within the cell so that they are responsive to the energy of afflictive emotions such as anger, fear and desire. It is all laid out in the cell - (1) the molecular patterns that take energy towards entropy and (2) the connector highways that take afflictive emotions to these same patterns. When these patterns and connections are put together, road blocks are created that deny the passage of one's awareness to inner consciousness. The purpose of meditation and the cultivation of a clear mind is to remove the blocks and cellular strands of information that pertain to the creation of entropy, negativity and chaos. Different forms of focus within meditation are in fact tonal designs or vibrational frequencies that correspond to a "deconstruct" program which attacks the tonal designs of entropic molecular strands built into the cell. The delicate surgery of removal and reversal of debris requires precision, for the vibrational frequencies inherent in a particular symbolic sequence can only go to work on particular molecular strands. The key is conscious breath as the means to deliver tonal chords to the cell in order to deconstruct particular molecular patterns that are embedded there. The attention to detail within the meditational sequence is important. Even more important is the foundation of stillness and emptiness that allows the surgery of deconstruction to take place. What is involved here is a paradigm shift to a more inclusive medical model (Lerner 1994; Dossey 1995; Chopra 1993; Moyers 1995; Prattis 1996; Rossi 1986).

My argument about the conjunction between the cell's physical and metaphysical properties may become clear through examining the effects of viruses on the cell, particularly the activities of retroviruses. Retroviruses have the ability to convert their R.N.A. to D.N.A. in cells they have entered, and place the manufactured D.N.A. into a chromosome of the host cell and thus direct the synthesis and reproduction of viral proteins (Verma 1990; Scott 1987). These properties of genetic adaptability and conversion need to be understood so that one may formulate a solution that prevents viral information being introduced to the human cell; otherwise this information is reproduced at cell division and multiplies throughout the body. The retrovirus gains entry to the human cell by keying on to a protein on the coat of the human cell, and delivers viral information to the host cell's cytoplasm. This information is embodied in a strand of the virus's R.N.A. whereas the host cell's genetic instructions are carried in D.N.A. Viral enzymes known as reverse transcriptase convert the viral R.N.A. to a strand of D.N.A. and help to fit that D.N.A. into the genome of the host cell. With this integration the retroviral D.N.A. is copied by enzymes in the host cell's nucleus and the retroviral D.N.A. then directs the synthesis of viral proteins and sends them out as messenger R.N.A.'s to penetrate new cells. The host cell's protein synthesizing capacity has been taken over by the viral messenger R.N.A.s (Velma 1990). Viral genetic material remains in the host cells until it is stimulated by any one of a variety of triggers. At the point of stimulation the retrovirus starts to replicate itself throughout the body.

The host cell receives the retrovirus because it assumes the entry signal from the retrovirus is legitimate. The retrovirus is an information-bearing structure made up of a set of energy frequencies or tones. We know from what I have said before about latent, underused parts of the cell that inside the human cell is a vast, unheard symphony of tones and frequencies. The manner in which the human cell can resist these intrusive and uninvited guests is to raise the vibrational frequency of the cell so that the virus encounters a tonal set of frequencies that does one or both of two things. The first is that entry into the human cell is denied. The viral "keys" that unlock the protein gateways to the cell are not allowed to fit -- it is as though the lock to the cellular door has been changed. Secondly, the altered tone of human cellular frequency causes the component structure of the virus to disintegrate, as it becomes confused as an information structured organism. The virus has the genetic adaptability and information to enter the human cell, and copy human D.N.A. structure. When this viral information encounters a cell vibrating with frequencies that deny access and replication, the viral information structure goes into a "Does not compute" mode and self-destructs. This self-destruct program is initiated by the raised tonal frequency of the human cell which causes the base connections of the viral D.N.A. structure to pull apart and destroy its replicative functions (Prattis 1996b).

Thus the solution to viral diseases that are species threatening does not entirely lie within pharmacology, drug or other allopathic therapies. These address and often alleviate symptoms, but do not fully deal with the cause of viral intrusion into the human cell. The overall solution lies with changing the tone, frequencies and connectedness of cellular templates, and developing the vaccines and procedures that facilitate this. One procedure that rarely commands scientific attention is the key provided by breath, meditation and symbolic focus. This works as a cathartic boost to the cellular activity of the body's immune system. Whenever a virus infects the human cell the body naturally launches an immediate counter attack of antibodies, made up of proteins, that target the virus for demolition. When one adds the conscious use of breath to the counter attack this promotes the activation of dormant frequencies and transport structures within the cell, which then greatly enhances the body's natural response through its immune system. So the act of changing the vibrational frequency of the cell through conscious breathing will lead to a more vigorous attack on the information strands being introduced to the human cell, first as viral R.N.A., then D.N.A., and finally as integrated messenger R.N.A.

Vibrational frequencies in the cell can thus be thought of as tones, much as a musical scale is composed of a sequence of tones. From this point of view it is possible to view the genome as a multidimensional set of tones. Each set of connections on the D.N.A. strand is held together by base pairs being pulled together by the frequency of energy that connects them. At cell division this frequency changes so that the D.N.A. strands separate and go their different ways into new cells. Each gene on the genome carries instructions for a single protein; the discrete vibrational frequency or tone for each protein catalyses hundreds of energy impulses. So conceptualizing tone and vibrational frequency as fundamental to the sequence and pattern of genetic structure is one step. The next step is to consider the effects of conscious breath in meditation on cellular frequencies and there are a number of implications to examine. For example, given that much cellular material is dormant, the process that activates, regenerates and connects latent cellular templates with active ones is meditation, which then communicates discrete energy pulses to particular locations throughout the body. This serves to mobilize and connect the previously unused latent parts of the cell and provide one with more players in the orchestra of the cellular dance. An array of tones is thus introduced to the cell through meditation that activates dormant cellular structures. The implication here is that one effect of conscious breath and focus in meditation is to raise the vibrational frequency of the cell so that it is performing with a full orchestra and an exhaustive supply of tones and frequencies are available to deconstruct viral intruders that seek to emulate human D.N.A. structure and invade the cell. The cellular nucleus is now armed with a vast array of detector devices and "destroyer" tones to be deployed automatically when viral information is introduced to the cell.

A common practice in meditation is to visualize breath coming in through the heart centre which is then directed by thought to different parts of the body, connecting to other energy centres. What takes place at the cellular level during this process is that a particular set of tonal frequencies is brought into the body by thought and experienced physically, as the vibration of the meditational sequence matches up with a corresponding tonal frequency within the cell. The emphasis on different symbolic sequences at particular stages of meditation may amplify a particular molecular frequency that already exists in the cell or activate a protein-ignited transport system that has been dormant. At other stages of meditation the consequence of conscious breath and focus brings a tonal set into the cell so that it can deconstruct entropic cellular strands which would otherwise diminish the body's potential as an efficient and effective cellular transport vehicle. Thus the use of conscious breath and meditation has far ranging effects on cellular activity -- it amplifies and boosts existing structures, plugs in latent transport systems and deconstructs entropic cellular strands of information.

As one continues the discipline of meditation using different forms of symbolic focus, the tonal frequency of the entire cell is raised. So when a retrovirus attempts to gain entry into a healthy cell, it is met by a heightened energy system that no longer allows it to key into surface protein entry points. The information that the virus tries to pass on is now rejected and the virus can no longer perform its designed function. This results in the confusion of the viral informational structure and it is unable to persist in its present form; so the virus deconstructs. An understanding of the effects of conscious breath on cellular activity has tremendous implications in the areas of molecular biology and energetics. As the conscious use of breath and symbolic focus in meditation is further accepted as a legitimate source of health promotion by western scientific communities, a whole new arena for scientific investigation may find the answers to otherwise fatal diseases. In other words, if we shift or expand our present medical paradigm we then ask different questions. The present pharmaceutical and medical research which develops drugs to interfere with different phases of a retrovirus's activity is essential. This, however, treats only the physical properties of cellular activity and ignores important axioms about synchronicity and science -- between the Universe, mind, body and cell -- and totally ignores the role of human awareness and consciousness. As one adopts the meditative discipline of conscious breath and focus, a physical and metaphysical synchronistic connection becomes evident because multidimensional levels of cellular activity are mobilized. What is introduced into the body through meditation is a set of tones which enhance the cellular transport system which then has further implications for the effectiveness of the bio-immune system and other still uncharted areas for medical science to research.

This assertion about synchronicity is not contradictory to present medical research into the development of vaccines that either repel the virus from the cell or interfere with the developmental stages of the virus once it is in the cell. This arm of medical science is essential;

it just needs to be stretched beyond its present boundaries. An extension of this medical model simply considers the increase in the body's efficiency and effectiveness which is caused by raising the vibrational frequency of one's cellular tones through the use of conscious breath. This boosts the immune system's capacity to recognize viral intruders and rapidly triggers an attack on them by mobilizing the antibodies already present in the body.

It is as though tidal waves of undiminishing energy are taken through the body by conscious breath to enhance the natural functions of the cell and furthermore remove debris. Tidal waves are more than a useful analogy. They are a phenomena in nature that have recently acquired additional scientific respectability as a worthy object of study. The tidal wave became known in science as a soliton, as it had properties that operated both as particle and wave and therefore a kinship with elementary particles like the photon and electron. In biology, scientists have begun to suspect that microscopic solitons move energy to and within the cell. A protein molecule is composed of a central group of atoms - carbon, hydrogen, nitrogen and oxygen - and it vibrates in accordance with the bonding energy between atoms of carbon and oxygen. In addition there are hundreds of clumps of other atoms linked to the protein core. The total configuration provides each protein with a distinctive vibration. The energy of a single protein, once it is activated, generates countless reactions and processes in the cell and does not dissipate in intensity as one would expect. This kind of behaviour is usually attributed to tidal wave pheonena. So, these protein waves of undiminishing energy pulses may well be the force that breaks the double helix apart both at cell division and whenever parts of the genetic code need to be replaced or replicated. These solitons in the cell also have the power to deconstruct retroviruses, and I would argue that they can be activated by the meditative process.

These activated solitons travel through the cell and trigger once dormant frequencies which then attack those genetic structures which were programmed to take energy towards entropy. It is akin to an express train that encounters debris on its tracks yet it smashes through without pause and the debris disintegrates. Nothing then can block the movement of important information from one part of the cell to another. The principle of the soliton is a Universal principle, and therefore must exist at all levels; on the oceans, in fibre optic cables, in the Universal formation of quasars, and in the cell. With the characteristics of wave and particle the soliton as energy pulse clears debris and continues in undiminished form, seemingly unaffected by the laws governing entropy. At the cellular level this is facilitated through conscious breath. All that is necessary is the entry of the clear mind into the cell.

This is what is at stake when one contemplates the mind and the soul in the cell. It is necessary that the mind, viz. -- human awareness -- enters the equation in a totally conscious way, so that one's birthright of connecting the mind and the soul in the cell takes place and one keeps the preordained appointment. The first step toward fulfilling that appointment is simply recognizing that the entire structure of the Universe is present at the level of the cell. The conscious focus of one's mind directs awareness toward accessing one's inner consciousness, the soul in the cell. This is the meeting place of the clear mind with the soul in the cell. The meditational structure one uses directly corresponds to a particular vibration which is then introduced into one's cells. The purpose of this is to engage with one's inner consciousness at yet deeper levels. The stillness of one's mind in meditation facilitates this as one reaches further within, touching yet deeper levels of what is commonly referred to as Godself, Krisna consciousness, the Buddahood within All, or other metaphors denoting the same cellular frequency and level of consciousness. They all refer to inner movement in the same direction. With practice one learns to recognize the specific tone associated with particular meditational structures. The cell, with its vast panorama of tonal sets, has only a portion of them activated at any one time. Meditation is a process that helps to bring those dormant tones of the cell into song, so that the master choreographer at the core of our being -- the cellular nucleus -- now has a full scale of tones to play with.

A further thought -- if much of the cell is asleep, this implies that the evolutionary potential of our species lies dormant. Focused breath is the catalyst to make manifest that which is latent, to bring potential into form. This energy is transformative, as information of a different quality and quantity is now available to be released and experienced within one's own life. So, as cellular transport systems are continually opened up and made available, information that once was dormant can now be engaged with cognitively. The entire cellular structure, now operating at a higher vibration, is able to choreograph a cellular dance that facilitates our evolutionary potential, which I feel is not so much in the area of physical change, but lies in the enhancement and change of our mental capacities.

The biology and physics of the cell is a fascinating area of study in its own right, yet it alone can only take one so far (Thomas 1974). The cell becomes an even more remarkable area of study when the necessary metaphysical perspective is considered (Prattis 1996b). Through symbolic focus, one draws on constructs and metaphors that allow energy to go from symbolic frequency to bodily vibration, to cellular impulse. The body, responding to the cells, provides one with an internal information source that is precise. This is why it is very important to "listen" carefully to one's body while in a meditative state of stillness. To come back to my opening remarks on the cell -- the soul is in the cell. The mind has to get there, and then it meets itself in the soul. There is ultimately no difference between the phrases, "the soul in the cell" and "the mind in the cell". This is where one ultimately moves to in meditation.

The cellular arena is quite extraordinary (Watson 1989). There is much taking place that has both physical and metaphysical correlates. For instance, the approach to species threatening viruses is clear: change the vibrational frequency of the cell. Enhance the process through the discipline of conscious breath from a place of stillness and emptiness. Cellular destructive diseases have been reversed through a process of meditation that defies scientific explanation, yet they can be understood if we include a metaphysical perspective on the cell. The "miracles" within medical history are not a mystical illusion. They are an indication of what is possible when we put metaphysics and physics together and look at the cell with new eyes, with a different perspective. In other words, we entertain a new paradigm.

Conclusion

The discussion of paradigms and science has been taken into a different discourse about the significance of the OM mantra and expanded in my discussion of the cellular dance. I have introduced new concepts and perspectives that reduce distortion in perception and enhance our understanding of events.

The understanding that comes with increasing self-awareness often does not appeal to the logic of intellect or to the linear form of reasoning that is the *modus operandi* of our present global civilization. Logic, intellect and linear reasoning do have their place, but it is within a different level of understanding. One that sees connections between different levels of correspondence and seeks the significance of those connections by listening in stillness for inspiration and insight. With the overall context of understanding placed in this domain, then the logic of intellect and linear reasoning become essential mapping devices for connections to be organized and ordered through what one's mind and intelligence can do. With that awareness, insights are revealed that are astonishing. Great scientists and thinkers have always operated thus, but rarely made it public as their audience and system of support would not hear of it. Yet not a single scientist, musician, politician or public figure who has made radical connection a point of transformation has done so without insight from higher intelligence.

A progression of consciousness is thus required to absorb all that has been presented so far. The conceptual dance of science is to the choreography of synchronicity that treats internal and external, physical and metaphysical as levels of correspondence that reflect a common unifying structure. The false separation between scientific and reflective domains is unsatisfactory and leads me to suggest an alternative emphasis on the evolutionary potential for science and civilization that is provided by the inner journey of meditation. This leads to the idea that the fundamental nature of reality is a synchronistic structure of formations derived from connecting self-awareness to inner consciousness, and brings attention to the power of conscious breath and symbolic focus in meditation. This is the paradigm shift which this work explicates.

Bibliography

Barker, J.A.
1985 The Business of Paradigms. Minneapolis: Charthouse International Learning Corporation

Barysenko, J.
1994 Fire in the Soul. N.Y: Warner Books Inc.

Bohm, D.
1980 Wholeness and the Implicate Order. London: Routledge and Kegan Paul

Bohr, N.
1938 Natural Philosphy and Human Cultures. Nature V. 143:268-272

Campbell, J.
1968 The Masks of God IV: Creative Mythology. N.Y.: Viking Press

1986 The Inner Reaches of Outer Space. N.Y.: Harper & Row

Capra, F.
1979 Dynamic Balance in the Subatomic World. Parabola V. IV, 2:60-65

1983 The Turning Point. N.Y.: Bantam Books

Chopra, D.
1991 Creating Health. Boston: Houghton Mifflin Company

1993 Ageless Body, Timeless Mind. N.Y.: Harmony Books

Clifford, J. and Marcus, G.
1986 (eds.): Writing Culture. The Poetics and Politics of Ethnography. Berkeley: University of California Press

Dossey, L.
1992 Meaning and Medicine. N.Y.: Bantam Books

Fiess, M.
1989 Remarkable Repairs: DNA 35 Years Later. Research V.9, 1:4-6

Grof, S.
1993 The Holotropic Mind: The Three Levels of Human Consciousness and How They Shape our Lives. San Francisco: Harper San Francisco

Iyengar, B.K.S.
1966 Light on Yoga. N.Y.: Schocken Books

Kuhn, T.
1970 The Structure of Scientific Revolutions. Chicago: University of Chicago Press

Lerner, M.
1994 Choices in Healing. Cambridge, Mass: M.I.T. Press

Moyers, B.
1995 (ed.): Healing and the Mind. N.Y.: Doubleday

Noel, D.L.
1990 (ed.): Paths to the Power of Myth. N.Y.: Crossroad

Prattis, J.I.
1996a Reflexive Anthropology. In The Encyclopedia of Cultural Anthropology. N.Y.: Henry Holt and Company Inc.

1996b Living Breath (Forthcoming)

Rappaport, R.
1994 Humanity's Evolution and Anthropology's Future. In Borofsky, R. (ed.): Assessing Cultural Anthropology:153-167. N.Y.: McGraw-Hill Inc.

Rosenau, P.
1992 Post-Modernism and the Social Sciences. Princeton: Princeton University Press

Rossi, E.L.
1986 The Psychobiology of Mind-Body Healing. N.Y.: W.W. Norton

Scott, A.
1987 Pirates of the Cell. Oxford: Basil Blackwell Books

Thomas L.
1974 The Lives of a Cell. N.Y.: Bantam Books

Tyler, S.
1987 The Unspeakable: Discourse, Dialogue and Rhetoric in the Postmodern World. University of Wisconsin Press

Saraydarian, T.
1990 The Psyche and Psychism. V. II. Sedona, Az: Aquarian Educational Group

Verma, I.M.
1990 Gene Therapy. Scientific American V.263, 5:68-84

Watson, T.D.
1989 The D.N.A. Gold Rush: D.N.A. 35 Years Later. Research V.9, 1:7-10

Wilbur, K
1985 Physics, Mysticism and the New Holographic Paradigm: A Critical Appraisal. In Wilbur, K (ed.): The Holographic Paradigm:157-186. Boston: Shambhala

Weber, R.
1985 Dialogues with Scientists and Sages. N.Y.: Routledge and Kegan Paul

Young, D. and Goulet, J.G.
1994 (eds.): Being Changed by Cross-Cultural Encounters. The Anthropology of Extraordinary Experience. Peterborough: Broadview Press

Chapter 12

Issues of Inner Ecology

Introduction: *Silent Spring* and Traditional Ecological Knowledge

Rachel Carson was a remarkable American woman. The publication of her book *Silent Spring* in 1962 was the major catalyst that transformed the fragmented and docile environmental movement of the 1950s into the more politically attuned and ecologically informed environmental movement of the present day (Norton 1991:120). She single-handedly shifted attention away from problems of land and resource protection, which had been the preoccupation of American environmentalists since the turn of the century, and focused on the more insidiously dangerous second and third generation problems of pollution. More dangerous, that is, to the health of the general population.

Her scientific credentials were impeccable, an important point to remember particularly in light of the chemical industry's attack on her credibility in the 1960s. She trained as a zoologist at the Pennsylvania College for Women, graduating *magna cum laude* in 1929, and earned a master's degree in zoology at Johns Hopkins University specializing in genetics (Logan 1992:66). She then worked as a career biologist with the U.S. Bureau of Fisheries and the Fish and Wildlife Service. In her published works she created a new vocabulary to talk about environmental issues and brought her understanding of ecological concepts into the discourse of public policy (Norton 1991:120). She wrote beautifully and graphically, yet initially not polemically. Her earlier works supported an ecological view of humility as the appropriate human response to the natural landscape that was inhabited, and in this she followed Albert Schweitzer's beliefs about reverence for the interconnectedness of all things.

> Life outside a person is an extension of the life within him. This compels him to be part of it and accept responsibility for all creatures great and small. Life becomes harder when we live for others, but it also becomes richer and happier.
>
> Frontispiece of M.F. Fox: *The Soul of the Wolf* (1980).

From the beginning her work was imbued with deeply held humanitarian and spiritual principles which became more explicit in her later work - particularly *Silent Spring* (1962). This book was written in a deliberately polemical style - not just to espouse ecological perception in its own right but to demonstrate in politically clear terms the threat to human survival caused by the indiscriminate use of pesticides. This publication evoked a huge controversy in the 1960s and as Norton points out,

> That controversy has set the parameters, as well as the tone, for much of the subsequent debate regarding environmental regulation and environmental policy (Norton 1991:121).

This book is based on sound and meticulous scientific research and it reveals in graphic terms the deadly effects of synthetic pesticides as they move through the webs of life into human bodies. She was taking on very large and powerful commercial interests and immense economic stakes -- which involved a forty-million dollar a year chemicals and agricultural industry. And of course the chemical and agricultural industry reacted in a predictable manner with threats of legal action against Carson's publishers, public relations exercises to attack the book, attempts to discredit Rachel Carson and a media campaign to persuade the public about the advantages of chemical pesticides. *Time* magazine in its September 29 issue in 1962 carried a caustic review of *Silent Spring* and in derogatory terms designed to undermine her credibility referred to Carson as a mystic, which was worse in that era than being labelled a communist.

Subsequent studies have, however, validated Carson's thesis beyond any shadow of a doubt. In October 1993 Professor J. Cummins, a geneticist at the University of Western Ontario, presented a paper at the public meetings of the International Joint Commission on Great Lakes Water Quality. He had traced the effects of atrazine, a herbicide used for over thirty years to control weeds in Ontario's corn fields. In a study with similar overtones to *Silent Spring* he considers atrazine to be more dangerous to human life than the long banned D.D.T., as it has been washed into ground water, streams, rivers and drinking water reservoirs, eventually making its way into the Great Lakes then through the St. Lawrence seaway to the oceans. Atrazine kills plankton, algae, fish populations and humans, and has been identified as the most common waterborne carcinogen to affect human bodies.

The U.S. Wildlife Fund published a set of scientific papers in 1992 edited by Theo Colburn. Scientists from very separate disciplines were arriving at similar conclusions about the devastating effects of synthetic pesticides on animal and human reproduction. Drawing on this earlier work, Colburn in 1996 went much further. Her book, *Our Stolen Future*, researches and documents how the toxins and chemicals used in industrial processes impersonate hormones and then disrupt the reproductive, nervous and immune systems in both animals and humans. She shows how the human endocrine system which controls cellular activities and bodily motor functions is at risk, as is the fertility of the human population. She cites studies that demonstrate a drastic decline in sperm count and the increasing infertility of college educated males in their twenties and thirties and concludes that human fertility in the twenty-first-century is clearly compromised. Colburn writes about the build up of synthetic pollutants and chemicals in the human body to the point that they can do an end run around the body's defences. Furthermore, researchers are identifying a growing number of synthetic chemicals that possess the ability to mimick hormones and then disrupt the neurological, immune and reproductive systems in both humans and animals. Singled out in particular are chlorine based substances, in addition to the toxic byproducts from pulp and paper mills (dioxins and furans), and the group of chemicals known as phthalates that are increasingly used in the plastics industry. These are all considered to be endocrine disruptors and are thought to be linked to embryo damage and breast cancer. Given their self-interests, it is hardly surprising that many industrialists, and scientists are openly dubious about these implications and conclusions, but in the 1990s writers such as Colburn cannot be readily silenced, thanks largely to the pioneering work of Rachel Carson in the 1960s. Al Gore, the Vice-President of the U.S.A., wrote the forward to Colburn's book and says of *Our Stolen Future* that it raises urgent and compelling questions that must be addressed.

Although Rachel Carson did not have this level of support, it is evident that her work has stood the test of time. Despite being attacked by the media she remained absolutely clear-headed. In *Silent Spring* she states:

> It is not my contention that chemical pesticides must never be used. I do contend that we have put poisons and biologically potent chemicals indiscriminately into the hands of persons largely or wholly ignorant of their potentials for harm (1962:22).

Underlying the contradiction between the popularity of Carson's *Silent Spring* and the counter-attack by the chemical industry and its media lackeys was a fundamental disagreement in basic values. To Carson the issue of pesticide use was a moral one whereas to manufacturers it was purely economic. This schism underlies most, if not all, environmental conflicts on the planet today where moralists converge in battle lines to oppose the phalanxes of economic self-interest

(Naess 1989:72). Carson's philosophical perspective is, however, very clear:

> We have subjected enormous numbers of people to contact with these poisons, without their knowledge. If the Bill of Rights contains no guarantee that a citizen shall be secure against lethal poisons distributed either by private individuals or by public officials, it is surely only because our forefathers, despite their considerable wisdom and foresight could conceive of no such problem (Carson 1962:22).

The moral issues invoked by Carson are clear in terms of citizens' rights. In her view they are not open to compromise, nor can they be brushed aside by the greed and logic of industrial capitalism that seeks maximum surplus value and profit irrespective of other considerations and consequences. The chemical and agricultural industries were equally clear in that the issues were strictly economic involving production costs, profits and jobs. This tension is larger than the specific issues around pesticide use. This moral versus economic schism is a template that surfaces everywhere as we are increasingly forced to examine the payoffs and costs that economic self-interest has for questions of environmental health and quality of life. What is becoming abundantly clear in this polarized debate, however, is that our present methods of production and consumption have simply become unsustainable.

In 1996 the U.N. Environment Program released a report called *Taking Action* which in stark and drastic terms demonstrates a rapid deterioration in every category of environmental quality from the water we drink, the food we eat, the air we breathe, the pollutants we ingest, to the oceans and forests that sustain life. The report warns that the planet is experiencing a mass extinction of life that is happening far faster than the worst-case scenarios of environmental alarmists. The industrial excesses of the human population are calculated to eliminate some two-hundred species of life every twenty-four hours (U.N. 1996), and at the same time these industrial processes pose an extreme threat to human existence itself. Schumacher (1973, 1977), Naess (1989), Russell (1988) and many other contemporary writers have, in different ways, amplified these points. They make it very clear that the global economic system relies on an impossible and unsustainable model of growth in political, social and ecological terms. The tension between their particular advocacies and the defenders of economic self-interest is very real and palpable. Although the specific issues vary, the template for conflict is remarkably similar and constitutes the cathartic crossroad for our global civilization to choose which way it is going to turn.

There is much more to Rachel Carson than I have briefly alluded to and I cannot do full justice to her impact, yet I would like to establish a number of fundamental premises that run through her career and work. In her own life and livelihood, Rachel Carson can perhaps be characterized as having a key spiritual quality of responsiveness, which is grounded in a personal sense of responsibility (Logan 1992:67). This she saw as one hope for the future. After *Silent Spring*, Carson wrote *The Sense of Wonder* (1965) which was published one year after her death. This volume is very reminiscent of Joseph Campbell's work on mythology, particularly the first function of myth -- which is to inculcate in the individual a sense of awe in the universe (Campbell 1988). In a similar vein Carson considered a sense of awe and wonder towards nature as an essential core element in human spirituality. It was as though she had internalized from some source the aboriginal ecological belief that humans are inextricably a part of nature. Just before her death Carson appeared on the CBS program entitled "The Silent Spring of Rachel Carson" (CBS 1963), and spoke of human maturity correlating with a profound attitude shift whereby humans are only a small component of a vast and incredible universe. Logan states:

> In her view for humans to declare war on nature is to declare war on ourselves. Our challenge is not to conquer nature but to come to terms with nature; "to prove our maturity and our mastery, not of nature, but of ourselves" (Logan 1992:69).

This is particularly poignant for me given my personal interest in wolves and dolphins, to mention only two species that I feel closely connected to. I have been dismayed and appalled at the systematic destruction and slaughter of these two particular species through human activity, as I believe that human beings and other species are not only of one globe, but share an interconnected essence that demands symbiotic relationships based upon respect. As we push these species into the endangered zone, humankind becomes in my mind no less endangered. In other words I would argue that we are physically and psychologically interdependent with nature and notions of human superiority serve to separate and alienate humans from the environment they live in. The seeds of potential entropy and destruction are sown in our concepts, attitudes and values. Thus we do not see the web of interconnectedness as it is because our worldview, our current paradigm, sees the environment and its resources in terms of how it can satisfy the needs of economic self-interest. The true morality of being fully human is necessarily lost and in claiming the world for ourselves in this way, the environment has become an extension of human egocentric needs and values -- an *egosphere* rather than an *ecosphere*. Similar themes underlie Carson's *The Sense of Wonder* which incidentally first appeared as an article titled *Help Your Child to Wonder*. She was certain that there was something deeper and transcendent beyond the boundaries of human existence and this infused her entire approach to ecology.

In quite explicit terms the concepts underlying Rachel Carson's work are expressed in statements of the traditional ecological knowledge of aboriginal populations. Chief Seattle's alleged communication to the president of the United States in 1852 is a sterling example of a Native American cosmology that unites human beings with the land and the universe. It finds a reflection in the work of Black Elk (Neihart 1972), Joseph Campbell (1988) and the mystical moralistic strain of environmentalism from John Muir through Rachel Carson to Arne Naess (Norton 1991). While questions have been raised as to whether the text can be totally attributed to Chief Seattle, it does stand as a blueprint statement of traditional ecological knowledge. It is as important to environmentalism as "*The Desiderata*" is to human hope and survival, irrespective of source. The text is worth quoting in its entirety.

The President in Washington sends word that he wishes to buy our land. But how can you buy or sell the sky? The land? The idea is strange to us. If we do not own the freshness of the air and the sparkle of the water, how can you buy them?

Every part of this earth is sacred to my people. Every shining pine needle, every sandy shore, every mist in the dark woods, every meadow, every humming insect. All are holy in the memory and experience of my people.

We know the sap which courses through the trees as we know the blood that courses through our veins. We are part of the earth and it is part of us. The perfumed flowers are our sisters. The bear, the deer, the great eagle, these are brothers. The rocky crests, the juices in the meadow, the heat of the pony, and man, all belong to the same family.

The shining water that moves in the streams and rivers is not just water, but the blood of our ancestors. If we sell you our land, you must remember that it is sacred. Each ghostly reflection in the clear waters of the lakes tells of events and memories in the life of my people. The water's murmur is the voice of my father's father.

The rivers are our brothers. They quench our thirst. They carry our canoes and feed our children. So you must give to the rivers the kindness you would give any brother.

If we sell you our land, remember that the air is precious to us, that the air shares its spirit with all the life it supports. The wind that gave our grandfather his first breath also receives his last sigh. The wind also gives our children the spirit of life. So if we sell you our land, you must keep it apart and sacred, as a place where man can go to taste the wind that is sweetened by the meadow flowers.

Will you teach your children what we have taught our children? That the earth is our mother? What befalls the earth befalls all the sons of the earth.

This we know: the earth does not belong to man, man belongs to the earth. All things are connected like the blood that unites us all. Man did not weave the web of life, he is merely a strand in it. Whatever he does to the web, he does to himself.

One thing we know: our god is also your god. The earth is precious to him and to harm the earth is to heap contempt on its creator.

Your destiny is a mystery to us. What will happen when the buffalo are all slaughtered? The wild horses tamed? What will happen when the secret corners of the forest are heavy with the scent of men and the view of the ripe hills is blotted by talking wires. Where will the thicket be?

> *Gone! Where will the eagle be? Gone! And what is it to say goodbye to the swift pony and the hunt? The end of living and the beginning of survival.*
>
> *When the last Red Man has vanished with his wilderness and his memory is only the shadow of a cloud moving across the prairie, will these shores and forests still be there? Will there be any of the spirit of my people left?*
>
> *We love this earth as a newborn loves its mother's heartbeat. So, if we sell you our land, love it as we have loved it. Care for it as we have cared for it. Hold in your mind the memory of the land as it is when you receive it. Preserve the land for all children and love it, as God loves us all.*
>
> *As we are part of the land, you too are part of the land. This earth is precious to us. It is also precious to you. One thing we know: there is only one God. No man, be he Red Man or White Man, can be apart. We are brothers after all.*

Charlene Spretnak has remarked that the exploration of such a nature-based philosophy as expressed in Native American spirituality made her realize "how very far our society is from comprehending, let alone abiding by, the deepest levels of ecological wisdom" (Spretnak 1986:18). For although Chief Seattle's alleged text is often referred to by environmentalists, the template offered is frequently ignored. We fail to realize that the balance between Mother Earth and the Creator, between the planet and the universe, is maintained by human beings choosing to retain a spiritual connection both to the Earth and to the Universe. So the global pollution crisis is not so much about the industrial excesses of our civilization, it is much deeper than that. It is about the absence of the sacred in our personal lives (Mander 1991).

Global pollution is about the absence of the spiritual connection so eloquently described in Chief Seattle's speech. Put very simply -- there is an external environmental pollution crisis because there is an internal pollution crisis in humankind. I would argue that the remedy is not to be found in North-South pacts, agreements on sustainable development or in international conferences on the environment. I think the remedy can only be found in a consciousness that deals directly with internal pollution. So the task is to transcend and move on from the internal garbage bags we carry around in our field of awareness, as these are the catalysts for the ills of our contemporary global civilization. This pile of garbage has been placed there by our judgments, fears, conceptions and confusions; all derived from the ideology and social structures within which we act. It colours all that we think, do and feel and has a colossal impact on the internal and external environments that we then create. So it is really not surprising that we live in an age of environmental crisis, of global pollution, for our garbage bags are taken from inside and dumped onto the world with our thoughts and attitudes. The logic of this argument leads to the assertion that our global environment will be restored to balance once our thoughts, values and attitudes shift and no longer sustain and feed our internal pollution. Thus recognition of our internal garbage bags and the manner in which they are dumped out on friends, family, loved ones and the planet is a first step and a supreme responsibility.

From Deep Ecology to Inner Ecology

This takes one into the area that has been defined as deep ecology by the Norwegian philosopher Arne Naess (1973, 1989). His claim that deep ecologists are a special breed of ecologists separate from shallow ecologists is not one I can accept. The position I advocate is that environmentalists do hold common ground expressed at different levels through diverse strategies. I prefer to avoid the pejorative aspect of Naess's comparison although I do believe the critical component to focus on is that of human consciousness. That can be expressed on many different levels as awareness changes and evolves and citizens respond to environmental issues in the best way that they can at the time. Although the deep ecology position has subsequently been softened (Fox 1986), I choose to focus on human consciousness but not in a manner that is pejorative to an audience that may not agree with my position. I think it is incumbent upon me as a citizen and a scholar to construct a compelling argument about the role of human consciousness with respect to environmental issues that may then provoke thought and a possible re-examination of entrenched positions.

The deep ecology I subscribe to has a much older tradition than Naess's writings and is found in Buddhist texts such as the Diamond Sutra which speak of interconnectedness and respect for the environment we are placed in. Thich Nhat Hanh, the Vietnamese Buddhist master, expounds on the Five Wonderful Precepts of the Buddha in his book *For a Future to be Possible* (1993). He shows how every Buddhist practitioner must be a protector of the environment and that the task before us is:

> to change society from its root, which is our collective consciousness where the root energies of fear, anger, greed, and hatred lie (1993:74).

He is concerned with the survival of our species on this planet and addresses this in his exposition of Buddhism. In this way he brings to the reader's attention an argument about moral conduct with respect to the individual, community, and the planet.

The question of interconnectedness has in fact gained a certain credibility in scientific and political circles. International and government agencies of the world's richest economies have been bombarded in the last decade with reports that demonstrate that there is a single ecosystem on the planet, and that discrete political and cultural systems, whatever their relative strength and power, are mere subsystems within a single ecosystem. If the ecosphere collapses then so will the dependent subsystems and it may be the wealthier nations that will have the greatest difficulty in adapting and surviving because poorer nations, closer to the margins of subsistence, are better equipped to survive a larger ecosphere collapse. It is also becoming more apparent that the planet we live on has the characteristics of an organism that includes us as an intimate part (Russell 1988: 6). This leads us ultimately towards the Gaia hypothesis of James Lovelock (1988), but first a diversion into my own activities, questions and dilemmas.

An Environmental Education

I have been an environmentalist all my life, long before I knew what the word meant. No one taught me to be so. It emerged from an intrinsic love of nature and rapport with animals. As a child I would often be late for school as the flowers and songbirds in the hedgerows would captivate my attention, particularly in springtime when creativity and new life exploded into being. I once attempted to explain my lateness in these terms to my schoolteacher. I was kept in at recess for my troublesome nature and made to write out one-hundred lines of "I will not be late for school." I adorned my punishment schedule with drawings of birds and spring buds and was then made to repeat the punishment. I did not understand this adult world, nor did I like it at the time. Something in me persisted, however. I redid my lines and once again drew birds on branches opening their beaks to sing joyously. I was kept in at recess for an entire week for my stubbornness yet refused to let go of my feelings for nature. Eventually the teacher gave up on punishing me for my drawings. I was eight-years old and that is when I learned to mistrust authority figures solely concerned with control and power. I was a relatively late starter in this recognition -- I realized at the age of eight that there was no point in telling the truth to an adult world that refused to listen. In looking back I am grateful to that particular adult because it is clear that my intimacy with nature and the environment was forever forged through the experience.

Yet what a transformation would have been created for the entire class had the teacher acted with sensitivity and wisdom and responded differently. He could have said,

> Class, I want you to listen to the wonderful things Ian saw and heard about nature on his way to school this morning. Perhaps you might all see and hear similar things. Maybe you'll all be late for class one morning and may even take me for a walk! Our studies this morning will be about the birds and animals and flowers that caught Ian's attention this morning.

As a child I had special relationships with wild animals -- in particular with one otter and a family of hedgehogs that I kept under my bed (the hedgehogs, not the otter). My parents were long suffering over the stray animals I brought home, however their patience was severely stretched over the hedgehogs. The hedgehogs had to be returned to the hedgerow when I became infested with their parasites and fleas which I passed on to my immediate family and classmates, and also to a particular school teacher that I was delighted to so infest!

My passion for nature was solitary; it had no encouragement from any quarter, perhaps because it needed none. I have subsequently made studies of wolf and dolphin behaviour, and was adopted by a wolf who lived with me in my home in the forest. I gave the wolf hybrid the highly original name of "Wolfie"! He had beautiful red fur with white markings. When I first met him he was running free in the interior mountains of British Columbia, and he immediately claimed ownership -- I was his! After showing me his mountain habitat and uncannily appearing every time I visited this area of British Columbia, he chose to live with me in my home in the forest. His presence of gentleness, patience and above all -- his loving heart -- were felt by everyone he encountered. On April 6, 1994, I was in the Arizona desert with an Apache medicine man, undergoing a ritual purification in a Native American sweat lodge. The third cycle of this ceremony was the round of the Red Wolf. The intense energy of this symbolic focus supported me in releasing internal patterns and I felt Wolfie's presence -- he made me smile. Unbeknownst to me during this round of the Red Wolf was that my red wolf in Canada had died from a heart attack at exactly that time. The news did not reach me in the desert for several days. The synchronicity and symbolism of this was shocking yet full of wonder and awe, for I know at the deepest level that he gave himself for me -- his life for the purification of my life journey. I celebrate his heartfelt love and the awesome gift he has bestowed on me. I trust this manuscript is a fitting tribute both to his great spirit and to the legacy left by Rachel Carson.

The fascination with dolphins lead to many adventures studying and swimming with them in their oceanic habitat. I was always exhilarated and totally humbled by their magnificent presence. Later on there was a turning point in my education about the environment and it occurred several years ago in 1990 when I decided to work for a number of environmental organizations as a canvasser. Usually my engagement with organizations was as a consultant, but one summer I decided to join the front line environmental workers in terms of educating the general public on their home doorsteps. I had already begun a process of talking to kindergarten and grade one and two classes about environmental issues and canvassing seemed to be a step in the same direction. It was, however, a re-education of myself about environmental issues. The summer I chose to step out in this manner was exceedingly hot and humid, and as I progressed through approximately ten-thousand homes in Ottawa and Kingston I was encouraged by how generous the general public was, irrespective of class, ethnicity, gender or occupation. As I stood dripping sweat on people's doorsteps talking about the environment, over 80% of the people canvassed contributed to the organizations I represented. Ambassadors, shop assistants, new immigrants from Korea, out of work labourers, politicians, school teachers, taxi drivers -- all were equally generous according to their means.

Yet something was missing, and I spent more and more time reflecting on what it was. My discussions with individual householders were about both local and global environmental issues. Recycling boxes, Great Lakes pollution, acid rain, rainforests and nuclear waste were all on the agenda as I had studied all of them, and more, in preparation for this job. But still I knew there was a major part of the jigsaw puzzle missing. It had two main components. The first was a lack of individual responsibility both for and towards the issues of environmental pollution. For the most part, members of the general public were happy to contribute generously to Friends of the Earth, Greenpeace, Pollution Probe or to kindred environmental groups, but there was no determination to dramatically shift their own patterns of product consumption or attitudes toward the environment. By and large they contributed to environmental groups so that some other body would take action and responsibility. Concern for environmental issues ended with their financial contributions. The second issue that struck me very forcibly was that hardly anyone I met that long, hot, humid summer were aware of any spiritual underpinning about how they and the environment interconnected. It is notable that this spiritual dimension was almost completely absent from the environmental organizations that I represented.

I spent considerable time thinking about this and about my own activities as an educator and an environmentalist. I knew it was important to step out and be visible and vocal as an environmentalist, yet most environmentalists I knew were exceedingly angry and violent individuals in their expressions to industry, government and the general public. This was not my way, and as a canvasser on the streets of Ottawa and Kingston I received an education about what was really at stake. The paramount issue was the internal pollution crisis that affected everyone in society -- environmentalist and industrialist alike. I knew it was essential to step back inside and examine this. Thus I started to lecture to university classes about inner ecology and to participate in play groups with young children along similar lines though expressed differently. At the same time I had to "put my money where my mouth was", as it were, and so I renewed my own internal journey through meditation, seeking out from within the patterns of inner ecology that polluted my own consciousness and awareness of the highest qualities within myself. From this change in direction in how I spoke and thought about environmental issues I created this manuscript, and I am grateful for students and children providing feedback over the last decade that enables me to better complete the jigsaw puzzle I am putting together. I received quite an education as a canvasser, not the least being the realization that despite all we are doing to the earth, the crisis is not with the planet. The crisis is with us - *homo sapiens*.

Attitude Shifts and Gaia - The Spiritual Dimension

The Canadian scientist, David Suzuki, wrote a very forthright column about these issues in the *Toronto Globe and Mail* newspaper in 1989 (Suzuki 1989). He referred to the massive changes necessary for us to be environmentally responsible. He stated:

> Such a massive transformation will only take place when our own attitudes, values and beliefs have been changed. Recognizing this a few scientists with impeccable professional credentials are beginning to use words like ‘spiritual’, ‘religious’, ‘love’ and ‘God’ -- words once unthinkable in a scientific discourse.

The scientists he refers to include Harvard University’s Edward Wilson, a world authority on biological diversity, Stanford University’s Paul Ehrlich, a noted ecologist, and the 1989 co-winner of the Templeton Prize, Sir Charles Birch, a brilliant scientist from

Australia. Wilson has long argued a thesis of interconnectedness within ecosystems, a theme echoed by Birch but taken further by him to ponder on creation, the relationship to God and the power of Love. Ehrlich has made the argument that biosphere destruction will come to an end only when there has been a "quasi-religious" change in human beings. Their emphasis on the nature of interconnectedness was to find an end to separation through an internal transition within human cognition and perception, so that we form our knowledge of ourselves and of the world through different and clearer perceptive filters. Suzuki concludes with reference to these notable scientists:

> ... in trying to resolve the global crisis, they identify the spiritual dimension as the key place to begin the personal revolution that will trigger the needed transformations in our social and economic systems (Suzuki 1989).

These issues of personal transformation, attitude and value shift and the significance of the spiritual dimension take me to a particular strategy for change. First of all, it is clear that we have to examine, then change, our models of self and society and transcend all the attendant and stubborn mental sets associated with the old models. Secondly, to set about doing this involves an inner journey, through meditation and self-healing practices, so that a universal self beyond our individual bag of bones, organs and flesh is experienced. In other words the orthodox perspective of ourselves and our location on the planet and in the cosmos has to be challenged and rethought. The many difficult and alarming crises of our times can be viewed as a T-junction, one fork leading to breakdown in all domains, the other directing us to a breakthrough to a new evolutionary level of consciousness as a species. This new postulated level has nothing to do with further physical evolution of the human frame but lies in a quantum leap of consciousness -- and this has to do with the human mind.

Here I draw on a provocative perspective on human evolution written by Peter Russell, *The Awakening Earth.* He charts the current crises of our times, yet considers the possibility that they constitute an evolutionary catharsis for our species. He characterizes *homo sapiens* as having evolved to an ability to self-consciously affect itself and its environment (1988:38). This self-reflective consciousness is now the spearhead of human evolution (1988;97); particularly as these abilities are set within a framework that has no evolutionary precedent. He outlines three main factors - (1) the exponential acceleration of scientific knowledge, (2) the growing complexity of our global society, and (3) the immense diversity yet interconnectedness of the current information era. All this places us in a twilight zone of evolution more powerful than either the Neolithic or the Industrial Revolutions. It is more powerful because the changes are not in the realm of technology and differential adaptation to a deteriorating environment. As Russell points out,

> The real problem lies not in the physical constraints imposed by the external world, but in the constraints of our own minds (1988:114).

Our current model of reality, our existing paradigm, is drawn from the Cartesian revolution and the onset of industrial capitalism. It is of a relatively short duration and it no longer works -- this centralized focus zeroes in on the individual ego's self-interest. It is essential to shift individual consciousness to a universal focus and Russell goes as far as to argue that such a change has now become an evolutionary imperative (Russell 1988:142). All the major evolutionary indicators of human diversity, organization and interconnectedness are in place in that there exists on the planet at this time the critical combinations of complexity that are the necessary catalysts for a new level to emerge (1988:86). What would this look like and what kind of planetary context would be involved? Let us pick up James Lovelock's Gaia hypothesis.

The Gaia hypothesis is one of the most fascinating in the earth sciences. I do not intend to explore Lovelock's argument in detail but draw on a particular set of implications. He outlines how the planet operates with such powerful forces in the biosphere that homeostatic control mechanisms are produced whereby the chemical, physical and biological processes of the planet are brought to conditions of equilibrium that are optimal to support life and continuing evolution. The emphasis is on supporting life in general, not necessarily the life of an organism, such as *homo sapiens*, that alienates itself from a habitable econiche on the planet. From this perspective one can posit that the planet is in fact very robust.

Reports to the U.N. by concerned world scientists that the earth is in grave danger (Union 1993) miss the point of understanding Lovelock's conception of Gaia as a self-regulating homeostatic mechanism. For the Earth itself is not in danger. Despite the ravages of industrial civilization, or more correctly because of them, a new equilibrium is being created. Human instrumentality in destroying the biosphere has belatedly been recognized, as it took until 1995 for the U.N.'s World Meteorological Organization to explicitly connect global warming and ozone layer decline to human industrial activity. The impact of increasing ultraviolet radiation on crop yields, human health and economic sustainability is still fiercely debated, but it is clear that a different equilibrium in the earth's biosphere is being created. What is problematic is whether a particular organism with self-reflexive consciousness can change rapidly enough so that these trends can be reversed, enabling it to continue occupying a niche on the planet's surface.

Lovelock pointed out in 1987 that the Gaia hypothesis had been neglected rather than criticized by the scientific community (1987:93). He did not have long to wait. In 1988 the American Geophysical Union held their annual meeting in San Diego and the main item on the agenda was the ramifications of Lovelock's treatise on Gaia. Their prognosis was largely negative and the major papers were published in the British science journal *Nature* in 1988 (V.336). However, the lasting and most effective word on the Gaia hypothesis did not lie with the American Geophysical Union. Shortly afterwards, Apple computers produced a fascinating software program called "Sim-Earth - The Living Planet". The programme's designer, Will Wright, relied totally on Lovelock's assumptions to construct the software, so despite the best efforts of the American Geophysical Union, the Gaia hypothesis has extended into public consciousness through the medium of a computer game that anyone can play. A vote of approval by the American Geophysical Union would not have had the same effect!

Conclusion

A further examination of Gaia and the crisis management strategies of a disintegrating global system (Thompson 1987:26) leads Francisco Varela, a noted biologist and philosopher at the Ecole Polytechnique in Paris, to state very bluntly that,

> the chance of surviving with dignity on this planet hinges on the acquisition of a new mind. This new mind must be wrought, among other things, from a radically different epistemology which will inform relevant actions (Varela 1987:49).

Varela, Thompson, Capra and others have been sculpting this new epistemology under the rubric of New Science. My own thoughts on this current are contained in my essay on Paradigms (Chapter 11), where I demonstrate that present conceptions of science do not recognize that our evolution and cognition are intricately linked with all that takes place within the wider ecosphere of our planet. Our consciousness is not separate from it, but first we have to recognize that this is so by moving to a radically different perspective towards the incredibly beautiful planet we live on.

We have to realize that we are part of a web of life, and are not the masters of the earth. We need to relate to ourselves and the earth within a sense of wonder and humility; in a spiritual manner rather than an exploitative one. In this way our knowledge will fuel wisdom rather than create structures of dominance and control. Yet our attitudes, concepts and values must radically change before that prognosis has the possibility of becoming a reality.

Dedication

For Rachel Carson, 1907 - 1964

Acknowledgement

Michael Sharpe, Kevin Karst and Tim Olaveson provided critical readings of earlier drafts of this work. There was so much I wanted to include but they very cogently argued for cuts and refinements and their suggestions greatly enhanced the rewriting of this chapter.

Bibliography

Campbell, J.
1988 The Power of Myth. N.Y.: Doubleday

Capra, F.
1983 The Turning Point. N.Y.: Bantam Books

Carson, R.
1962 Silent Spring. Boston: Houghton Mifflin Company

1965 The Sense of Wonder. N.Y.: Harper and Row

C.B.S.
1963 The Silent Spring of Rachel Carson. N.Y.: CBS Reports, April 3.

Colburn, T.
1992 Chemically Induced Alterations in Sexual and Functional Development: The Wildlife/Human Connection. Washington, D.C.: World Wildlife Fund

1996 Our Stolen Future. N.Y.: Dutton

Cummins, J.
1993 Atrazine Effects, Environmental Catastrophe. Paper presented to the International Joint Commission on Great Lakes Water Quality, October 1993

Fox, M.F.
1980 The Soul of the Wolf. Boston: Little, Brown and Co.

Fox, M.W.
1986 Approaching Deep Ecology: A Response to Richard Sylvan's Critique of Deep Ecology. Environmental Studies Occasional Paper #20. Centre for Environmental Studies, University of Tasmania, Hobart, Tasmania

Hanh, Thich Nhat
1993 For a Future to be Possible. Bath, U.K.: Gateway Books

Logan, J.W.
1992 A Scientist's Reverence for Life. Chrysalis, V. VII, 1, Spring 1992

Lovelock, J.
1987 Gaia, A Model for Planetary and Cellular Dynamics. In W.I. Thompson (ed.): Gaia, A Way of Knowing:83-97. Gt. Barrington, Ma: Lindisfarne Press

1988 The Ages of Gaia. N.Y.: Bantam Books

Mander, J.
1991 In the Absence of the Sacred. San Francisco: Sierra Book Club

Naess, A.
1973 The Shallow and the Deep, Long Range Ecology Movement: A Summary. Inquiry 16; 95-100

1989 Ecology, Community and Lifestyle. Cambridge: Cambridge University Press

Neihardt, J. B.
1972 Black Elk Speaks. Richmond Hill, Ontario: Simon and Schuster

Norton, B.G.
1991 Toward Unity Among Environmentalists. N.Y.: Oxford University Press

Russell, P.
1988 The Awakening Earth. Harmondsworth: Arkana

Schumacher, E. F.
1973 Small is Beautiful. London: Abacus Books

1977 A Guide for the Perplexed. N.Y.: Harper and Row

Spretnak, C.
1986 The Spiritual Dimension of Green Politics. Santa Fe: Bear and Company

Suzuki, D.
1989 When Scientists Start Using Words Like Spiritual, Love and God. Toronto Globe and Mail

Thompson, W.I.
1987 (ed.): Gaia, A Way of Knowing. Gt. Barrington, Ma: Lindisfarne Press

Time Magazine
1962 Review of Rachel Carson's Silent Spring. September 29, 1962

Varela, F.
1987 Laying Down a Path in Walking. In Thompson, W.I. (ed.): Gaia, A Way of Knowing. Gt. Barrington, Ma: Lindisfarne Press

Union of Concerned Scientists
1993 World Scientists' Warning to Humanity. Cambridge, Ma: Union of Concerned Scientists

U.N.
1996 Taking Action. N.Y.: U.N. Environment Program

Chapter 13

Myth, Meditation and Transformation of Consciousness

Introduction: Scepticism and Mythology

David Brower, the noted American environmentalist and a co-founder of the Sierra Club, tells a macabre joke that is an apt metaphor both for the environmental crises of our times and the response of national and international authorities to these same crises. He tells of the first night of a Broadway musical. The concert hall is packed and just before the curtain goes up a fire breaks out. This produces panic and pandemonium as people rush to the exits. Then the piano player steps in front of the curtain, tells everyone to stay calm and return to their seats, that everything is under control and there is nothing to worry about. He then starts to play the piano. Everybody calms down and returns to their seats. And they all burn to death!

Despite the fire much scepticism remains over the issues I have raised in discussing paradigm shifts and environmentalism (see Chapters 11 and 12). Can one be sure about synchronicity between levels, the interdependence of physical and metaphysical? Does the environmental movement really have a future particularly after the Rio conference in 1992? Is inner ecology a fanciful idea totally unrelated to daily realities? There are many unanswered questions and a great deal of scepticism, particularly about the burden of proof. Can the assertions made in the previous essays be substantiated and held firmly in a convincing and plausible manner? Not directly perhaps, but at a particular level of correspondence there is the most convincing evidence of all to draw on. That is the evidence from mythology.

These sacred narratives that lie outside of time and space provide blueprints and symbolic guides for an inner journey of personal transformation, and in doing so provide insights as to the interpenetration of levels. I maintain that if one understands the myths from the inside and can discern the guidelines for the inner journey, one then knows what steps to take (Prattis 1991, Chapter 2 this volume). There are a body of myths worldwide that deal directly with environmental issues. I refer to the Tree of Life myths that connect the planet, the universe and human beings in a template that is repeated with astonishing similarity in culture after culture. As Joseph Campbell (1949, 1960, 1962, 1968, 1974, 1988) and Claude Lévi-Strauss (1969, 1973, 1978) have demonstrated, there are no accidents in these sacred narratives. My views on myth have been made clear in other essays and publications (Prattis 1995, Chapter 8 this volume) and will not be repeated in this essay. I do, however, want to show how the unfolding of the Tree of Life myths in countless cultures bears eloquent testimony to all the claims I make for mythology.

The Jewish mystics, the Kabbalists, have the sefirotic Tree of Life central to their conceptions about creation, and the Divine Tree is the intermediary between the world of human beings and God (Halevi 1968:9). This same inexhaustible metaphor appears in the Norse myth of the Universal Tree - *Yggdrasil* (Davidson 1969). The mighty ash - *Yggdrasil* - is centred as the *axis mundi* and connects the planet, humans and the universe, as long as human beings, represented as gods, choose to locate at the centre within themselves. Otherwise chaos and destruction ensue. All the cycles of existence are played out and orchestrated within *Yggdrasil's* domain. For the Lakota Sioux the central pole of the Sun Dance lodge is known as the sacred tree, the centre of everything, the connector, the Great Spirit. This kind of symbolism is found in *every* myth about the Tree of Life. What is it telling us?

Jesus of Nazareth was crucified on the Tree of Life, placed at the centre of the world and the universe. The four directions of the cross connect the earth, humankind and the universe in the most powerful symbol of our times. On this Tree of Life Christ provided human beings with an example of God's truth incarnate that speaks to every human heart irrespective of particular religious tradition. The Tree of Life as a source of life is also found in Revelations (22:13-14):

> I am Alpha and Omega, the beginning and the end, the first and the last. Blessed are they that do his commandments, that they may have right to the Tree of Life, and may enter in through the gates of the city.

Moyra Caldecott collected these and many other myths in her remarkable book - *Myths of the Sacred Tree* - yet the one that illuminates my argument more than any other is her account of Siddhartha Gautama and the Bodhi Tree (Caldecott 1993:38-39):

> At Bodh-Gaya he sat under a tree and did not move from there for forty-nine days. Time passed and did not pass. He could feel the great tree drawing nourishment and energy from the earth. He could feel it drawing nourishment and energy from the air and sun. He began to feel the same energy pumping in his heart. He began to feel there was no distinction between the tree and himself. He was the tree. The tree was him. The earth and sky were also part of the tree and hence of him. When his companions came that way again they found him so shining and radiant they could hardly look at him directly... He could have said, "There is no distinction. There is no suffering once one experiences the wholeness of things. There is only suffering if we think in terms of separation: I and Thou, this and that, before and after, here and there. There is only suffering if we desire what we think is outside ourselves, not realizing that we have everything because everything is contained within the "I". These things if he had said them would have gone some way to explaining what he had learned, but not far enough. To know in

> part is to know nothing. He took a leaf from the tree and looked at it. In it was the whole essence of the universe. He held it out to his disciples. They saw it glowing with the same radiance that he saw.

The Tree of Life in mythology is constantly referred to as a sacred, symbolic vehicle of communication representing the Cosmic Axis, the centre of the Universe. It is the metaphor through which human beings connect to all worlds and dimensions, natural and supernatural, Universal and planetary. The underlying motif throughout the various expressions views humankind as being physically grounded within the synchronistic heart beat of Mother Earth, for it is through this planetary vascular system that humankind connects to the experiences of life-sustaining forces; seasons, renewal, nurturing and creativity. On their own each of these qualities remain unfulfilled. It is the conjunction between metaphysical Father — the Universe — with the planet — Mother Earth — that permits the harvesting of fruit on the sacred Tree of Life. It is at this juncture of balance that the individual integrates with the Creator, self meets God and part meets Whole. That is the message of the myths, to locate at the centre of being and retain a spiritual connection both to the Universe and to the planet; otherwise disorder and chaos will ensue.

Karma, Genetics and Conditioning - Inner Ecology

The lessons and directives from the Tree of Life myths are abundantly clear yet something prevents this collective wisdom from being implemented in human lives. What is it that keeps our self destructive attitudes, values, and activities intact? I would argue that it is our negative patterns of inner ecology -- from karma, genetics and conditioning -- that obscure a clear vision of who we basically are, and cause us to ignore the very clear lessons from the Tree of Life myths. Of the three sources of negative patterns none is as significant as karma.

Karma has precision. Its imprint prescribes for human experience a conditioning from genetic predisposition to select genes that then attract a corresponding conditioning from social and cultural existence. All this reinforces the separation frequencies set in motion by karma. I believe that negative karma establishes the design in the cell for genetic selection and cultural conditioning to respond to. It is the common and necessary experience of being human to know separation. This in a sense defines the species, and all life, history and personal evolution is the story of how that initial separation is either compounded or transcended. It is how one journeys through separation to the wholeness that is one's own to reclaim that describe the various paths of self-awareness.

For the present, we have to realize that our beings have become internally polluted with negative patterns from social and cultural conditioning, genetics and karma, and they find comfort zones within us and imprint their patterns within this false security. The silence and stillness of meditation is the vehicle to shatter the security of such comfort zones, providing no hiding place for negative patterns which are surfaced to awareness and released through conscious breath. It is those patterns that support negative karma and all its consequences that are endangered in meditation. The most difficult pattern of inner ecology to dig out is karma, yet the Tree of Life myths provide the guidelines to step beyond karma's cyclic embrace so that one may experience liberation.

In Eastern mysticism and much aboriginal symbolic thought, negative karma is a known and recognized force that functions at different vibrational levels throughout the energy spectrum (Ikeda 1985; Waters 1977). In these symbolic systems negative karma is conceived of as patterns that pollute. These patterns are activated by thoughts, words and actions that derive from afflictive emotions such as anger, greed, desire and jealousy. The answer to karma is to deal directly with afflictive emotions in order that they are robbed of energy and ultimately transcended. This means inner work and scrutiny of one's being so that one continually surfaces, clears and releases negative patterns that block one's access to inner consciousness. As one chooses to fill oneself with love, compassion and wisdom and actively takes steps in this direction, there is simply less room for fear, ignorance, anger and reactive emotion to take root (Hanh 1993). I believe that moving beyond negative karma is an essential step for the continued presence of humans on this planet. There is no longer the time scale to consider long therapeutic remedies for global environmental ills and the fate of the species.

One must rapidly step beyond karma to indicate that one is finished with the associated patterns of a maladaptive inner ecology.

Meditation

The discussion of myth and karma provides an entrée for the last sequence of dance steps in the choreography I am weaving. In the last few chapters I have referred to meditation without being very specific, as I wished to construct an argument through Rachel Carson, the Gaia hypothesis, my own experience as an environmentalist, new science, mythology and karma, so that a foundation is established for meditation and consciousness changing that is unshakable (see Chapter 11 on *Science and Sages*, Chapter 12 on *Issues of Inner Ecology*). I trust I have done this, to locate the problem of pollution and environmental degradation where it belongs -- inside us. One implication of the arguments presented is that commitment to inner cleansing and self-healing through meditation has major effects on the individual, their immediate household, community, nation and on the local and planetary environment.

We have to return to what is missing from the human-environment equation. We need to step back inside and acknowledge the necessity of changing our individual consciousness by removing the negative barriers of inner ecology. In dealing with inner ecology, by surfacing and clearing our old "stuff", we build a climate of clarity that is shared with others taking similar steps. In this way we can eventually take care of the external environment because the internal environment has been properly cared for. In other words, as consciousness changes, negative patterns of inner ecology dissipate and we see things more clearly and holistically. Furthermore, we recognize that our own minds, bodies and souls are interconnected components of an entire web of planetary life. This kind of vision is denied until we clean up internal patterns, as this process is the pre-requisite for the emergence of a new mind that will have the necessary clarity and perception for solutions to global pollution to emerge.

The key to all this is conscious breath and symbolic focus in meditation. The different techniques of focus in meditation at some point bring to one's awareness the recognition that the mind and body is moved by the same energy that pervades the planet and the entire Universe. The science of breath in the body is part of the respiration of cosmic breath, and the discipline of meditation is geared to bringing the two into a balanced harmony (Iyengar 1966). Mastery of the science of breath enables one to still the mind and turn inward. Without such mastery one is subject to the bondage of the mind's attachments and projections. There is no secret to meditation. It simply takes commitment, discipline and courage and is based on the desire to transcend one's current level of consciousness. However, factors of social and cultural conditioning, genetic heritage and karma so influence the ego and personality that barriers and blockages create an internal ecology that prevents one's awareness moving beyond one's present consciousness. Part of the journey embarked upon through meditation is to seek out these blockages and remove them so that one's thoughts, words and deeds become consistent with higher levels of internal consciousness and a congruence between thought, speech and action evolves. There are any number of meditation techniques that can facilitate this. It matters only that breath, light and stillness are brought into the body with special reverence. Meditation is a beginning, an initial process of guidance to adjust one's awareness and mind to be in tune with one's body. Ultimately there is a progression to the point where the heightened sense of stillness and awareness experienced within meditation is taken out into each moment of one's life.

Meditation also has a destructive role, a dangerous aspect. It constitutes a danger to anyone who chooses to remain in an unaware and shallow life, for its purpose is to shatter all the psychological refuges and hiding places where illusions of Truth and negative patterns of inner ecology are embedded. The destructive force of stillness in meditation make's one aware of the barriers to Truth that must be transcended. The barriers and repressions are erected by the ego so that it does not have to surrender to the Grace of the constant soul, and so one remains trapped and driven by unintegrated shadow material. The inner movement beyond these ego-derived frontiers of consciousness through the fireball of Truth and clarity is what meditation brings.

The experience in meditation is also of death. The death of pettiness, negative thought and the dictates of ego. The tempest of meditation takes one into silence, stillness and a vast emptiness that is beyond time, space and structure. It is a way to the wholeness that is already there, only one's vision of such wholeness is obscured by the barriers of afflictive emotions, the negative patterns of inner ecology erected by the ego. As a way of life meditation destroys such barriers and provides a propulsion into wholeness. Yet it is one step at a time.

The first step is the choice to take responsibility for one's state of being, Teachers, gurus, and sacred teachings are there to provide guidelines and signposts only. It is the individual, choosing to be self-aware, who does all the work. This choice firstly, calls on each of us to take full responsibility for our own place on the planet, so that both the individual and the species may evolve to a higher order of consciousness. Secondly, self-liberation involves reaching deep within one's stillness and accessing a higher order of Universal knowledge. What is important is that steps are taken to conjoin all that remains separated — physically and metaphysically -- to put back together what the Cartesian revolution tore asunder. The result is that one may rediscover what many ancient and tribal wisdoms knew—that being fully human was simply being in harmony with oneself, with each other, with the earth and with the Universe. Meditation also brings one to an integral connection with the planet and all upon it. Not only does one feel the universe as part of one's body, one feels the planet in a similar way. Just as the Buddha felt no separation between himself, the Bodhi tree and the earth, so meditation puts us in touch with the same sense of interconnectedness. Rachel Carson's sense of awe at nature, Francisco Varela's new mind, and my insistence that we clean up inner pollution through meditation all converge on this point.

Conclusion

This all too brief overview of meditation is simply to provide a flavour for what stepping back inside to deal with the negative patterns of inner ecology is all about. Stepping out in one way or another on the environmental stage is only one part of the dance. It cannot be fully effective until the internal choreography is in place.

That is how we ultimately get at global issues of environmental pollution and degradation; through healing ourselves in a discipline of meditation. That is an initial responsibility.

This brings me full circle to the principles that imbued Rachel Carson's work on environmental issues, particularly the key spiritual qualities of responsiveness grounded in responsibility. The personal sense of responsibility for what we create and what we are part of was Carson's main hope for the future. Antoine de Saint-Exupéry, in his wonderful book *The Little Prince* was particularly explicit about this (1961:21):

> Now there were some terrible seeds on the planet that was the home of the little prince; and these were the seeds of the baobab. The soil of that planet was infested with them. A baobab is something you will never, never be able to get rid of if you attend to it too late, it spreads over the entire planet. It bores clear through it with its roots. And if the planet is too small, and the baobabs are too many they split it into pieces... "It is a question of discipline," the little prince said to me later on. "When you've finished your own toilet in the morning, then it is time to attend to the toilet of your planet, just so, with the greatest care. You must see to it that you pull up regularly all the baobabs, at the very first moment when they can be distinguished from the rose-bushes which they resemble so closely in their earliest youth. It is very tedious work," the little prince added "but very easy!"

We deal with our internal toilet and pull up regularly all the baobabs of our inner ecology through meditation and self healing; then attending to the toilet of the planet will be very easy, to extrapolate from the Little Prince.

The purpose of meditation is to heal, and to transform ourselves, our communities and our planet. It is a progressive movement towards wholeness and integration and requires that we look deeply into ourselves and into the environment we are located in and the environment we create with our thoughts, attitudes and values. In the process of meditation we liberate ourselves from internal resistances and blockages created by maladaptive patterns of inner ecology. Thus we transform by personally experiencing different cognitive and perceptual levels that enable us to transcend our internal baobabs. This step inwards to raise consciousness enables us to create solutions from a foundation of wisdom and confidence in our clarity. Yet it is clear that changing our consciousness comes first, then out of this solutions can be created. His Holiness the fourteenth Dalai Lama expressed this very succinctly in an interview with James Thornton (1993:44). He said to Thornton:

> As an environmentalist you already have the right view. What you need to do is to become confident and positive, and help other environmentalists to become confident and positive. The long-term solutions we need for our global problems can only arise from the confident and positive mind. They can never arise from the mind of anger and despair.

Our afflictive emotions and negative patterns of inner ecology do shape our experience and reality by creating structures of thought and practice, society and ideology that are maladaptive. That is until one moves to a level of consciousness whereby these patterns can be cast off. At the same time one must also acknowledge the value of these same patterns. The ecological decline of the planet caused by our industrial practices *has* galvanized many people to actively take steps to transform themselves. We now, more than ever before, recognize how interdependent we all are, as our resources in the air, water, and on the land become mutually poisoned through neglect and greed. We are learning very quickly about impermanence, the illusion of separateness and the necessity of changing our perceptual mind states. Although the odds may appear to be stacked against us -- *it is* an exciting time to be alive. When you take a steady look at ecodoom, it does lead to an abandonment of the trivial and a choice to step onto the razor's edge of putting our consciousness and intentions to the test. That is where we are right now, on a razor's edge. It would be wise to wake up before we are sliced and dismembered by the consequences of our present attitudes, values and structures.

We talk about compassion, love, interconnectedness, trust and transformation, yet are we brave enough to practice it? I do think we are and agree wholeheartedly with Joanna Macy when she says: "...give it all you've got. Use that sense of being on the brink to come alive, to discover who you really are, to let all the falseness that we imprison ourselves in be stripped away" (Macy 1993:51).

It does take great commitment, however, and I am drawn to a wonderful quote by Goethe:

> Until one is committed there is hesitancy, the chance to draw back, always ineffectiveness, concerning all acts of initiation (and creation). There is one elementary truth the ignorance of which kills countless ideas and splendid plans; that the moment one definitely commits, then Providence comes too. All sorts of things occur to help one that would never otherwise have occurred. A whole stream of events issues from the decision, raising in one's favour all manner of unforeseen incidents and meetings and material assistance which no man could have dreamed would have come his way. Whatever you can do or dream you can, begin it. Boldness has genius, power and magic in it. Begin it now.

Right now is the time to be bold and confident -- internally and externally. Begin it now. I have chosen to do so and life's lessons have helped to liberate me from some of the prisons of my own making. It is not easy to face the inner hiding places but I personally would not have it any other way. My commitment is to be at the forefront of change within myself and from that I can truly be of service to myself, the planet and all upon it.

It has taken time, crises and many false starts for me to be convinced of this path, and I see that my career as a professional anthropologist has been part of the learning experience. Being an anthropologist is also an excellent cover for what is really important -- making the world a better place, both environmentally and in terms of shifts in human consciousness. So be bold and confident; take care of the environment you inhabit and the environment you create.

Bibliography

Caldecott, M.
1993 Myths of the Sacred Tree. Rochester, N.Y.: Destiny Books

Campbell, J.
1949 The Hero with a Thousand Faces. Princeton: Princeton University Press

1960 The Masks of God I: Primitive Mythology. N.Y.: Secker & Warburg

1962 The Masks of God II: Oriental Mythology. N.Y.: The Viking Press

1968 The Masks of God IV: Creative Mythology. N.Y.: The Viking Press

1974 The Mythic Image. Princeton: Princeton University Press

1988 The Power of Myth. N.Y.: Doubleday

Davidson, H.R.E.
1969 Scandinavian Mythology. London: Paul Hamlyn

Halevi, Z'ev ben Shimon
1979 A Kabbalistic Universe. Bath, U.K.: 1979 Gateway Books

Hanh, Thich Nhat
1993 The Blooming of a Lotus. Boston: Beacon Press

Ikeda, D.
1985 Buddhism and the Cosmos. London: MacDonald

Iyengar, B.K.S.
1966 Light on Yoga. N.Y.: Schocken Books

Levi-Strauss, C.
1969 The Raw and The Cooked (trans. John and Doreen Weightman). N.Y.: Harper & Row

1973 From Honey to Ashes (trans. John and Doreen Weightman). N.Y.: Harper & Row

1978 The Origin of Table Manners (trans. John and Doreen Weightman). London: Jonathan Cape Ltd.

Macy J.
1993 Schooling our Intentions. Tricycle; The Buddhist Review, Winter 1993

Prattis, J.I.
1991 Parsifal and Semiotic Structuralism. In I. Brady (ed.): Anthropological Poetics:111-131. Savage, Maryland: Rowman and Littlefield

Prattis, J.I., D. Blair,
L. Grigas and O. Krassnitsky
1995 "Reflections" as Myth. Dialectical Anthropology V.20, 1:45-69

de Saint-Exupéry, A.
1961 The Little Prince. N.Y.: Harcourt, Brace, Jovanovich

Thornton, W.I.
1993 Radical Confidence. Tricyle: The Buddhist Review, Winter 1993

Waters, F.
1977 Book of the Hopi. Harmondsworth: Penguin

About the Author

Ian Prattis was educated at London, Oxford and the University of British Columbia. He has been at Carleton University since 1970. Fieldwork amongst North-West Coast American aboriginal nations and North Atlantic fishing communities from Norway to Newfoundland was an early focus. Over the past twenty years an interest in native land claims has lead to ongoing fieldwork in Indian and Inuit communities with an emphasis on training native leaders to conduct their own research process. He has worked with groups as diverse as Native Americans, modern dancers, business executives, environmental organizations, Gaelic communities in the Hebrides and Quebec, Inuit craft co-operatives and New Age healers to mention only a few, and has a passion for doing anthropology. "It's better than having a real job" he says "the only limits are your imagination and self discipline". His career trajectory has curved through mathematical models and economic anthropology; development studies and applied anthropology; hermeneutics, poetics and symbolic anthropology to reflexive anthropology, new science and consciousness studies. The intent was always to expand, then cross existing boundaries, to renew the epistemological freshness of the anthropological endeavour and to make the discipline relevant to the individuals and cultures it touches. His recent and highly acclaimed television course on Culture and Symbols draws on his original research and novel perspectives and Ian is exploring the possibilities of delivering the twelve videotapes of the course through an Internet homepage which will be a prototype for the Electronic University of the Future - no boundaries. Click on:

http://www.carleton.ca/~tolavesco/cspage.html

One assignment requires students to watch the Star Trek series as modern myth, then create a dream or myth or storyline for a Star Trek episode, and analyze it with the theories discussed in class. In keeping with this theme he was "beamed off" at the end of the last televised class. His home is in Kingsmere, Quebec, in the middle of Gatineau Park where he had a pet wolf. The lakes and hills of this incredibly beautiful area are the locale for his graduate tutorials, whether by trail, canoe or front porch! The necessary progress reports transform into theses with Nature's blessing and a great deal of hard work. His interests include cross-country skiing, hiking and canoeing. He also enjoys Tai Chi, dancing, dining out, playing baseball, and swimming with dolphins. The basic commitment he holds is to make the world a better place - environmentally and in terms of shifts in human consciousness. Being a professor of anthropology provides an excellent cover for both activities! He teaches meditation and travelled to France to study with Thich Nhat Hanh in 1996 and to India in 1997 to pursue his interests in meditation with Rishi Prabhakar.

Author Index